I THOUGHT I WAS THE ONLY ONE

I THOUGHT I WAS THE ONLY ONE

GRANDPARENT ALIENATION: A GLOBAL EPIDEMIC

AMANDA

WITH A FORWARD BY GLENN ROSS CADDY, PHD

 iUniverse®

I THOUGHT I WAS THE ONLY ONE
GRANDPARENT ALIENATION: A GLOBAL EPIDEMIC

iUniverse books may be ordered through booksellers or by contacting:

iUniverse
1663 Liberty Drive
Bloomington, IN 47403
www.iuniverse.com
844-349-9409

ISBN: 978-1-6632-2433-0 (sc)
ISBN: 978-1-6632-2434-7 (e)

Print information available on the last page.

iUniverse rev. date: 06/14/2021

CONTENTS

DEDICATION

This book is dedicated to our precious grandchildren. Granma and Poppy started AGA because we wanted you to know how hard we tried for so long to be back in your lives.

We wanted you to know that we would never give up.

Our prayers were answered, and our grandchildren still love us.

This grandmother has been blessed by a guardian angel.

ACKNOWLEDGEMENTS

The pathway forming Alienated Grandparents Anonymous Incorporated has been an emotional but rewarding road, and one that we could not have accomplished without the support, guidance, and passion from those who have contributed. Putting a name to this phenomenon - AGA, we did not know our journey would take us across the globe. The incidence of Grandparent Alienation is staggering.

First and foremost, we wish to thank the distinguished masters of knowledge in Parental Alienation Syndrome - PAS for providing us with an academic understanding of the complex dynamics of Alienation, and for agreeing to study the circumstances of Grandparent Alienation with us. Each has mentored us through these learning years. We are sincerely grateful to have such astounding scholars as a part of AGA. Your dedication and availability have meant so much to so many. It has been an honor and a privilege to work alongside those who know. Thank you for giving hope to the victims of family cut off. Your commitment to grandparents and to AGA has helped hundreds of families reunite.

It is with much appreciation for the insight, dedication, compassion, and participation of experts in the related fields of law, mental health, medicine, and religion who have imparted valuable knowledge; that AGA can offer suggestions from their advice to those who suffer such emotional devastation. On behalf of grandparents and grandchildren around the world, we thank each of our specialists for their active involvement, research, and writings.

We are grateful for the many thousands of personal stories communicated to us via emails, phone conversations, and at conferences and support group meetings for the past eight years. Thank you, grandparents and great-grandparents, for opening your hearts and sharing your emotional pain and struggle with us, so we could better comply with the needs of millions. You are the voice of our grandchildren.

We are thankful for the generosity of those who offered donations to our Non Profit, which has enabled our ability to help others.

Were it not for Team AGA and a guardian angel, our personal story, and those of hundreds of others thus far, would not have had a happy ending.

Amanda and Matthew, AGA Founders/Directors

I have always prayed for wisdom to help grandparents with shattered hearts.

I acknowledge that this is not an accomplishment of my own.

You have helped us empower grandparents, giving them give hope and a voice.

Without you, this book and AGA would not have been possible.

- Amanda

AGA Board of Directors

Carol Golly, PhD Doctoral Dissertation: Intergenerational Conflicts - Grandparent Alienation (2019)
James Karl, Esq.
Vickijo Letchworth
Suzi Krig, R.N. Grandparent Advocate

AGA Professional Consultants

J. Michael Bone, PhD

Glenn R. Caddy, PhD

Joshua Coleman, PhD

Charles Jamieson, Esq.

Rev. Dr. John Killinger

Abe Worenklein, PhD

Jason Holloway, Florida Legislative Assistant

A special thanks to Darryl Rouson, Florida Senator, Sponsor of Florida Grandparents Rights Legislation. We appreciate the efforts of AGA grandparents who advocate for Grandparent Visitation Rights in their states and countries.

Before AGA, my BFF, you were my emotional sanctuary. Thank you for your wonderful heart. You were constantly lending an ear and a shoulder, and lifting me when I was shaken to my core. Girlfriends, you know who you are, thank you for being there for me through the tough times. You continue to be in my prayers every day.

- Amanda

FOREWORD

This Book and the creation of Alienated Grandparents Anonymous (AGA) is the brainchild of two devoted Florida grandparents, Amanda and Matthew. These two people like many millions of grandparents in this country and around the world suffer the agony of estrangement from their grandchildren. The idea of this book was to provide an educational and self-help resource that would extend beyond the work that was already being done to help grandparents who were experiencing the agony of parental alienation.

Determined to do something to bring the tragedy of grandparents experiencing this cruel phenomenon into the spotlight, these two incredibly energetic and committed people founded AGA, Inc. in 2011 as a Florida based nonprofit corporation. They sought out experts in the disciplines of psychology, sociology, law, and even religion, and they created a scientific advisory board of both national and international experts in these fields and then they began to market AGA, Inc. as an educational and self-help support organization that also has the capacity to draw on experts to offer specific advice and support to grandparents who have been alienated from their grandchildren.

Beyond drawing on the advice of experts in the various disciplines that link to the tragedy of alienation, AGA provides professional quality education, consultation, and advice throughout the United States and now, through affiliates, in more than twenty-two countries for grandparents worldwide who suffer the agony of being cruelly alienated from those they love and miss dearly.

As of this book, what is contained in this volume is the first-ever effort to look in depth at the phenomena of grandparent alienation. With thirty-one chapters that range from a description of the complex dynamics of alienation to how to form a strategic alliance with AGA to legal issues to the enablers, gatekeepers, strategies for a hoped-for reunion, and so much more, this book is a treasure trove of information, resources, and hope for those grandparents who are facing the tragedy of alienation from their grandchildren.

Glenn Ross Caddy, PhD, ABBPP, FAPA, FAABM
Clinical, Forensic, and Health Psychology
Scientific Advisor, AGA, Inc.
Fort Lauderdale, Florida

INTRODUCTION

I'm Not the Only One!

"Take a look at this ad in the magazine. Get a copy of this book, then call to tell me what the last chapter says."

We couldn't believe what we were experiencing as we simply looked at the title, A Son Is a Son Till He Gets a Wife: How Toxic Daughters-in-Law Destroy Families. Then, reading Anne Kathryn Killinger's words, we realized for the first time that we were not suffering alone. It spoke directly to the anguish our souls.

"To a mother's heart," said Anne, "this is one of the most unbearable psychological burdens imaginable."

She was talking about the separation of a mother from her married child, and she wasn't kidding. And from the moment we each started reading, we felt a curious surge of hope. Here, we knew, in the pages of this book, we would find an answer to the confusing thought that kept assailing our minds: Why had we been abandoned by our own adult child?

We hadn't been able to understand it. We were loving and caring parents of a successful son and daughter. They had always been a loving son and daughter to both of us. We were devoted to our children's welfare. We were also devoted to — our precious grandchildren. Why had our loving son, after decades of bonding, broken off with us? Why couldn't we see our grandchildren anymore?

From the first, we had made a conscious effort to treat our son's spouse with respect and fairness. But now we couldn't help wondering if this was the person who had caused the fracture in our relationship. Anne Killinger had put her finger on the problem in the very title of her book. Our adult child's spouse was toxic; and, for whatever reason, was poisoning our own child against us.

After reading the book, I (the grandmother) called Annie. She talked with me for endless hours. She listened to my story without passing judgment on me. She had told in her book how she was going through the very same ordeal with her son and daughter-in-law. She had put her finger precisely on the problem that was causing me such grief and agony. She encouraged me not to blame myself. Someone else was causing the unhappiness, not me. I wanted seamless joy and good will in the family, but my child's spouse didn't.

Out of my conversations with Annie, Matthew and I made the decision to create Alienated Grandparents Anonymous, so that all of us mothers and fathers who were experiencing broken relations with our children could come together in love and understanding and support one another on this difficult journey. We were determined to be there for all the grandparents who were unjustly cut off from their grandchildren, so that they would know they weren't the only ones unable to hug and protect and teach and provide unconditional love to their children's children.

It has been our unwavering goal to be there for all the grandparents who need an Annie in their lives. Knowledge is power—at least a kind of power—and we wanted to help all the suffering grandparents by bringing together clergy, counselors, lawyers, psychologists, and others who could shed light on this almost universal problem that Annie's book had finally brought to our attention.

When Annie traveled to AGA headquarters during our early formative years to speak to an audience of 150 troubled parents, you could hear a pin drop in the room. She spoke from her heart and from her pain within. She became our role model. She was the kind of grandmother every child should have in their life. She was a great story-teller, passing on her legacy in an articulate and persuasive manner. Her tone was gentle and caring, and she was always ready to listen with compassion to anyone's plight.

It is our goal now to be there for grandparents who need an Anne Kathryn Killinger in their lives.

Annie will always be remembered by her many friends and relatives as a cheerful, outgoing, attractive, and humorous woman who was a gracious hostess, a splendid cook, a loving wife and mother, and a generous friend. She died in 2014 after a long battle with cancer. She had always been a healthy, vigorous person, and her husband, Rev. Dr. John Killinger, believes it was the stress of their unhappy family situation that caused her to have the disease.

It was in the last weeks of her life that her estranged son finally contacted her by phone. They had a brief conversation, and her son said she should not expect to hear from him again. She said she could hear his wife in the background telling him what he could say and not say. When she died, he declined an invitation from his father and brother to travel with them to her memorial service in Kentucky, which we attended.

1

The Phenomenon of Grandparent Alienation

"Nothing happened. For my wife and me it was sudden....like overnight. No notice. No explanation. No reasons. Still no reasons, for us or the OG's (other grandparents). For us, just sudden abandonment and alienation with little to no empathy. For the OG's, a little more gradual and less severe but devastating nevertheless. No arguments. No disagreements. We were all wonderful grandparents, always very respectful of them and their busy schedules, and we're still standing accused of... nothing. No one has a clear idea what is going on."

"No one can truly understand what is taking place in our lives. We were denied a reason why this is happening. This is more than shameful behavior by our own sons and daughters along with their toxic spouses. Parents actually lie to their own children by using cruel demeaning devaluing stories about the grandparents. This must be stopped before they totally ruin the grandparents' character. This teaches the child to lie, have no respect for others, and worst of all it teaches them how to hate. This is abuse, and needs to be taken seriously. Children are not born to hate."

"My husband and I were speechless. Accusations went back and forth for about a year, and there is no communication now. I sent my son a nice card a month ago, and he returned it unopened. I have called him two times in the last year, and asked if we could see the girls, and he said he would talk to his wife and call me back. He never called me back."

Amanda

"We learned of our grandson's birth, from my sister-in-law, three days after he was born. Our grandson is three years old, and we have never seen him."

"We will never give up. One the most incredible things that my dear wife said after being alienated for a couple of years is, 'If we cannot be with our dear daughters, their husbands, and our grandchildren while we are on this earth, then we'll see them in heaven. We are committed to not ever giving up in our quest to reconcile. We pray we can help others as well."

"His wife is very domineering and she told him it was her or us!! He said this in an email to my daughter. He had to make a choice!"

"I have not seen my eight grandchildren in seven years - no reason. My daughters just say they don't need a mother any more. What happened to honor thy mother and father?"'

"That's the thing we're all dealing with—a culture in which children think they can thumb their noses at their parents and get away with it, regardless of what the parents ever did for them. You and AGA are trying to shine a light on that culture and say, "Hey, everybody, this is wrong. It's unnatural and it's wrong. We need to start educating our children differently so that when they grow up, they'll know they should avoid behaving like this." Rev. Dr. John Killinger, author of From Poppy with Love...Letters from a Grandfather to the Grandchildren He Isn't Allowed to See).

A very serious problem affecting millions in our grandparent population has been uncovered. Our grands (grandparents and great grandparents) are being cut off from access to their grandchildren or have severely limited access to them, mostly for unknown reasons. The dynamics of the family are being torn apart by selfish choices made by adult children. As a victim of another person's malicious and devious plan, a human tragedy has resulted in the lives of grandparents and grandchildren. Grands who long to be actively involved in their grandchildren's lives are walking around our communities trying to make sense out of no sense, and needing help to cope from this willful intimidation. The middle generation is sabotaging this relationship, thus denying the unconditional love from the grandparents to their precious young ones. (Dr. Bone) This alienation of loving and supportive grandparents will have a negative impact on these grandchildren for the rest of their lives. The alienating parents are role-modeling poor behavior which often is an inter-generational transmission.

Being a targeted grandparent brings excruciating emotional pain. Grands are being treated like criminals by their own sons and daughters who turn against them. They are causing such deep hurt, predominantly with no justifiable cause. How could one's own sons and daughters intentionally inflict such pain upon their own parents who loved them so completely? To complicate matters, they use the grandchildren as pawns to punish grandparents for perceived wrongs. The grands are now the victims of double alienation. They have been cut off from their child and their grandchildren.

When children become adults and chose to disown themselves from their parents, it is one of the most painful things that families can go through. It usually occurs without justification or knowing what crime they committed. No dialogue is permitted, and questions remain unanswered. This toxic situation closes the door to grandparents, leaving them to wonder what they did wrong to have caused this level of cruelty? There is no balance in decision making in these families. There is no discussion, no dialogue, and no exchange of ideas. The family becomes just them, not us.

The cut off is usually sudden, but it can also come apart over a period of time. It occurs from what was once an existing loving grandparent-grandchild relationship, then is destroyed by the behaviors of an undermining daughter-in-law, daughter, son-in-law, or son. Whether it occurred as the result of a high conflict divorce, or the death of an adult child, or family rift, it is likened to amputating these precious children from their grandparents. Grandparents who have been cut off from their grandchildren call it a *living bereavement*. As each day passes without their grandchildren, they feel a part of them dies. Because these stories are so tragic, a lot of people (for varied reasons) don't share them.

Joshua Coleman, PhD, Co-Chairman of The Council on Contemporary Families stated, *"…it's not their fault because we have also socialized them to believe they should prioritize their well-being, they should be assertive, and not let anything interfere with their happiness. Sadly, we didn't realize that we would one day be one of the items on the menu that interferes with their happiness and therefore have to be eliminated."*

Alienated Grandparents Anonymous, Incorporated (AGA), has given a name to this bewildering experience affecting millions in our grandparent population. It appears to be a phenomenon of the baby boom generation, though it did occur in the past generation. This is a "give me" generation; give me, give me, and then I owe you nothing in return.

Being cut off from, rarely allowed to visit, or never having had the thrill of seeing and holding your precious grandchild is a roller coaster journey of excruciating emotional pain. It can happen to one parent or both parents, and the results for these grands is a devastation that is so severe it effects almost every facet of their lives. They become victims of the power and control of another person's devious plan, resulting in a human tragedy. Grands who suffer the isolation from their grandchildren and their adult child wonder what kind of life they have been left. With tears in their eyes and sadness to their hearts, they experience a loss of meaningfulness.

Our adult children can make choices, but our grandchildren cannot. The children's critical thinking skills are being stifled. The unjustified abusive behavior of our adult children is creating a lifetime of emotional problems for our grandchildren, and for grandparents. In Millennium jargon, *Ghosting* (completely cutting off someone) is already a common term. The cutting off of loving and supportive grandparents will negatively impact our grandchildren for the rest of their lives, and will affect generations to come.

This once hidden epidemic has resulted in a tragedy in the lives of grandparents and grandchildren. They are the victims of parents alienating themselves from their own parents. This incredibly destructive alienation creates an unnatural psychological distance between the grandparents, adult children, and grandchildren. While many grandparents will never experience the heartache that comes from not having contact with their grandchildren, it is important to keep in mind that it can happen in any family. The reality is that it effects millions. In practically every family there are sad stories of one degree or another. The worst cases, like these, are devastating, and our families are suffering. Society needs to take notice and deal with this.

This insidious and destructive abandonment by our adult children has reached epidemic proportions worldwide, affecting all populations regardless of socio-economic, educational, professional, or religious boundaries. Adult children refuse to let their parents see the grandchildren. They prevent them from sending special occasion cards and gifts, attending school functions, sports events, milestone and holiday celebrations, and the birth of their own grandchildren.

Those with severely limited contact do not even know how to talk to their own children any longer. They are walking on eggshells knowing that if they don't tolerate this treatment they are out. They are forced to put up with the abusive behaviors of their daughters-in-law, sons-in-law, daughters, or sons. No one should have to face this behavior. The alienators undermine and destroy the family unit they have worked so restlessly to create. If it were not for the deep love they have for their children and grandchildren, they would otherwise walk away. Instead, grandparents are burdened with the fear and anxiety that they are doing everything wrong.

The children are being withheld with little or no provocation. The grands are kept from playing a vital role in the child's life. Those who previously bonded with the young ones, now have had that love connection denied. The grandparents worry about the impact this cut off will have on their precious little ones. Their own adult children have turned against them, leaving a huge unimaginable hole in their hearts and in their day to day lives. The lifelong loving relationship they had with their son or daughter is now strained or broken. They no longer recognize their own son and daughter's behaviors, wondering silently how to love a child they don't like anymore. Our older population is trying to cope with their torment, grief, and anger. They are befuddled wondering if the relationship they once had will ever exist again, as they harbor the fear of losing them forever.

(Carstenson) Baby boomers are less likely to participate in community or religious organizations than were their counterparts 20 years ago. They are less likely to be married. They talk with their neighbors less frequently… Boomers report fewer meaningful interactions with their spouses and partners than did previous generations, and they report weaker ties to family and friends.

In correspondence with AGA Headquarters, Rev. Dr. John Killinger stated:

> What we're experiencing is a cultural phenomenon in which baby boomers, the generation of late-middle-aged-adults who were born in the aftermath of World War Two, are less integrally tied to their parents and society than those of us who were born before the great war. This can be read as a weakening of all societal ties,

or perhaps even a complete refusal of that particular generation of people to be intimately related to and responsible for fellow human beings.

Suppose this is a trend, and that the children of baby boomers, those born after 1970, are even less inclined to be obligated to or related to the generations that went before them.

While this possibility is disconcerting to imagine, it may help to explain why many of our alienated children have renounced all responsibility to and for the parents who brought them into the world and spent years nurturing them. Our very culture appears to be shifting into a new mode, one in which some of our children disown all previous relationships and can therefore casually reject us without any feelings of regret or failure.

They simply refuse to accept any moral responsibility toward those who gave them life and sheltered them through their early years, as if their relationship to those forebears is a mere accident of time and matter which they can disregard with full impunity. They have forsaken all the old guidelines about love and family and responsibility, leaving them free to live as they please, without any obligation to those who cared and sacrificed so much for them.

It is a frightening thought, but what we are witnessing is, in some measure at least, the breakdown of society as we have always known and understood it, where people honored their fathers and mothers and continues all their lives to acknowledge and indebtedness to them.

What, if any, are the conclusions we can draw from this enormous change in younger generations' sense of meaningful ties to the society that produced them?

For one thing, our own disrespectful sons and daughters are not at all unique in their rejection of us; they are merely doing what an increasing number of sons and daughters are now doing when they separate from their original families with the intention of becoming fully independent of them. Unless something happens to reverse this tendency, the dissolution of the family will only worsen as time goes by.

By the end of the present century, all human existence on this planet will be vastly different from the way it has always been in the past. We may well be entering a historical phase in which family relationships as we have known them will be completely abandoned in favor of a rootles unrelated society in which everybody is independent of everybody else, even parents, children, and siblings.

All I can say about this is God help us, for we are on the path to the eventual and complete destruction of the very feelings and understandings which from the dawn of time have made human life beautiful and meaningful.

In his writings regarding family cut off, Arthur Kornhaber, M.D. shows deep concern that family cut off is becoming more common in society. He views this as a growing tragedy with millions and millions of children being deprived of the love and adoration of one set of grandparents. His thoughts regarding the "intact" family, consisting exclusively of Mom, Dad, and the kids, "flies in the face of biological, psychological, social and spiritual directives". He says that a family which excludes grandparents is not intact at all. He states that a family with living but exiled grandparents is a dismembered family which is suffering, turning grandchildren into "grand-orphans". He affirms the concept that grandparents are the link to priceless family traditions and years of wisdom that can play a significant factor in the future success of a child; and that this American family heritage has become lost and forgotten for many.

Carol Hosmer Golly, *Pruning the Family Tree: The Plight of Grandparents Who Are Alienated from Their Grandchildren*, The International Journal of Aging <u>2016</u> states:

> Longer lifespans allow for intergenerational family relationships, yet many grandparents are prevented by the middle generation from seeing their grandchildren. Limited research suggests that this phenomenon may occur as the result of a divorce or death in the middle generation, intergenerational family conflict, or through Parental Alienation Syndrome (PAS). Alienated grandparents suffer serious consequences, including depression, anxiety, grief, suicidal ideation, and physical health problems. Grandparents may be helped through mutual aid and advocacy groups such as Alienated Grandparents Anonymous (AGA).
>
> There are currently 70 million grandparents in the United States, representing one third of the population (Breslau 2016). Life expectancy has increased threefold in the past two hundred years, allowing for the possibility of lengthy familial multigenerational connections between children, parents, and grandparents (Grandparents.com 2013). There are instances when these primary kin relationships are disrupted or severed, and in some cases, grandparents are suddenly cut off from contact with grandchildren for unknown reasons. This may occur as a result of a sudden event in the middle generation, such as a death or divorce, or the

adult child in the middle generation may actively alienate the grandparent from the nuclear family and children.

Older grandparents realize their years are numbered and are frightened by loss. The older and seriously ailing grands live in fear they may never see their own children or grandchildren again before they die. They are simply devastated. This relationship which has been so good for the well-being of the grandparent and so good for the grandchild and their development has now suddenly collapsed.

When grands should be delighting in their later days and years, the rocking chair is empty of joyful thoughts of their grandparenthood. Their minds are tormented with stress and depressing thoughts as they contemplate their future of disappearing hopes and dreams. Having been forced out of their families, their homes are places of quiet instead of the laughter of their children and grandchildren. Holiday and birthday celebrations in the home they made for them are now vacant of happiness. Feelings of emptiness and loneliness have set in.

How many grandchildren are entangled in inter-family disputes? How serious a dispute would warrant the permanent denial of a grandparent – grandchild relationship? Severing the bonded GP-GC relationship causes the children to go underground with their emotions. Typically, children want to please their parents and receive praise from them. They realize if they defy their parents' wishes, there will be a penalty to pay. The fear of losing their parent's approval has new meaning. They now they live in a world of heartbreak and chaos.

"I hear her, Grammie. I hear her say bad things about you. Fix it, Fix it now!" says a five-year-old boy, red-faced and pacing.

Who is there to help these grandchildren? To whom can they turn? Our innocent confused children, the precious gifts in the lives of their grandparents, live with this chaos. The once close relationship causes deep emotional pain for the first and third generation when it is forcibly and unjustifiably removed. The grands celebrated their moments of joy, comforted them in trying times, and provided them with unconditional love and self-esteem building. Now these little ones are the pawns in an outrageously wicked chess game.

If death takes a grandparent from and grandchild that is a tragedy. But if family bickering and vindictiveness deny a child the love of a grandparent, that is a shame. The dynamics of a family are being torn apart by selfish choices made by adult children. It is a damage that can take years to repair, and often never gets repaired. Grandparents and great grandparents experience profound grief and loss; this complicated grief, a grief without closure, is felt 24/7. The person they are grieving is still alive. The lost ones are physically absent but psychologically present in the mind of the grandparent who is grieving with the continuous hope of reuniting with their precious grandchildren.

Alienation is considered by the experts to be a severe form of child abuse, and a severe form of elder abuse. Abuse is never acceptable; abuse is never okay. Abuse is against the law. This particular form of abuse tends to escalate without the grandparent making sense of what is occurring. The emotional abuse limits communication with you, and the psychological abuse threatens you and uses family members against you. Psychological abuse is most pervasive and includes behaviors that harm an older person's self-worth or well-being.

Studies show the abuse of older people is on the rise. For the millions of older people worldwide, this has serious individual and societal costs. We must do more to prevent and respond to the increasing frequency of different forms of abuse. Despite the frequency and the serious health consequences, elder abuse remains one of the least investigated types of violence in national surveys, and one of the least addressed in national plans to prevent violence. By 2050 the number of people aged 60 and over will double to reach two billion globally. If the proportion of elder abuse victims remains constant, the number of people affected will increase rapidly due to population ageing.

Elder abuse is rarely discussed in policy circles, less prioritized for research, and addressed by only a handful of organizations. Governments must protect all people from violence. We must work to shed light on this important societal challenge, understand how best to prevent it, and help put in place the measures needed.

Denying access not only brings tears to the eyes and sadness to the hearts of loving grandparents, but it hurts the children being deprived of all that affection and belonging. Because they have deep love for their children and grandchildren, they tend to allow abuse to continue. If it were not for the fact that they have loved and supported their child unconditionally for decades, they would have walked away. There is this tie that binds them. If someone other than their own child treated them so cruelly, they would have walked away.

Grands are hurting non-stop, and they want answers. They want to know why this is happening to them. They want to know what more they could do to try to fix this. AGA heard this cry loud and clear, thus contacting the leading international experts in the field of Parental Alienation Syndrome (PAS). AGA was the first organization to connect the dynamics of PAS to Grandparent Alienation (GA). AGA has looked at this from the varied aspects associated with this phenomenon. Realizing that knowledge is power, we wanted to study and find answers for the grandparents who suffer this otherwise silent disease.

The one thing AGA continually hears is, "I thought I was the only one going through this." Discovering that you are not suffering the devastating emotional trauma of being cut off, does bring some comfort. Realizing that you have not been singled out as the one and only worst parent/grandparent in the world, but are instead part of a social phenomenon does help. There are millions globally experiencing alienation, estrangement, or isolation.

Grands from around the world continue to express their profound appreciation for the dedication of the AGA Board of Directors and the AGA professional consultants who have agreed to study GA with AGA Headquarters. Luck favors those who are prepared. Therefore, AGA strives to provide hurting grands with suggestions from the advice of these experts in this new specialized field of study. AGA does not want traumatized grands to suffer one day more than they already have. AGA Headquarters' communication with many thousands of grands worldwide, allows AGA to continually provide updated insight and strategies for a hopeful reunification. AGA also reminds grands to apply their personal instincts, as they best know the history of their own adult children.

Human behavior makes sense if you understand what is driving it; thus, it is very important to understand that being cut off is not about fairness and that the grandparents must be the ones who have to try harder than the middle generation. Anything worth having is worth working for, therefore AGA encourages grandparents to empower themselves with the accumulation of knowledge. Educate yourself, become informed, acquire wisdom. A disease known is half cured. Hopefully though knowledge gained, we can continue to reunite the generations and prevent others from reaching an escalating level of alienation.

2

The Role and Feelings
of Grandparents

"You and I have a history. I held you only minutes after you were born and kissed your sweet little rosebud lips. You felt right in my arms - so small and vulnerable, yet communicating to me, even then, a strength of character and determination. OH, darling girl, I loved you from the moment I saw you; I love you still, even though I am prevented from holding you...I will continue to write letters to you with the hope that someday, somehow, we will meet again. Until then, please leave a secret spot in your heart for us, and understand how much we love you and always will. If we could move heaven and earth to see you again, we would begin right now. With hugs to last a lifetime, Gram"

"I should have begun my letters to you when you were five years old, instead of waiting until you would be capable of reading and understanding them. So, I am starting two years later, hoping that when/if you should ever get to read my words, you will look back on that time when you first began to forget us."

"The really sad part is that my grandson and now the baby I never met live about 20 minutes from me. *I have tried everything I know of to reconnect with my daughter, but they have managed to block every way to connect with them. Cards and presents are sent back. Phone numbers and Facebook have been blocked.*

"I have no idea what they told my granddaughter to explain my sudden and complete disappearance. That they were willing to hurt their own child came as a shock to me."

"It's a daily and nightly yearning to see her again."

"It feels sad and painful from the moment you wake up until you drop off to sleep…if your broken heart will let you. It is not possible to understand this unless you are unlucky enough to be in the position so many of us are in."

"The sorrow I feel from so many years of separation has been intense."

"The initial stages of estrangement were profoundly hurtful, in a way that was immobilizing."

"I honestly don't know what to do, we have been torn to shreds emotionally, humiliated, abused verbally and yet we are "the ones who are in the wrong'."

"I will not stop trying to have a relationship with my grandchildren until the last breath is exhaled from my lungs! I write this with a lump that feels like a basketball in my throat and what feels like the weight of an elephant on my heart, but I only want a chance to he heard."

"Every day that goes by I'm missing more of my grandbaby's life. I'm afraid I'll never see my child or grandchild again, and that there isn't enough time to change this."

"The word estrangement was never in my vocabulary before it happened to me seven years ago. And like many parents, I was ashamed and reluctant to talk about it."

"I am ashamed of being an alienated grandmother."

"The people I have met at AGA are distressed. They loved the people that have alienated them. They are hurting, and they are not ogres. The stories I have heard don't bring to mind a need to feel shame nor to hide. I don't feel a need to be anonymous, I don't feel guilty, and this situation doesn't define me. I don't walk around with a placard on my chest or a sign on my forehead announcing the fact that we don't see or talk to our son and his children. I don't talk about my personal health challenges with people I have just met either. Essentially all of our family and friends know about our situation, and we talk freely with them. I also think if you just don't want to deal with other people knowing what is happening, you have every right to remain anonymous."

"My grandson is failing with this alienation. I'm terribly worried about him. He has stopped talking to me the rare times I see him. I know I shouldn't have done it, but I started crying. I have so much to say to him but am afraid to say anything. The parents have shut me out completely. They say it is my fault. What have I done? My life has changed to something I don't know."

"I never thought I'd be part of any group of this nature, until my son married a woman who never liked me. I have to bite my tongue whenever she and I are in the same room. My granddaughter is now five years old and I have not been permitted to attend any holidays because my daughter- in-law doesn't want me around. My son feels it's better to comply then to fight with her. No one should have to endure this pain and embarrassment. This AGA group is a blessing."

"It's like a big secret, and we parents are the only ones not in on it. It is so bazaar and we are worried sick! We miss our son and daughter-in-law and our precious grandchildren. We wonder if they even care about us. Have they fallen out of love for us? We have come to believe that hope is out there somewhere; somebody will do something or something will happen, and we can be on the road to recovery. A light just may go on when the truth is finally told and known. We also need the energy and comfort that come from doing something and not giving up. Getting older, I am not ashamed, depressed, or vengeful. We are very healthy. We are simply devastatingly hurt."

"All we want is for our children and their children to be loved, respected, and valued. They are our priority even through the pain."

"There was a time when the family unit included grandparents, uncles, aunts, and cousins either close by or living in the home. It is tragic that we have drifted so far from this. I subscribe to the adage that it takes a village to raise a child. Most of my fondest childhood memories are of activities with my grandmother and her sister, my great aunt. I learned and was exposed to situations/experiences through them that I probably would not have had, were it not for their influence. I will be happy to do anything that I can do to help other children have a relationship with their grandparents. Hopefully, I will be able to get to know my youngest granddaughter at some point in her and my life."

"How I feel is lost. My days and nights are spent being sad and angry."

"Our grandchildren are in another state far from us, and our situation keeps getting worse. I cry a lot, but trying to let them all go. Our daughter-in-law is evil. And, so is our son. I don't know him anymore."

"I am 70 and so many bonding years with my grandchildren have past, leaving a big whole in my heart. I see other grandparents all the time with their grandchildren and think, they don't realize how fortunate they are."

"I feel totally devastated, violated, disappointed. I cry most of the time even though I try to take my mind to other places. It is not only the estrangement that I have to deal with, but also, I am constantly worried about my grandchildren's welfare. I don't even know where they are!

"My son seems to have reconciled to the fact that it is too much trouble to stand up to his wife's demands. I know in his heart he wants us to be their lives, but he has detached from us, his siblings, and his grandparents."

"I found out that my son had married a year ago. My ex discovered a baby girl was born two years later. I called the town clerk who informed me that there had been a birth at their address. There's been no contact and no pictures."

Amanda

"We and the OG's and have done nothing to deserve this, but that's the essence of Grandparent Alienation that occurs coldly, slowly or suddenly, and without any apparent cause. GA is a cruel epidemic. We are so hurt, beyond imagination. Beyond belief."

"As I sit here with tears streaming down my face, I'm wondering when I accept what's happening and get back to living."

"The last thing you need is someone looking at you like you've done something terrible."

"It is 'killing' us, and they seem to care less. It's very simple. I love my son and my grandchildren. I will love and honor his wife. They need to put this behind them, and allow me to become the most dedicated grandfather there ever was. A little positive communication from them would go a long way. A little understanding and empathy from anyone else would help immensely. The silence is deafening."

"They undermine and/or destroy the family unit we worked so diligently to create—the one we thought we knew. Indeed, the very fabric of what we called family is shredded by these interlopers—trespassers on our sacred land. Our own flesh and blood have turned against us for no apparent or justifiable cause. How is it that our own sons or daughters could intentionally inflict such searing pain upon the very ones who gave them life; who gave their all and loved them so profoundly?"

(Rev. Dr. John Killinger) "Love your children and allow us to love them, and them to love us. If you don't love your parents, at least honor them."

"Our own children cut us off at the knees. They bedeviled us with their intransigence. They were not willing to discuss their mean—spiritedness, nor to explain their contempt. Despite our resolve to persevere in our efforts towards a remedy, we found ourselves adrift in a sea of acrimony. What made matters worse was their indifference to our pleas. To this day, we do not know what we did to deserve the punishment of alienation."

"Heartbroken, my expectations about my involvement in her life were turned upside down."

"The silence is deafening. It has been five years now. I don't socialize like I used to do. I don't recognize any special days. Sadly, I have outlived my four best girlfriends- the ones you had years of history with and know you well. That compounds my heavy heart."

"In today's world, very different from yesteryear at the time we grandparents grew up, the cruelest form of GA, more common than you think, is fueled, as much as anything else, by parents who feel they have the legal 'right' to do almost anything they want with their children. They do so no matter what anyone thinks, how anyone else feels, or even what the laws may say about it. Even those who strongly disagree with these behaviors often say or do nothing, either because of fear or just plain weakness, while we remain in pain, and our little grandchildren suffer. We are hurt beyond belief. *Little children are conflicted and hurting. They should be the primary focus of everyone's energy, attention, and intention....* <u>all</u> *of us. If I do or say nothing from this day forward, we and other grandparents may never see our grandchildren again.*"

"I see you every night in my dreams. Time and space won't erase your face because love is not blind. She can take you away from my sight, but she cannot take you from my life. You are because I am, and I am because you are. I love you always from afar. Every heartbeat, every breath I breathe, I grieve. I would give what life I have to be, for one more hug your eyes to see. To my grandchildren, I love you until I am no more and forever after when my spirit soars, the sunlight on your faces, the breeze that kisses your little cheeks, is my love forever my promise to keep." (Seymor}

Amanda

"In the end, for me, it's like I've run into a cold, brick wall at the end of life. There's not enough time left for me to take my excellent health for granted, but there is enough time left to love my grandchildren."

"Hoping to see my grandchildren before I die."

Grandchildren are meant to be a blessing. They are a gift to grands from the moment they are born. 1.7 million Americans become grandparents every year. The number of grandparents in the U.S. has increased by 24% to 70 million since the turn of the century. They represent approximately one third of the population in the United States. With life expectancy increasing threefold in the past two hundred years, it allows for the possibility of lengthy familial multigenerational connections between children, parents, grandparents, and great grandparents

Entering perhaps the most exciting chapter of life's adventures, becoming a grandparent will allow us to fall in love all over again with feelings of happiness and enchantment. Instead of feeling old, there is a new twist in life. You change your mindset from: Grandparent = Old + Idle to Grandparent = Joy + Purpose. You are being given a gift of a little one who will transport you to a world of jubilance. This new-found love is boundless and unbreakable. The entire extended family of sisters, brothers, aunts, uncles, cousins, grandparents, and great grandparents welcome this new bundle of joy into their hearts. There are never too many people to offer love a child. Especially excited are the grandparents who will love their grandchildren so much, because they have loved their children so much. Our grandbabies grow to trust that their grandparents and others who love them will always be a part of their lives.

Should a troubled controlling adult child, daughter-in-law, or son-in-law enter that picture, you may never get to pick up the phone to learn you are going to be a grandparent; or, that your grandchild was just born. Instead you learn of the birth through social media, a contact person, or for many not at all. Your opportunity to be a part of your living legacy has been denied.

When a troubled adult child decides to severely limit or cut you off from "their" family, it affects the well-being of both the grandparents and the grandchildren. The impact of suddenly being cast out of the lives of their adult child and grandchildren is a tormenting endless grief. The fear of what is possibly being told to their grandchildren, with no opportunity to provide corrective experiences and remind the child that they really do love and adore them, is agonizing. The psychological wedge created between grandparents and their adult child has blindsided them. Their long-awaited desires to create memorable moments with their own grandchildren have been shattered. They have raised and invested time, love, and energy yet may never see their own children again.

Rev. Dr. John Killinger, pastor, prolific writer, and author *of From Poppy With Love…Letters from a Grandfather to the Grandchildren He Isn't Allowed to See states*, "Grands feel robbed and deprived because they are unable to grow old with the love and fellowship of their grandchildren, the way their parents did.

Many grandparents have mentioned how they observed warning signs during the dating stage. From the wisdom of their years they wanted to alert their child of this negative quality, and to a potential conflict. However, they realize that saying something negative about their son or daughter's choice of a partner might very well come back to haunt them someday. (Dr. Coleman) The more you take a position against their choice, the more they will feel obligated to embrace that person as a show of independence and autonomy.

In the cycle family relationships, the strongest bonding ever experienced is between a parent and a child. Possible exceptions include those with spouse or partner. When your child has children of their own, they now experience the strongest relationship they will ever know. When your child becomes a parent, you then become the second tier. If your relationship with your adult child is terminated, you lose your primary relationship and your adult child and your child loses their secondary relationship. In addition to loss of contact with your child, you lose contact with your grandchildren as well. Your loss becomes a double lose, with a huge emotional toll.

AGA's distinguished international professional experts agree grandparents play a particularly important role in the life of a child. To suddenly sever the children from their positive powerful attachment figures is traumatizing and makes their world a much less safe place. Removing grandparents from a child's life deprives the child from developing their identity, their social development, their cognitive development, and the safety and security in their world. It is definitely a severe form of child abuse.

Did you ever contemplate in your wildest dreams the possibility of being cut off from your child in the future? Did you think it possible that the child you raised, lovingly sacrificed for, taught to make good choices, and loved would sever all communication and keep their life a secret from you? Did you ever think a spouse would be so powerful that they could keep you from the child you raised? Enter the troubled spouse with their unresolved childhood issues!

The disruption of the grandparent-grandchild(ren) bond is a personal and tragic loss to each individual experiencing it. Grands expected their aging years would be a time of calmness. As they move into what should be the golden years…a time when relationships are of crucial importance and when a security system should be in place for them, being cut off from their grandchildren and adult child(ren) is emotionally devastating. They have been made to feel uncomfortable in the home of their own offspring, bewildered, and left wondering what they might have done wrong to cause this cruel out-casting.

With the wisdom of their years, grandparents think of themselves as problem solvers and rational. They are now being left alone to suffer because they cannot fix the unfixable.

They can't bear it, but they carry it. (Vagnoni) There's a primal bond between a parent and a child. When that's broken, parents feel they've failed as human beings.

Grands who have been cut off are faced with the reality of how short life is, and how few years may be left in their lives. Being of grandparent/great grandparent age is a realization that your remaining years are valuable. They frighteningly wonder how long the wait will be, and if it will ever be fixed. They are burdened with the knowledge that they cannot make up for what they have already missed, and are left to the lonely gloomy pathway of grief ahead. It breaks the hearts of grandparents denied, that these precious young children do not fully know how much their grandparents truly love them. Perhaps they have been told that their grandparents just abandoned them. The additional deep concern is for the well-being of their sons and daughters.

Most grandparents have remained silent about their loss supposing others would look upon them with thoughts of, "What did they do wrong", or "What monstrous things have they done to be punished so hardheartedly?"

Role of Grandparents

Without the daily pressures of parenting, grandparents and grandchild often develop a bond that is as close as it is strong. A close grandparent-grandchild bond does a world of good for both generations. Grandparents can and do make a difference in a grandchild's life.

A study from Brigham Young University which examined the role grandparents play in the development of children has confirmed what every grandparent knows (or hopes, at least), that grandparents are key to grandchildren's happiness! The results found the emotional relationship between grandparents and their grandchildren can significantly affect the children's academic, psychological, and social development. When grandparents are involved in their grandchildren's lives, kids are not only more social but also more engaged in school. Researchers also noted kids were more likely to develop pro-social skills essential for social development, such as showing care, compassion, and kindness for people who are not part of their inner circles. Grandparents matter above and beyond parents . . . and can significantly affect the children's academic, psychological, and social development.

(Zullo) The GP-GC bond is positioned second in emotional importance only to that of the parent-child bond. The studies found that children who enjoy close relationships with at least one grandparent feel accepted and adored as is, that they are more secure, and have a comfort in knowing they have a place to go to in times of need.

(Kruk 1995) The relationship between grandparents (GP) and their grandchildren (GC) is highly salient – significant- and an important component of grandparent quality of life and self-identity.

(Dr. Coleman) Grands perform a really important role in the life of a grandchild. Studies regarding this relationship show the importance to a child's social and cognitive development, and for their safety and security in the world. Depriving a child of this, suddenly taking this away from a child is a severe form of child abuse. These grands have been a positive powerful attachment figure to the child. If this attachment is taken away it is traumatizing to the child, and makes their world a mush less safe place.

Grandparents do matter. They are an intricate part of raising and loving unconditionally our youngest generation, and preparing them for society. They play a supportive role, and provide a balance in grandchildren's lives that no one else can replicate. Loving grandparents can affect the development as a care giver, playmate, storyteller, mentor, friend, buffer between parent and child, and can perform as outstanding role models of behavior especially if there is chaos in their home. If the parents are critical, rejecting, or too overwhelmed to give positive input; then grandparents can give them a different experience. Grands provide the children with another opinion about who they are, thus building their self-esteem.

Grandchildren surveyed about their relationships with their grandparents said they most valued their grandparents' sense of family history, the unconditional acceptance by the grandparent, helpful advice and wisdom, and help understanding their parents.

Dr. Kornhaber labels the love between a GP and a GC as the simplest and least complicated intense human love bond. He calls it, "I love you because you exist". His finds this unconditional love to be incredibly empowering for children, making them feel more secure and accepted.

Our grandchildren find comfort knowing they have a place to go in times of need or trouble. Grandparents give kids roots to the past, that link of belonging to a family history. Great-grandparents contribute an increased perspective for understanding the past, present, and future. The children gain an enhanced understanding of their world because of what the older generations have to offer. The grandchildren are provided with a moral compass to follow, aspirations for the future, and a good sense of self-esteem from belonging to this attachment.

(Sanders) The great-grandparent serves as the trunk of the family tree. It's a living trunk, and all those branches are tied together by that person.

Grands greatly enrich the lives of their grandchildren by providing special time for them, and breaks for the parents. They often supply assistance in getting the grandkids to their special activities, care for children of special needs, negotiate disputes, and are often called upon to provide financial support. If the parents are critical or rejecting or simply too overwhelmed to give positive input to the child, then grands can be there for them. They can assist with those complicated issues that arise in all human relationships, thus guide them how to make good choices. They can keep an eye on problematic or dysfunctional family behavior. They are an extra layer of protection. Keeping their grandkids safe is their top priority.

During these special times shared, they are giving advice in family values such as honesty, sharing, or fairness. Grands may also instill values of love and marriage such as supportiveness, friendship, trust-worthiness, or faithfulness in hopes of influencing their character. They bring a continuity between generations. Grands reported that they attain a sense of purpose of their own life by sharing their memories, life experiences, and advice with their grandchildren.

Grands pass values on to the next generation as they share stories about themselves overcoming hardships, and retell stories of family's positive moments and the ability to bounce back from difficult ones. Children learn life is adding the stories, challenges, and positives. Kids need to know what it is like to be part of a family and have a connection to the past. Grandchildren who have been cut off from access to their grandparents are being denied a wonderful heritage of their extended families.

Grands are an intricate part of raising and loving unconditionally our young ones, and preparing them for society. A grandfather and a grandmother can serve a far-reaching role by giving a sense of identity and confidence. The manner in which they tell stories about themselves as a boy or girl and how they grew up, communicates perseverance and sacrifice. They can convey family roots and traditions. Studies show the grandchild who knows a lot about the history of their extended families tend to do better when they face challenges.

(Duke) Knowing where their grandparents grew up, where they attended school, how they met, how the family came to this country, family traditions, illnesses that occurred in the family, difficult situations that members of the family had to face, and the story of the grandchild's own birth contribute to their core identities.

It is important for children to know about the ups and downs in the lives of family members. It teaches them that families stay together, even through difficult times. They need to acquire a sense that no matter what happens, a family works toward solutions and sticks together. This demonstrates positive examples of how to handle situations. It teaches compassion, and not to just cut off people who someone doesn't want anymore. With good role modeling, children come to learn that life is about adding new chapters to their story. They learn not to give up or eliminate. Learning sensitivities from being a part of an extended family, gives the child a stronger sense of control over their lives. It gives them a higher the self-esteem and an ability to better moderate the effects of stress.

Pursuing activities with your children such as holidays, vacations, family get togethers, traditions, and the sharing positive stories about yourselves of overcoming challenges and hardships are an important part of keeping the family together. A close GP-GC bond does a world of good for both generations. Grands can and do make a difference in a grandchild's life. The quality of attachment is very strong, and contributes to our grandchildren's sense of self.

Enter Grandparent Alienation. Once blindsided by this, a grandchild is denied the love, experiences, and closeness of those they love and trusted. Half of their heritage is sacrificed; the values the grands brought with them, heirlooms which our children deserve to inherit, have been disallowed. Grands are treasures deserving of honor and respect. Cutting them off robs our young ones of their innocence, and sends the wrong signals to them. Grandchildren want grandparents. Babies are not born to hate; they have role models.

Research shows a strong link between involvement of grandparents and well-being of children, teenagers in particular. Today's teens need information and accountability in potentially dangerous areas like drugs, alcohol, and sexuality. Often times they find it easier to open up to someone who cares about them, but who isn't the main authority figure in their lives. Be prepared should they come to you needing help in making good choices, while being cautious not to undermine the parents. As grands build a close relationship with the very young, they are forming the foundation that will do a lot to ease the strain once they reach the teen years. Grands can take the time to listen in a polite, effective, and less judgmental way.

Becoming a grandfather often opens a surge of sensitivity and love. It brings out this great need to secure their own legacy, and continue their heritage. Our grandchild is what we leave behind. The aging retired grandfather is often eager to help with child care. He enjoys the satisfaction from teaching a child how to master a skill as he helps shape the next generation in his family. This relationship is a powerful motivation to live and feel joy, and adds new meaning to his life.

Studies have shown that grandchildren who have a close relationship with their grandfather are likely to perform well in school, displaying emotional adjustment, have higher self-esteem, and a greater ability to develop and maintain friendships. A teenage boy will open up more readily to his granddad if they are working on a project together or doing something fun. This togetherness provides the grandchild with a way to bring up something that has been on his mind, and is a good scenario for the granddad to ask questions. Granddads become mentors. Let your grandkids know they can call you anytime, about anything.

Grandfathers who have been cut off from or have severely limited contact with their grandchildren are hurting. They hurt even if they appear not to show it to their spouse. Anger is a common cover-up for hurt. They are angry that this is taking place, and frustrated that they cannot fix it for their wife and grandkids. They deeply miss the father-son and father-daughter relationship they developed over the decades. Priding themselves always as problem solvers, they suffer because they cannot change the un-fixable. The answers are locked somewhere in the cold hearts of their adult child, where they fear may remain until it is too late

The truth is, if they did not cause this, then they alone cannot fix it. The adult child holds the cards, and they make the new rules. Grandparent Alienation is not about fairness. Surviving this emotional trauma includes the importance of understanding how fortunate the grandma and grandpa are to have each other. Think how much worse it would be if they didn't have this person in their lives. It is time to be grateful for all those who do love and care about you. Without them, life would be worse.

GRANDPARENTS HAVE FEELINGS

SHOCK REJECTION HELPLESSNESS NUMBNESS BEWILDERMENT HOPELESSNESS ISOLATION HURT DISAPPOIONTMENT TORMENT GRIEF DEPRESSION FEAR BETRAYAL FRUSTRATION CONFUSION ANGER RAGE USED REGRET ABUSED SAD SORROW DISRESPECTED SICK GUILT SHAME HUMILIATED DESPAIR LOSS

Having a D-I-L, daughter, son, or S-I-L who makes you feel these emotions is toxic to your well-being. The definition of toxic is that something is harmful to your health or lethal if consumed in sufficient quantities. Understanding how negative family members affect your health, this word makes sense. Toxic family members cause a lot of stress on you. Their manipulation, criticism, jealousy, lack of empathy, and other negative traits can drain you emotionally. No matter what you do, they say and do things that make you feel bad about yourself and your relationship with them. People you love should make you feel great about yourself. You shouldn't find yourself unable to speak up when you normally have no problem saying what's on your mind. You shouldn't have to walk on eggshells around people you love.

Being cut off from grandchildren can be agonizing, especially when there has been frequent and close contact between the grandparent and grandchild. Each September some 70 million American grandparents celebrate National Grandparents' Day, but countless numbers of us will not. Ironically, the official flower of this holiday is the forget-me-not. None of us want to be forgotten, yet millions of grandchildren are being kept from a relationship.

Grandparents expected the so-called golden years would be a time of calmness. In place of this are the grown children who opt to strictly limit or cease contact with one or both parents. They bestow intense complicated and predominantly unanticipated grief, ambiguous loss, and emotional trauma upon their own parents.

The cut off is profoundly hurtful in a way that can be immobilizing. Alienation is not a mutual parting of ways. The one left behind often feels guilty of perhaps having done something wrong, but has not been granted an opportunity to discuss what the reason might be. (Dr. Coleman) Mothers particularly tend to be more vulnerable to guilt and worry which causes a great deal of agony. They suffer a crisis of identity and the loss of a child. Having been their child's sanctuary, made sacrifices for them, trying to be close to them growing up, offering them opportunities they themselves never had as a child; now feel they are a failure at parenting, and leaves them questioning who they are at this point in their lives.

Their adult child has made a choice, but their innocent grandchildren are not granted a choice. As minors, they have no choice. The decisions have been made for them, at least for now. Grandbabies, toddlers, youth, and teenagers are being denied the unconditional love, attention, and support system they should been entitled to have. The grandparents are being denied their so-called golden years.

Grands become immersed in thoughts of not being able to face life ahead without their precious grandchildren. Their own offspring are causing this suffering. Grands, deep in their hearts, continue to hold onto hopes. They pray that one day their precious grandchildren will come back to them. Even though hurting grandparents have tried to set boundaries to protect their broken hearts, they continue to yearn for their grandchildren. All along, the innocent grandchildren are being denied the love, attention, and support system they deserve. Remaining is the emotional trauma, and the destruction of the family unit.

Grandparents who have been abruptly cut off from their families experience intense and unanticipated grief. In the beginning stages, there is shock and disbelief. AGA grandparents speak of physiological symptoms such as shaking, anxiety, nightmares, sleepless nights, and crying. Some were diagnosed by their physicians with Post Traumatic Stress (PTS). Anger, disappointment, and contemplation persist for years. They wonder why the they were rejected, and why they were the one picked to be betrayed. They are angry because these conflicts put them in an impossible and stigmatized position.

As they move into the years when family relationships are of crucial importance, and when a security system should be in place for them, they instead find themselves victims of crazy-makers in their families. With the breakdown of a supportive relationship between family members, grandparents find themselves the victims of those who were supposed to be caring and sympathetic of them in their final years. Those who should be on their side, aren't. This willful intimidation and vindictiveness cause grandparents to feel emotionally devastated.

As they keep picking up uncomfortable signals that they are unwelcome in the home of their own offspring, they feel insignificant, disempowered, and excluded as though they no longer belong to the family. They are determined to do everything they can to correct this madness, but always feel like they aren't doing enough. No matter how hard they try, the denigration increases.

Worried that the grandchildren do not fully know how much their grandparents truly love them; they worry that they have been told that they just abandoned them. Concerned about the well-being of their precious grand-kids they wonder: Who will she become? What will he be like? What kind of world will she live in? They struggle to cope wondering for how many more years will there be an empty spot on their counter for cards they never receive for special occasions, or thank-you notes for presents they are forbidden to send.

For the vast majority, they do not know why they were cut off. They have no idea why this cruel punishment has been handed out. Whether severely limited to access or isolated, they feel confused and frustrated. They feel blamed for things that they either never did or said, if in fact they ever learn what has been said about them behind their backs. If they have committed a "crime", they don't understand why it wasn't fairly balanced out by all the loving and dedicated things they did over the decades of parenting. You can be a loving, devoted parent who sacrificed everything for your child, only to find yourself being treated as though you are the worst person in the world. Having invested time, love, and money to form a solid basis for their kid's happiness and successes, has resulted in being excluded from their grown children's lives. It is bewildering. Living with alienation is excruciating and heartbreaking. The more you care about someone, the greater the trauma of losing them.

(Dr. Golly) Some grandparents are afraid to be angry, so they get depressed.... walking on eggshells around their adult children.

The conflicts are mainly between grandmothers and their daughters-in-law. With manipulation and mind control occurring in the family, grands fear if they don't kowtow to their daughters-in-law, they risk having their grandchildren disappear. Thousands have shared heartbreaking stories with AGA of family ruptures because of unyielding frictions over food, gifts, napping schedules, baby-sitting, or angered false accusations.

Millions of mothers-in-law feel excluded from their sons' lives by controlling wives. It is the power struggle that blights so many marriages. Most choose not to complain to their sons about the pattern of behavior in the M-I-L / D-I-L relationship. The M-I-L tends not to reveal the insulting angry outbursts of the D-I-L to the son. They believe it is wise to keep things to themselves. They feel if they complain to a son, the more likely they are to escalate tensions and trigger the very alienation they fear. They presume the son will feel obliged to side with his wife for the sake of his marriage. Realize though, there are times when even with intact family relations when it is best to keep close-mouthed.

With these deep feelings, having been rejected by their sons or daughters and deprived of the core of their being - their children and grandchildren, they see no end in sight. They do not want to jeopardize or interfere with the marriage by telling their son or daughter about this treatment they have been receiving from the D-I-L or S-I-L. They do not want to place more pressure on the marriage. AGA experts state that Grandparent Alienation is about a troubled marriage, a marriage of power and control.

Back in the day when grandmothers were raising their own children, they wore many hats. Whether a stay at home mom or out in the working world, their greatest achievement was being a mom. Women who are denied the ability to define themselves as good mothers often experience not only loss, but a crisis of identity: "If I'm not a good mother, then who am I?" 24/7 they were dedicated to providing love, nurturing, understanding, advice, a shoulder to cry on, and an ear for listening. They were the dedicated nurse when the kids were sick, and the teacher at homework time, chauffeur, soccer mom, cook, confidant, negotiator, sounding board for their woes. As parents they lovingly sacrificed for them, and provided opportunities for them. Now these emotional bonds have been severed by these same children. They pick up signals that they are unwelcomed and placed in a position of marginal importance; never imagining such a thing existed, at least within their family. It is now inferred that they were a failure at the most important reason for their existence. These moms find themselves wondering who they are, and why they have been so harshly rejected.

Grandparents try to make sense where there is no sense at all. The heartache of sudden rupture is a shock to their systems which creates enormous emotional pain, and possible physical side effects. They speculate that this is something that happens to other people who may have been awful parents. It is hard to admit the child with whom they had a loving relationship for decades is no longer talking to them. Even with the wisdom of their years, grands find themselves not knowing what to say or do in front of their own child.

Just because it feels like your adult child hates you, it doesn't mean that they do. In the majority, your alienating adult child still loves you. They may not be behaving as such or realize it at this time, but there is a connection of the heart.

It is difficult to admit to others that your grown child is no longer speaking to you. Perhaps it is time to place the blame on the other side. Grandparents should not be embarrassed by this cut off from their own children. Instead, realize that each of you is likely dealing with an unresolved childhood issue or a level of underlying personality disorder such as narcissistic tendencies, bipolar disorder, paranoid personality disorder, or borderline personality disorder.

Grandparents in situations of contact loss with grandchildren are mostly either too ashamed or guilt-ridden to confess their circumstances, even to their doctors and clergy. Often, they blame themselves for having failed. In their hearts, they know that they have been good, decent, loving, and giving parents and grandparents. They just cannot accept the catastrophe that has shaken them to their core.

Dr. Coleman explains guilt as a feeling that we have done something wrong, while shame is the feeling or experience that we are inherently bad or flawed. He discussed how nothing creates more bad feelings than to be rejected by our own child, since our identities are so closely tied to our perceptions of ourselves as parents. This holds especially true for mothers. Studies show that motherhood moves to the top of the list in terms of how women think of themselves. Therefore, a rupture in the relationship causes a crisis of identity.

Fathers surely are hurt or angered by cut off. They may not show it, but they do suffer. They have anger that they cannot fix this for their wife who is in tormented. Unfortunately, men are not as likely as women to seek counselling for an emotional trauma. Many grandfathers do accompany their wives at AGA support group meetings. They realize how important their relationship is to one another. They have been distanced for a son or daughter, but appreciate having of their spouse in their life. Frustrated by the cruel disassociation cast upon them, many divorced fathers/ grandfathers attend as well.

AGA grandparents talk about this alienation becoming a pattern for the future of their families. They wish they could just get their kids to meet with them so they could say, "Don't do this! You're teaching your own child that it's okay to get rid of their parents!"

While grandparents are not being given the dignity of discussing why this has happened to them, their adult children are being abusive in their blame, coldness, and lack of empathy. With all the real problems of the world, why do our own offspring bring such agony into our daily lives? Society, in this regard, is moving in the wrong direction.

3

Feelings of Grandchildren

"I hear her. I hear her say bad things about you. It's sad Gramma. Fix it; fix it now!"

"Come to my house, Grandma. You can come over. It's OK with my dad; it's just not OK with my mom."

"I've NEVER done ANYTHING to my daughter-in-law but be courteous and kind. I am practically 100% innocent, but not nearly so innocent as her children. "See Mommy, Granddaddy IS here", her exact words, i.e. 'not where you told me, Mommy', right in front of me (her mother in a chance encounter). How a mother can see and hear this, and not display empathy and human understanding instead of fear or anger, is baffling to me!"

"For well over two and a half years we have discreetly, patiently, professionally and tactfully tried everything we know to address our personal tragedy as privately as possible. We have left them completely alone for months at a time, though I did once speak to my grandchildren without prior permission in a chance encounter; and, the grandchildren painfully spoke volumes to me, but their pleas have fallen on their parents' deaf ears, and vice versa. Sad truth from those who now offer us little more than silence and a cold shoulder."

"Do you know why I cried every time I saw you?? I said I did NOT know why. My mommy said that if I got into the car with you, you would hurt me, you would hurt my daddy, and you would hurt my mommy. But you don't hit, do you??? I said that I did not believe in hitting anyone because that would be wrong."

"This is the second time I have been alienated from these three grandbabies. The times we would see them they would wrap their little arms around my husband and me and say, "I love you grandma, I miss you". So, although I am being told they have not asked once about seeing me, I know the truth is they love me and know I love them."

"When my granddaughter was in the first grade, she came to stay with me once a week. I would help her with her homework. Her mommy told her that I could NOT help her because I was NOT smart enough, that I did not know enough. I told my granddaughter that I taught the first grade for many years, and I was also a school principal. My granddaughter said that she did not know this information, and now I could help her."

"Please send me the AGA Dear Educator letter as I need to get this information to my grandson's school. I'm hearing that he is having behavior issues now. I'm not surprised. We practically raised him for five years, and now he has been alienated from us. The other grandparents and they are raising him. My hope is that he will get counseling at his school, because I believe he needs an objective party to talk to if he will."

"My grandkids find ways to connect. They too are very confused. What parents don't realize is how they are sowing distrust."

"Children have neither voice nor choice in their environment. They have no rights. They cannot conduct research into the reasons their lives have changed or the people they love have suddenly disappeared. When they ask questions, they must settle for the lies they are told. And they know when they're lied to!"

Every child wants a Grandma and a Grandpop, even children who were never allowed to meet them. Children want grandparents who would love them unconditionally and bring love and attention their way. Currently millions of children across the United States and millions around the world are missing out on one of the greatest loves of their lives, the grandparents. It is cruel to deny these children the love and attention that a grandparent is longing to give them. A grandparent's s whole purpose is loving. A once bonded GP-GC relationship becomes a deep loss; the children's lives may never be the same again. Some go into a serious depression, have anger issues, or tend to rebel. Many suffer from low self-esteem issues.

The unjustified abusive behavior of our adult children is creating a lifetime of emotional problems for our grandchildren. When grandparents are suddenly taken away from a child, it is traumatizing to them. Removing this support system causes the child to feel less safe in their world. When this severe form of child abuse is taking place, it is a time when the child(ren) should have a grandparent there to provide them a sanctuary. These children will become adults who do not trust those close to them. Who is there to help our grandchildren?

Research needs to be done on the long-term impact on children if their grandparents are prevented from seeing them. However, we do know the effects on a child when a targeted parent is alienated from a child regarding Parental Alienation.

- Low Self Esteem
- Depression
- Drug and Alcohol Problems
- Lack of Trust
- Alienated from Their Own Children
- Divorce

Alienation has deep effects. The little ones are left wondering why grandma and grandpop are not coming to visit with them anymore. Grandchildren who have been alienated from the loving grandparents may have anxiety of lose or death of a parent or grandparent. The grandchildren may feel powerless and hopeless about being unable to communicate with their grandparents. It is cruel to deny these children any knowledge of their extended family. They may feel guilt or responsible for not being able to stop the alienation. They become confused not understanding why this is happening, and get mixed messages about what family relationships should be in a "normal" environment. It may cause them to create fantasies. Children who experience alienation of family members may believe that alienation is acceptable.

(Dr. Baker) …such parents employ and manipulate their children to serve this need by inducing them to abandon the targeted parent. These children quickly learn that their rejection of the targeted parent is the price to pay to for feeling acceptance and love from (or not to banished by) this alienating parent. The child has the ever-present fear that if one parent can be banished, they can be abandoned, too. To avoid pain, the child anxiously maintains a close relationship with the alienating parent.

(Dr. Golly) When you erase family from children's lives, you pay for it. The attachment of a grandparent when broken by these parents is a very sick thing. It is considered by experts a very severe form of child abuse.

(Dr. Bone, Dr. Caddy, 2017 AGA presentation) Alienation positions children as objects whose connections with grandparents can be controlled solely by the parent, without regard for the ill effects of separations. These children are being used as accomplices in the war of power and control. The alienator enmeshes the children into beliefs of their own. The grandchildren are forced into a limited circle of family to whom they can turn for support.

Unless there are very sound reasons for denying access to grandparents, leading experts in the field of alienation state that it is an act of emotional and psychological abuse of both the grands and the grandchildren.

Breaking this bond is considered a severe form of child abuse, and a severe form of elder abuse. Alienating parents use outrageous claims (to the grandchildren) to distance the child from the grandparent. The worse the alienator, the greater the risk for the children.

(Dr. Golly):

> Grandparent Alienation affects our grandchildren's own ability to trust their own perceptions, their instincts, or to feel entitled to protect themselves from destructive people. The children may form a negative picture of the formerly loved grandparent from whom they are kept separated.
>
> Alienating parents are role-modeling that the way to deal with anger and conflict is to sever all connections. The lesson learned is that the response to family and other relationship issues is to shut down the heart, and walk away. They become adults who do not trust those close to them. They learn that the only family members that really matter are their parents, and that parents are the only ones who really care about them. This can create an undesirable and unrealistic dependence on parents. The children are not developing their critical thinking skills. They are living in a cult-like environment.

(Kubler-Ross & Kessler) Children often fill in gaps with thoughts like, 'It must somehow be my fault." Children are old enough to grieve if they are old enough to love; they are the "forgotten grievers". They often lack the words to put to their emotions, and since their lives are just beginning, how can we expect them to understand life's endings?

(Dr. Caddy):

If you begin to see the alienation process, become informed. Try to help the grandchild gain access to the other healthy people or relatives. Talk to the child. Tell the children you love them, and you will always try to be there to talk and listen. With age-appropriate children say, "I'm glad you are smart enough to see the difference between right and wrong, and that you strive to do the right thing." Do not criticize the alienating parent. Say, "I'm sorry you have to hear these things. I love you."

After bonding with your grandchild for several years, your grandchild's love for you is paramount and solid. Given that your grandchild was with you during the very significant and formative years, their brain developed and "fired" thru love for you. The attachment bond is fairly well completed by age 3 to 5, and happens neurologically thru the bond between caregiving grandparent and child. The toxic mother cannot erase this.

(Dr. Bone) Kids learn not to trust those close to them now and in adult life. They are being brainwashed (cult-like) to banish those who truly love them and they love without provocation.

International leader in research for PAS, Amy J. Baker, PhD, has brought some of our cult-related insights into the field of family environments in which children need to maintain total loyalty to one parent at the cost of a relationship with the other parent. Likewise, with Grandparent Alienation, the alienator's spouse and their children are being manipulated to target the rejection of the grandparents. Psychological harm can result. Low self-esteem, guilt, depression, and lack of trust may be the after effects of this alienation process.

Children of alienation have feelings of anger and fear. These young victims suffer from anxiety of lose. Forbidden to have good relationships with their grandparents, grandchildren are most certainly torn emotionally, and the longer this goes on, the more chance there will be long-term ill effects. As they try to survive this childhood trauma of the sudden disappearance of their grandparents who have loved them unconditionally, they need to talk about their feelings. Who is there to help these children as they live with this chaos?

(Dr. Baker) Grandchildren often come to realize that their rejection of the grandparents is the price they must pay for feeling acceptance and love from the alienators. Unfortunately, this alienation negatively impacts not only on grandparents, but extends to the children who miss out on the love and attention that could be coming their way.

We as adults can seek help in many directions, but who can the children turn to as they experience the chaos in their homes, and the questions in their minds? What can these confused broken-hearted grandchildren do? When the child's welfare should be everyone's priority, these poor children are forced to deal with their deep intense feelings on their own.

The true, loving, supportive presence of EVERY family member is ESSENTIAL to the healthy development of every child. Family cannot come and go (Joan Luby, MD, psychiatrist).

Grandparents play a vital role in the lives of grandchildren. Grandchildren deserve grandparents, and the grandparents should be there for the safety and well-being of their grandchildren. Severing the bonds in a GP-GC relationship is certainly not in the children's best interest.

Doesn't the alienating parent understand that their children learn this lesson from THEM, and then will most likely repeat this in the next generation! Don't they realize forbidding the children from having a good relationship with their grandparents and other members of the family, being isolated from people who love them most, is harmful to the child?

(Golly 2016) A parent's decision to terminate a GP-GC relationship as pawns in a diabolical psychological chess game is detrimental to the children. Studies found that grandchildren who reported greater closeness to grandparents experienced fewer problems.

Grandchildren may be told stories of misinformation. Therefore, they may appear uneasy, nervous, frightened, or act strangely around you. Should your grandchild have an unexpected encounter with you, the child may demonstrate negative reaction.

(Dr. Bone/ Dr. Caddy 2013 AGA presentation):

> When he grandchild doesn't spend quality time with us, this sometimes-horrifying information on a neurological level can produce an anxiety-based response of "Fear, Fight, Flight" when they see you; especially if the alienating parent is present. When they go into this automatic nervous system response of Fight or Flight, their body may interpret this event "not okay", and may perceive this encounter as threatening. The grandchild who was previously loving and excited to see you, may now act negatively toward you. They now have feelings of anxiousness and fear knowing if they defy their alienating parent, there will be a penalty to pay. These precious grandchildren do not have the resources to help them cope with such emotional turmoil. They are victims.

The child is frightened and has no one to go to. He must live with these alienating parents.

The deliberate misunderstandings about timing of the grandparents' visits are common. When visitation is permitted, parents often exert some kind of negative pressure on the situation, making the children feel strange about being friendly toward their grandparents. Should you have an unexpected rendezvous with your grandchild, especially if the parent is with the child, the child may have a strange negative reaction toward you. If they seem uneasy, anxious, or frightened in your presence it is because their behavior is being controlled. They know they must comply with their parents' wishes. They know that if they defy the position of the alienating parent, if they show love and attention toward you, there will be a penalty to face. These children are truly victims.

The Fight or Flight response is something that occurs in everyone's body. If you are in a situation that you interpret as threatening, your nervous system's reaction is to fight or flee. We have a strong physiological response to stressful situations. Your heart rate increases, your breath rate quickens, you begin to sweat; you are ready for battle, or you are ready to run. Children only know they feel bad, or sad, and have no control over their circumstances. Tension from alienation in the family is felt by these children. They may even internalize this as having done something wrong themselves to actually cause the estrangement.

If you have ever experienced this negative reaction from your grandchild, understand that they are only protecting themselves. Stay calm, and tell the child you love them. Depending on their age, tell them that you are glad they know the difference between right and wrong.

(Dr. Bone):

The frightening stimulus triggers the Fight or Flight response in the child's brain. Driven by the amygdala (part of the brain involved in emotions and fear) and weakens the sensory response in the frontal cortex. He has a startle response. The structure of the brain encourages this. We are quick to develop a bias, especially if it has to do with danger. Anxiety response, or the fight or flight response is important for our survival. We are hyper-focused, more vigilant. So, when the child is told all kinds of alarming stories, it creates a response we see on a neurological level. Stories become reality in the child's mind and they become visual images in the child's mind/. The child can recall an experience as memory when, in fact, it has a very different source, well, the alienating parent.

(Dr. Caddy) advises:

Do not hold your grandchild accountable for inappropriate and disrespectful behavior in this predicament. These situations are not normal circumstances. Children are literally being placed in a situation where in order to be loved by the parent, they must reject the grandparent.

> If you do get to spend time alone with your grandchildren, given time with you they will thaw from their fear, and the from the brainwashing attempts. They will come to know your kind gentleness. If you get the chance to be with them, just tell them you love them, that you are truly a good person, and that you are glad they know the difference between right and wrong. Do not say anything negative about their parents. Just show love and tenderness toward them. They will remember how they felt when they were with you.

> Say, "I am glad you are smart enough to see the difference between right and wrong, and that you strive to do the right thing. I am sorry you have to hear these things. I love you."

> If you have been isolated, try to find a bridge person who can pass along your messages of love and trying to be with them. Try to help the child gain access to other healthy people or relatives.

(Dr. Golly) Your grandchildren might SAY they don't want the visits, and protest; however, they don't really want you to stop trying to see them.

Currently, they likely HAVE to conform to what the alienator says, in order to avoid a loyalty bind. But deep inside, they are dying to see you.

Of course, grandparents cannot know what is being said about them out of their presence, but when previously affectionate grandchildren become distant or fearful, that could be a red flag. When parents deny their children contact with others whom they care deeply about, *anger* can become a problem outside of the home. The *child's* behavior can become aggressive. Grandchildren who suffer with anger issues due to a very controlling parent have a sense of helplessness. They can sense when things are not fair or right. It is troublesome for grandchildren to feel mixed emotions when their true feelings are being denied expression. They may be unable to protect themselves from the control of the parent. If the parent's mood often changes from rage to loving, this chaos may cause children to be afraid and lack trust in authority figures. They may feel it is not safe to love or attach.

Those who alienate want power and control. They set the rules for the family. When the alienating parent is a bully in the home, they are role-modeling bad behavior in front of their impressionable children. Children learn from what they witness.

Generally speaking, grandchildren who have bonded with you and knew you by age 3 -3 ½ still adore you under it all. The underlying bond flows through based on emotion. If an opportunity presents itself, there are things you can say to them depending on their ages. Using your intuition, knowing your own family best, tell the children you love them and that you will continue to try to be with them to talk and listen.

4

Schools

"The kids' school counselors don't want to deal with a matter like this. Again, they cite privacy issues. People don't think the way you do. They don't care and do not want to get involved. Parents can rear their children however they wish, unless they are being physically abused."

"If I go to the school, I could be causing more problems for my grandson if they call my daughter-in-law."

"My grandson is acting out in pre-school. I feel so helpless. Wish I could be there for him."

"His first-grade teacher said she has six boys in the class with anger management issues."

Grandchildren living in chaos may have difficulty focusing and learning, and their grades may decline. AGA's form letter *Dear Educators* (available at end of book) for school staff may be copied and sent to the superintend of schools, school administrators, guidance counselors, and nurses. You may choose to do so anonymously. It brings awareness to this issue and asks that they keep an eye on our precious grandchildren whom we are not allowed to observe and protect. We must inform those who can help.

So many stories have been shared with AGA about the psychological trauma to the young ones who have abruptly had the relationship with their loving and caring grandparents severed. There are children sitting in classrooms filled with anger issues who know no other way than to act out in the preschools, middle schools, and high schools.

Due to the Right to Privacy laws in several states, the school system is unwilling to confront these policy issues and the effects of Grandparent Alienation on students. When approached, they are not considerate of the emotional needs and rights of the children. They will be startled to learn the dynamics of Grandparent Alienation, but are unlikely to cross legal barriers. Nevertheless, it is important to educate the school staff.

(Rev. Dr. John Killinger):

> AGA does not seek intervention from the school district, but rather our purpose is to identify a situation that in some cases certainly interferes with the schools carrying out their mission to educate our children.
>
> Educators are well aware that emotionally upset children will not be able to benefit fully from their work. Our intention is to make teachers, counselors, psychologists, nurses, and administrators aware of a problem to which most are unaware. Parental Alienation Syndrome PAS and Grandparent Alienation GA can tear a child's world apart. The frequently sudden and complete removal of a loving and caring family member is quite emotionally traumatic. Behavioral problems, acting out, depression, and unwillingness to participate can be signs of this traumatic separation. Our goal is to make the school staff aware of this alienation as a possibility when a child presents with an emotional/behavioral problem.
>
> Our schools need to become aware of the human tragedy of alienation. There are literally millions of children growing up without the opportunity to know and love one half of their family.

Our youth, our grandchildren, have no one to turn to regarding the emotional chaos. Staff members must become aware of the plight of so many children of all ages.

The school system might assist the children regarding awareness, prevention, and counseling by possibly offering a confidential "go to" person for grandparents to inform the school of any immediate or ongoing trauma.

Schools place an emphasis on character, family, inclusion, and community. School is a place where bullying of children is not tolerated. Bullying by students is unacceptable, but if by the middle generation? It is not entirely a question of whether anything is legal or not, but rather if it is right and in the interests of our children. How are innocent grandchildren going to feel when their teachers innocently or casually ask them about their family and their grandparents? Imagine their confusion. The school system should be there to assist children who are suffering from this emotional trauma.

As a grandparent, investigate what kind of contact would be permissible at the school. Public and private schools each have different criteria regarding your visitation. Find out what the perimeters of your visit would be. Ask specific questions about your attending sports activities, school plays, concerts, holiday performances, graduation ceremonies, possibly volunteering, and even standing outside the building or at the bussing area to see the children.

You may schedule an appointment with the administrator to bring awareness to PAS/Parental Alienation Syndrome and Grandparent Alienation. Anonymity is your choice. At the appointment, lead with AGA documents to validate your position.

AGA grandparents have taken or sent a gift, card, fruit basket, or flowers for a birthday surprise. The school officials might call the parent, who may disapprove of your attempt. However, some get very lucky. Sometimes the gift is delivered to the child's classroom. In some cases, they actually call the child to the front office so you can hand the gift to your grandchild. It is worth a try. This method may work one time only, until the parents put a stop to it. But, think of the joy the two of you just shared! Think how very meaningful this would be for your grandchild to actually witness how hard you tried to be with them.

Professional consultant to AGA and family law attorney Charles D. Jamieson presenting at AGA International Conferences 2017 stated:

> Do not allow fear to be your guide. Decide what you think is the right thing to do for the well-being of your grandchild. When you take action, attend an event at a school, or whenever you attempt an unannounced visit to your grandchild or adult child, always have a witness with you.

> Schools can offer an opportunity for GP-GC contact. Elementary teachers are drastically underfunded in terms of providing supplies to their classroom. Consider donating supplies, or becoming a classroom sponsor or volunteer. If you can't get into your child's classroom, then volunteer in other areas of the school. Become involved in the school's clubs. You can either volunteer your time or your money. Sponsor signs around the school. Sponsors of school activities often have a recognition banner on the school grounds or within the school itself.

> Middle school and high school teachers are also in need of supplies. Communicate with each individually and ask how you may assist them, which in turn would be helping your grandchild. Perhaps

you can obtain a copy of the school's yearbook, newspaper, or bulletins. See about becoming a sponsor, volunteer, or participant of your grandchild's extracurricular activities. Attend all school events in which your grandchild participates.

Find out in which clubs, sports, or other activities in the community they participate. If it is a community-based recreation program, then volunteer or become a sponsor. Do not be afraid to coach. If they have private lessons or tutors in studying music, find out when the music recital is going to occur. If some event is going to take place such as equestrian, recital, weight-lifting meet, etc.; try to obtain a schedule of games or completions and attend each one. Obtain a copy of the practices and occasionally show up to watch. Do not approach the parent when you do so.

Numerous AGA grandparents have shared the advantages they have gained by hiring a private detective to answer questions they alone have not been able to accomplish. Try to get recommendations for this investment.

Attorney Jamieson discussed dealing with authorities. He encouraged grandparents to always remember that school officials, including teachers and school administrators, do not wish to become involved in an interfamily squabble. Therefore, he suggests you not try to get the teacher to take sides or believe in your story.

Attorney Jamieson's final words at the AGA International Conference 2017 were, "Don't give up. Keep trying anything and everything."

5

Complex Dynamics of Grandparent Alienation

"We have been going through extremely difficult times since the birth of our grandchild. I know the old saying "things could be worse" could apply here, but to us, it is as bad as it gets."

"My daughter had always been the ideal daughter. She was caring and never mean-spirited, selfish or demanding. She had many friends, a sunny disposition and was fun to be with. But now, in four years of marriage, she no longer has these attributes. In fact, she has become like him."

"His wife is very domineering and she told him it was her or us!! He said this in an email to my daughter. He had to make a choice!"

"First she convinced our son to move to the state of her mother. Once the baby was born, he was completely controlled."

"I found out that that my son and his wife had a baby. We were dying to see our grandbaby so we drove over a thousand miles to where they now live. We showed up on the front porch asking to see our son and they baby. Or son came outside, did not invite us in, and demanded that we leave the property or he would call the police. I stood my ground as he summoned the police. After telling the policeman our story he said," Madam, wait here a minute. Your son is going to talk to you." He went inside and made our son come out on the porch to talk. Unfortunately, he was adamant about not letting us see the baby. We had to turn around without accomplishing our mission."

53

"I did not know about gas-lighting and her propensity to control, manipulate, and coerce. I know better now."

"Our S-I-L is exerting negative pressure when we are allowed to visit."

"My D-I-L often deliberately tells me there are misunderstandings about the timing of my visits."

"Knowing that my son is in the middle of some horrible mind-controlled game, I am constantly between being so angry at him that I want to scream at him and being worried that he will someday harm himself. What are my grandchildren going through? I haven't seen them in five years."

Abandoned Parents, the Devil's Dilemma, Wildey) The person your adult child marries is hell bent on building a successful family (in their own narcissistic image) and that means no interference from anyone is tolerated. "This statement helps explain why all hell broke loose when the baby was born. I was going over there every two weeks to deliver groceries or diapers until one day she said, 'You can only come over when your son is here.' I have not been back since."

"I believe these little texts and coming out to see me is like he is coming up for air while underwater. When she sees him trying to reach out to me, she yanks his chain and pulls him underwater again."

'I feel so frightened for my grandchild that I'd gladly give up ever seeing her again if only my daughter would wake up and begin acting in her best interests, and start meeting the little one's needs instead of her husband's. I get "secret" texts and updates from my daughter occasionally, but they scare rather than comfort me."

"The signs were on the wall in the early stages of their relationship."

"Our daughter-in-law emailed that we were welcome to come over for birthday cake after the birthday dinner, and that we were to arrive at 5:15 and could stay till 5:45." They make a lot of petty rules that only become more difficult, and seem to have no purpose but to upset us."

"My little grandson lived with me for four years because my daughter had a drug problem. When she qualified to get him back, she cut me off."

"We felt more and more uncomfortable every time we were around them. We felt so sad for our daughter to have this new husband acting disrespectful to her. Our good deeds for them were turning sour. Tactics were being used to cause wedge issues for the purpose of alienating us from our daughter and grandson."

My D-I-L is obsessed with food control. I ask what I can feed them, only to have her get angry with me for serving it. I oblige her wishes, but the list keeps changing."

"She lies, tells half-truths, changes a story to fit her need, and gossips and slanders our other children and us. She is insecure, immature, and has cut off all ties with our other children and us. She has also cut off ties with all of my son's friends."

"My daughter cut off our relationship before she had children. Then she would come back into our lives until someone said or did something that she didn't like or agree with, then she would be gone again."

"The more I talk with clarity and not emotion to others, the more I hear similar stories. Families have become fragmented at a dear cost to the kids who need the stability of loving grandparents in their lives. There is a new sense of entitlement and unreal expectation in some of our children. The opposite of how we were. We were raised to honor, respect, and look out for our parents even when we thought they were humanly flawed."

"*I am a mental health professional. My practice specialized in abuse and violence. So, when my daughter became interested in her now husband, I felt I needed to caution her. I saw him as a controlling man. Only once my husband and I talked to her to let her know our concern, that his controlling behavior was a red flag for domestic violence. We did our best to be supportive. We established a relationship with them, and babysat regularly for the grandkids. We put up with his verbal abuse. Guess what, all my professional experience proved to be correct. She is now totally estranged from us and her siblings.*"

Entering the Baby Boomer era, the television industry helped create a stereotype of the American nuclear family. What these baby boomers imagined for their futures never included a thought that someday they would be cut off from their grandchildren by their own sons and daughters.

The way in which different social classes of families growing up in America were portrayed on the popular TV series back in the day, has changed dramatically. Over the years, the perfect nuclear families have become more inclusive. The traditional family structure in the United States is created at birth and establishes ties across the generations. The extended family can hold a significant emotional role for the nuclear family. In the recent decades, alternative family forms have become more common, causing families to adapt to influential changes.

When a couple marries, everyone roots for their happiness. Families gather to celebrate at the wedding, intending to remain part of their lives forever. As newly married couples seek independence, it should not mean that they severe the emotional bonds with parents and extended family. (Dr. Bone 2017) The failure to manage these bonds puts the marriage at risk, as highly charged tensions of conflict with in-laws spread to marital conflicts.

Research shows that in-law relationships are a key determinant of marital happiness. Balancing loyalty to a spouse with the lifetime bonds of attachment and obligations to parents and the extended family members, can hold deeply felt worries. The effort to accommodate a spouse's family would greatly benefit a marriage. Doing this would confirm that you are committed to the feelings and needs of your spouse. You do this because you love your spouse. By staying on good terms with your spouse's relatives, you are honoring and promoting your relationship.

(Dr. Bone 2017) When a toxic spouse succeeds in cutting off contact with family members of their spouse, they most likely feel they have settled by making some sort of peace in their own home. They have chosen to protect or at least align with their spouse for a variety of reasons. As the times and distance between the targeted son or daughter and his parents increases, the influence of the alienating spouse becomes stronger and more insistent. The balance of power and control gained, leaves the alienating spouse to rule the relationship, placing the other more accommodating spouse in a secondary position. Should your child make attempts to be with you, the toxic spouse will most likely come down harder on them with a cycle of denigrations.

We have all been involved with toxic people at some point in our lives. These are the people who make you feel bad about yourself, or are critical of you. If you challenge their impressions, they will blame you and declare everything your fault. Toxic people can destroy your relationships, wear down your self-esteem, and cause you to feel so bad after being around them.

Sometimes toxic people aren't immediately identifiable, but eventually their true nature shows through. As a bully, they thrive on dominating and humiliating those they perceive as weaker than them. They systematically destroy your sense of well-being, happiness, and peace.

(Dr. Caddy 2013) Grandparent Alienation is a sign of a troubled marriage. When our adult children exist in unhappy marriages, they may not want us to see the ugliness in their lives. These unhealthy minded adult children may not want for their parents to be happy.

The majority of alienated grandparents have reported to AGA that they had a good relationship with their adult children prior to the marriage, or moving in with their partner. Yet, many grands have stated that the signs were there during the dating years, or when the ring was placed on their finger.

(Dr. Baker) When a young person with limited prior relationship experience choses a charming manipulator, he or she may not be able to recognize it until it's too late to get out of the relationship. People who present themselves as loving, honest, caring, and committed but are actually selfish, deceitful, controlling, and manipulative chose a trusting mate who doesn't realize to whom they are truly attaching themselves. You don't just marry the person; you marry his or her family. You marry the dynamics of your spouse's history growing up in that environment. Unaware of a possible disaster waiting to happen, they fall victim to domestic abuse in which their spouse systematically cuts them off from friends and family.

(Dr. Bone 2013) A spouse often takes on the personality of the alienating spouse. When your son or daughter marries, they are marrying the psychology of that person and their family. Therefore, issues they had with their own parents can become the issues they will have with you. They may have felt over-controlled, rejected, devalued, or abandoned. They may convince your son or daughter that you as a parent are much more critical and rejecting than you are, or were when raising your child.

(Dr. Baker) In order to gain advantage in the relationship and exercise their control, they prey on the other person's fear of abandonment, fear of anger, or inability to stand up for themselves.

Grandparent Alienation is mind control within the family (Bone/Caddy AGA Presentation 2013). Brainwashing is the theory that a person's core beliefs, ideas, affiliations and values can be replaced, so much so that they have no autonomy over themselves and cannot think critically or independently. The first step towards brainwashing begins with isolation because having friends and family around you is dangerous to them. The last thing a brainwasher wants is for someone with a different opinion to theirs questioning what you are now being asked to believe. The isolation could start in the form of not allowing access to family or friends or constantly checking where someone is and who they are with.

Neuro Linguistic Programming is a common dynamic of GA. It is mind control within the family. It is "behind the back" constant indirect criticisms and lies. The alienating spouse undermines the grandparent by telling your son or daughter day after day, month after month, and year after year pathological lies about you. (Dr. Bone 2012) Eventually, the mind automatically forms a pathway so that when your child hears the words, "Your mother", your adult child automatically thinks, "My mother is crazy!" Your child now often believes the lies about who you are. This is classic triangulation. Once established, it can result in the alienating spouse using your son or daughter as the bully to keep away you and others they do not want in the family.

(Dr. Bone 2017) Grandparent Alienation is a matter of power and control which begins with the undermining daughter–in-law, daughter, son-in-law, or son. Grandparents become the victims of classic triangulation when a spouse sets up and uses their partner as the bully to get rid of those they no longer want in the family. They put your adult child into a loyalty bind.

The targeted spouse tries to manage this reality by staying in the middle of a situation which contradicts their own value system. The targeted spouse is befuddled as how to maintain two significant relationships, one as the son or daughter and one as to the husband or wife. Your son or daughter must abide by the rules to prevent chaos.

(DiSalvo) Once they are certain of the story, they stop listening to the part of their brain that says it might be wrong. A schema of the family becomes embedded in the person's mind, and information that does not fit that schemata is selectively ignored and actively rejected. Di Salvo explains how neuroscience has uncovered the basis of their not wanting to change their point of view. He states that being uncertain is an extremely uncomfortable place for our brains to live, and that the greater the uncertainty, the worse the discomfort. In this way the negative message the alienating parent wants you to absorb about the targeted (grand)parent sticks to their brain.

Grandparent Alienation is not just about family relationship issues. Leading international experts in the field of Alienation who collaborate with AGA state that these isolating adult children frequently have personality disorders. They include but are not limited to narcissism, anti-social personality disorder, borderline personality, anxiety disorder, and delusional disorder.

(Dr. Caddy 2013):

> Alienating spouses try to rewrite the history of their spouse by telling stories which are magnificent in their absurdity. This dynamic involves stories/untruths that are absurd and outrageous; causing someone to believe, as fact, something that is not existent in reality. The dynamics may involve traits of anti-social behavior, borderline personality disorder, narcissism, paranoid personality disorder, or unresolved childhood issues. The spouse and others

who want to 'belong' play along becoming enablers. As one parent denies access, the other remains passive to keep peace and balance in the relationship. The husband and wife do a pathological dance together, deeming another person pathological. Alienators believe the "stories" and abandon rational assessment (Stockholm Syndrome). They no longer have the ability to rationally interpret their world. It is cult-like thinking. It cannot occur without this isolation, or without the ability and use of control. Fear is an important aspect of this situation and relationship; and, it is necessary to sustain it.

Grandparent Alienation often shows its ugly face when grandchildren arrive. Becoming a Grandma or Grandpop has taken on possible new concepts. Unfortunately, these all too often include devastating emotionally traumatic results.

(Dr. Caddy 2017) Grandparent Alienation exists when a GP-GC relationship is transformed to reject a formerly loved grandparent due to programming by the alienator - NLP. Neuro Linguistic Programming is the result of one or more persons actively working to turn an adult child against their parent. It exhibits itself through jealousy, raging, secrecy, pathological lying, or the twisting of truths to improve their position in cutting off the grands. GA is about insecurity, some level of personality disorder, or unresolved childhood issues. Brainwashing, mind control, and neuro-linguistic programming are used to perpetrate this cruel and destructive behavior. Alcohol and drug use can exacerbate the problem. Alienators manipulate their universe and use cult-like thinking as they play out this tragic game.

(Dr. Coleman 2019 AGA International Conference) Generally, men have fewer friends. They consider their wife as their friend. If their only friend is rejecting of them, the wife becomes more powerful in the relationship. The son has to buy into his wife's characterization of the targeted grandparent. She might be making accusations such as, "You are such a Mama's boy; you need to separate from her."

The psychological stress of holding the belief of the toxic spouse along with their own value system keeps them stuck in the middle. To escape this would mean they would have to face the manipulating spouse who holds the power and control. When a toxic D-I-L is the controlling spouse, she "forces" her husband into a position of pathological adaptation. He must play along abiding by her rules to keep peace and balance in the relationship. In order to get himself out of the middle, to reduce his discomfort, and restore balance in the relationship he gives up his attitudes, beliefs, and behaviors leaving the grandparent with the insufferable feeling of being defeated by the betrayal. (Dr. Bone 2017) Pathological Adaption is necessary to get out of the middle – to lessen the cognitive dissonance. The spouse therefore takes on the personality of the alienating spouse.

Cognitive dissonance is the dynamic of Grandparent Alienation which results in the targeted spouse having to reduce their discomfort and restore balance. It is particularly evident in situations where an individual's behavior conflicts with beliefs that are integral to his or her self-identity. (Dr. Caddy 2013) An example of cognitive dissonance occurs when one spouse acquires the personality of the manipulating spouse resulting in a joint delusional dance. The psychological stress of holding the belief of the toxic spouse along with their own value system keeps them stuck in the middle. To escape this would mean they would have to face the manipulating spouse who holds the power and control.

(Dr. Caddy, AGA International Conference 2019) Alienation has extreme power. It is mind control. Alienators manipulate others and control their universe. People get manipulated into situations. The more stable spouse only balances and maintains their marriages by figuring their place in the system. If a person experiences manipulation and inappropriate or extreme mind control too much, great harm can be done. If not dealt with, there is a risk of progression. "Honor thy father and thy mother", and "Thou shall not bear false witness" gets lost.

Adult children who are being manipulated by their controlling spouse can tell themselves that a short life filled without their parents is better than a long life devoid of their children. When there are conflicts between thoughts, beliefs, and opinions, they take steps to reduce the dissonance and feelings of discomfort. When there is an inconsistency between attitudes or behaviors (dissonance), something must change to eliminate the dissonance. They can go about doing this by decreasing the importance of the dissonant cognition. They will find some way to justify their behavior. They may achieve this balance by believing that their parent is the guilty party, or that they must place their husband or wife in the primary relationship position. Changing the conflicting cognition is one of the most effective ways of dealing with dissonance, but it is also one of the most difficult, particularly in the case of deeply held values and beliefs.

The targeted spouse wants to seek relief and keep a likeness of peace in the home. They are not willing to lose the love of their children by going against or divorcing the alienating personality. They do not want to become the victim of Parental Alienation Syndrome.

(Dr. Coleman 2019) The husband acknowledges her power and reconciles by taking on the belief system of his wife. He shuts down when out-classed by his wife, the gatekeeper. The wife makes him as in-defensive as possible.

(Dr. Bone 2013) When a powerful alienating spouse succeeds in cutting off contact with family members, the targeted spouse most likely feels they have settled by making some sort of peace in their own home. They have chosen to align and protect their spouse for a variety of reasons.

As the time and distance between the targeted son or daughter and his or her parents increases, the influence of the alienating spouse becomes stronger and more forceful. The balance of power and control gained leaves the alienating spouse to command the relationship, placing the other more accommodating spouse in a secondary position. There are numerous tactics that manipulators use to maintain their power and control. Should your child make attempts to be with you, the toxic spouse will mostly likely come down harder on them with a cycle of denigration that is unjustified or exaggerated. Failure to manage these bonds puts the marriage at risk.

(Letchworth 2011 AGA Elder Abuse presentation):

> Any type of abusive relationship is about power and control. You may not think the relationship you have with your alienator was abusive, however there are two ingredients that an abusive situation is made of - power and control. Power and control consist of coercion and threats, intimidation, privilege, isolation, minimizing and blaming, emotional abuse and /or humiliation, and will turn children and/or friends against you. All of these aspects are horrible, but they are effective in obtaining this power and control over the victim.

> Alienators often tend to be the most charming people. They will slowly gain control over a period of time. Because they are so manipulative, most people won't realize what is going on. If this behavior had presented itself in the beginning of the relationship, you would have done some things differently.

> The emotional abuse can be so arresting of the person's spirit that it becomes more bearable to give in to it then to fight it. Abusers prohibit any non-supporting opinions, undermine a person's confidence, and punish by arousing humiliation, isolation,

guilt, and anxiety. These tactics can be creating fear in both the grandparent and the grandchild, enough fear to cause the desire to contact each other to be stifled.

The parents use an authority privilege against the grandparent and the child. Children do not always see the abusive behavior, but they are very sensitive and are usually aware. They observe the tone and demeanor of the parents. They can feel powerless and hopeless, possibly thinking they have created a cause for the separation. The grandchildren are confused, and don't know how to act. What was right before, is unsure to them now.

Coercive control, the psychological influence which aims to overcome the individual's critical thinking abilities and free will, plays a significant role. The victims usually lose their ability to make their independent decisions. Their critical thinking, defenses, cognitive processes, values, ideas, attitudes, conduct and ability to reason are undermined. The victims become unable to make the normal, wise, or balanced decisions which they most likely or normally would have made had they not been unknowingly manipulated. These tactics make the person re-evaluate the most central aspects of their experience of self and prior conduct in negative ways. Efforts are designed to destabilize and undermine the targeted person's basic consciousness, reality awareness, world view, emotional control, and defense mechanisms. The targeted one is guided to reinterpret his or her life's history and adopt a new version of causality.

People who need to exercise their control over another person are engaging in abusive behavior. In Dr. Baker's book, *Surviving Parental Alienation...A Journey of Hope and Healing* she throws light upon abusers as having a sense of entitlement, a characteristic of narcissistic personality with a right to treat others as he or she wants with no regard for others' rights or feelings. She explains a sense of entitlement being pervasive in the alienation process. She reveals how personality disorders such as narcissism, borderline, and anti-social provide a psychic platform for alienation in her book *Adult Children of Parental Alienation Syndrome: Breaking the Ties that Bind*.

Dr. Baker notes that the nature of a person with narcissistic personality predisposes them to be unconcerned with the feelings or needs of others. She examines their possessiveness, the limiting of time, attention, and contact toward others as being motivated by difficulty in sharing the loved one with others. She explains how their feeling of superiority and being justified with their lack of empathy paves the way for the alienation. Their feeling of superiority over their target affords them the confidence that they are right, and that the targeted person's thoughts and feelings are no longer important. They do not take responsibility for the harm that their behaviors have caused. Baker states, "Once future alienators give themselves permission to deny the consequences of their actions and to disregard the feelings of their spouse, they have no internal constraints on their behavior. They have free rein to act as they please, regardless of the pain they are causing to their spouses."

Grandparents are shocked when they discover what is being said about them. Many have shared with AGA the horrendous tales being told, but most grandparents never learn of these absurd stories. In most cases the grandparents don't hear of these accusations against them for several years. They had no idea this was happening at the hands of the alienators in their family. Once discovered, they cannot stop the flow of lies and negative comments, because they do not have a platform to defend themselves. This is coupled with the targeted spouse being unable to believe the grandparent, because that would mean they have to look in the mirror. It would make them feel guilty and feel the emotional pain that their own parent is right!

(Dr. Baker) The art of persuasion is so compelling that the person experiences the implanted idea as authentic rather than as forced upon the from an external force. This is mind control within a family and the manipulation by a highly influential person who can play on others' underlying insecurities. The targeted spouse eventually takes on the personality of the toxic spouse becoming the enforcer and family spokesman.

Dr. Baker describes those who alienate as behaving like misguided cult leaders. She explains how couples who cut off try to influence others to join their cult-like behaviors. She states that oftentimes the cut off does not sever just one relationship, but relatives are also coerced to choose sides. Those who cut off try to convince others that they are right, and the grandparent is wrong. Those who do not join in the delusional dance are cut off.

(Wildey)There are cult-like families who target others in order to keep their own members in their group, and make clear to outsiders what their fate will be, should they defy the matriarch.

(Dr. Coleman) Your child's spouse, a family member, or some other person may be powerfully motivated and successful in persuading your child to have a negative opinion of you. This may not only distort their view of you in the present, but may cause them to rewrite their childhood.

Explaining this cult-like phenomenon Dr. Coleman states, "It has become clear that cults come in a number of shapes and sizes ranging from group membership with a powerful leader to a dyadic cult, where an estranged child is unduly influenced by a single person such as a spouse. Even a parent using Parental Alienation Syndrome can have many similarities to a cult leader."

Dr. Coleman explains that grown children who rid themselves of family members who challenge their perspective, have an interest in constructing a world where they feel safe and with less anxiety. The mother-in-law and father-in-law often become targets.

He describes this campaign by the alienating spouse to destroy the couple's relationship with the targeted grandparent as a cult-like behavior. The alienators decide who is in and who is out. The grandparent(s,) and oftentimes other family members, no longer belong, seeking to take away your support system by advocating on their own behalf.

These extremely manipulative alienators convert others to share in their delusional beliefs. This gain causes them to feel more justified in their behavior toward the targets. Having more control makes them feel more powerful. Dr. Coleman stated, "Alienators try to make you and those around you think you are "crazy" with all of their pathological lies. They target extended family members, close friends, and in many cases the alienators keep separate the two sets of grandparents."

(Golly) Research shows that when men marry, their wives are far more likely to bring them into their family fold than sons are with wives. The mother-daughter dyad in these dynamics can often be a powerful force against the son's parents. Men tend to be more likely to go along to get along rather than take a stance against their wives that results in more frequent fighting.

AGA grands have reported that these alienating adult children, who have come from loving families, have now become abusive, showing no empathy. They question why their own grown child is so determined to keep them out of their present and future. They wonder endlessly how they can be so cruel, so heartless to their own devoted parents. They don't recognize their child anymore. Would it make them feel so guilty that they cannot provide an explanation, or allow for an open dialogue? Over and over the grandparents think," Why won't they let us try to fix this?"

(Dr. Bone) Grandparents question, "How could my adult child believe this about me, his/her own parent! It is mind control which compromises the relationship with the targeted grandparent. The adult child develops a delusional system as a result of this programming, and come to believe something that is untrue and invalid. The first thing to understand is that parents who do this have a strong tendency to distort, exaggerate or even manufacture false claims about the target other alienation. They lie. Sometimes they do it intentionally, and other times they believe their own distortions and technically become delusional.

Grandparents face the obstacle of trying to make sense out of no sense. Commonly, grandparents are cut off without knowledge of why this catastrophe has occurred. They feel like their own child has broken up with them, and is no longer available. (Dr. Coleman) Most adult children don't want to talk about the estrangement because they know they wounded the parent, and don't want to be reminded of that.

(Dr. Bone, Dr. Caddy 2017 AGA International Conference) The alienators stand outside oneself and critique one's behavior so they blame someone else. Ultimately, these delusional systems create an imaginary 'reality' that is highly difficult, if not impossible to challenge, as that will destroy the false reality and cause the 'house of cards' to crumble. In effect, without the delusional system, they would have to look at themselves, which they cannot do. Thus, the delusion continues and anyone who is not susceptible or challenges is deemed destructive and alienated. Too much contact with any healthy person is therefore seen as destructive. Grandparents who are alienated should disconnect from these delusions, negative statements, and thinking. You must keep in mind that fact that you own the truth! Repeat the truth to yourself, and when appropriate, possibly to others to whom the alienator has told to not like you. Tell yourself, "I am a good and loving person."

(Letchworth 2012 AGA presentation) Alienation is frequently an escalating condition. This is clearly a matter of power and control. Power and Control is the driving force behind abuse and domestic violence. Never underestimate the power of someone to influence the situation. The goal of someone abusing a child or another relative, is power and control over them. The abuser uses any form of control they need to accomplish power and control over the victim.

Eventually, restrictions without explanation are placed on the grandparents with little regard as to the substantial risk to grandchildren. Many adult children simply declare the relationship over with no recourse to strike a compromise or discuss the matter further.

Some grands are told there will be no unsupervised visits. Others revealed that they were not permitted to hold their own grandbaby. The more destructive the alienator, the greater the risk for the children. The grandchildren are often taught not to like the grandparents by using outrageous claims. The grandchildren become the collateral damage as victims of alienation. Picking up signals that they are no longer welcome to be part of their family, grands find themselves trapped in an unfixable situation.

Stopping a bully means standing up to them. Unfortunately for the targeted grandparents the grandchildren, the targeted son or daughter does not stand up to their controlling spouse/partner to do the right thing. Though many are independent and successful in their work, they are weak at the hands of the spouse. Your adult child should compassionately explain that they have enough love for both their wife or husband and their mom and dad. They should explain how both of these relationships are important to them. If they do stand up to the alienating spouse, it may result in a threat of divorce. This can set into motion the realization how their alienating partner has succeeded in cutting their own parents off from the family, and will eventually poison their own children against them, too (PAS). Hopefully at some point, the alienating spouse will back off with the threats and agree to new ground rules for grandparent visits.

Dr. Golly's 2018 survey of AGA grandparents shows the majority who deny access to the grandchildren are female. Cut offs are mostly caused by the undermining daughter-in-law at 43%. Close behind is the daughter at 28%, followed by the son-in-law at 15%, then the son at 13%. The daughter-in-law is a powerful force against her husband's parents. Aware of the power she holds over this husband who loves her, she limits and creates restrictions for the targeted grandparents.

Continuing with the toxic D-I-L scenario, pre-isolation tactics include controlling visits and any form of contact or communication the paternal grandparent may have with the son. The D-I-L instructs how often the grandparent may send messages, and to whom the grandparent may send these messages. Frequently, the D-I-L demands that the only communication to her husband will take place through her.

AGA found that many grandparents have been told to comply to a written list of demands should they ever want to see the grandchildren again. Included in these lists are false accusations. Most who have complied with this humiliating ultimatum have reported that they just kept upping the ante. The list does however demonstrate the point of view of the alienators. The power and control dynamic taking place once again. This is just one more way the insecure controlling spouse feels they can gain more control over you. Do your best to comply. Carefully consider each word you write in response. For demands you are not guilty of, respond with something like, "I am sorry you feel this way; I had no idea you were thinking this. What can I do to improve this situation?"

The insulting announcement that unsupervised visits are no longer allowed is common. Demands on how grandparents must behave and how they are to conduct themselves with the children are common. With some, touching or holding the baby is off limits. In numerous cases, Grandpa can touch the children, but Grandma cannot, or visa/versa. They are told what and how many gifts are permissible. Stringent rules for foods for the grand-kids are commonplace; once agreed upon, the food demands are then changed. If these demands are not met, then isolation is the result.

Some adult children need to stay mad no matter what you say or do. It is your choice whether to sat boundaries limiting the stress from the emotional abuse you endure. The D-I-L may stay mad at the M-I-L or F-I-L no matter what they try to do to appease her, holding onto the grudge rather than forgive. She wants to stay comfortable in her territory, the place from which she can intimidate people. Unfortunately, if following these rules is the only way to spend time with the grandchildren, it may be worth doing for a while just to prove to them that you are not this demon that they are making you out to be. All the while, strive to form a better relationship with this gatekeeper. The prize is worth it.

Since young women usually have had more experience talking about their emotions with their mothers than sons did, it leaves the young husband more vulnerable to their wife's control and less likely to contest the argument. With alienation, the wife knows the power she has over this man who loves her. She can be quite persuasive, or make your son's life so uncomfortable that he gives up trying to have a relationship with you. Because the husbands' best friend is often his wife, he wants to avoid the loss of her affections. (Dr. Coleman) To fend off repeated arguing, sons tend to go along with their wives' stance. She decides who is in and who is out. Loyal becomes regulated by the wife as the husband frequently hands over the moral compass to their wives.

Studies in the United Kingdom and Australia report there is a substantial and growing issue of emotional and psychological abuse perpetrated by the young child's mother. In western cultures where the mother is generally perceived as the primary care giver and women are frequently responsible for negotiating family relationships, this result is unsurprising. AGA's survey also concluded that the highest percent of cut off was initiated by a daughter-in-law, followed by the daughter.

When a daughter-in-law feels threatened by the mother-son bond, she tries to weaken that kinship. They place intimidation tactics for the purpose of putting a wedge between them and us. Insecurities lead her to believe that time, attention, or love that is not directed toward her is being taken away from her. Factor in the husband's feelings of masculinity if the wife makes accusations of his dependency tie to his mom. The scenario becomes one of, "The children and I are your family now; we come first." As incidents build up over time, the message can escalate to, "Them or me; you chose. You don't get to have both!" Remember, never underestimate the power of those who alienate! They can cause terrible damage in their pathway. Just know that if she is treating you this way, she is treating others this way as well.

The majority of grands reported how uncomfortable they felt when they were granted a visit. Deliberate misunderstandings about timing of the visit are common. Grands have received actual invitations to visit the family, then upon arrival were told they had never invited them stating, "There must have been a misunderstanding". Not finding their voice or words to respond, they turn around defeated, humiliated, and in shock. Imagine having the wisdom of your 50, 60, or70 years; yet, not knowing what to say to your own son or daughter.

Grands find themselves walking on eggshells in the presence of their own child. The message received is that that they are not worthy of being treated with honestly and respect.

(Dr. Coleman) Little binds adult children to their parents these days, beyond whether the relationship feels good to them. Within this generation of parents there is a very strong sense that if a relationship, including a relationship with a parent, doesn't make you feel good about yourself or makes you feel guilty or bad that completely cutting that parent out of your life is a reasonable decision.

Grandparents live with the shame of their own children not wanting to be with them, and not being allowed to be with their precious grandchildren. Grandparents, YOU own the TRUTH.

The stories that are told radiate irrationality. Disconnect from those delusions, negative statements, and negative thinking. Unfortunately, we cannot be responsible or control what others say and do; we can only control our own thoughts and actions. Thereupon, repeat the truth to yourself, "I am a good and loving person." Do not let the unhealthy minds of others take away from you who you really are. Remind yourself of your accomplishments and all the good you have done in your lifetime. You have the healthy mind; you are the one who wants repair this.

No parent is perfect. If you did the best you could at the time, then do not shoulder all the blame. Stop blaming yourself for actions you did not cause, and attempt to make amends for actions you feel responsible. If you did not cause this alienation, then you alone cannot fix this. Ask yourself, "Were my actions really worthy of the penalty of permanently being denied the grandchild-grandparent (GC-GP) relationship?" Those who have become alienated as a result of an active campaign of denigration by family members have fallen victim.

Grandparents are confused. They ask themselves, "Who is this person?" This is not the child I raised. The suffering is so profound that they come to question, "How can I love a child don't like anymore?" These thoughts are compounded with the belief that their adult child is not suffering as well. As Dr. Baker has stated, "Grandparents, in the majority of cases your child does love you. They may not realize it at this time or behave in such a manner, but there is a connection of the heart."

It is the grandparent who must try harder to repair this relationship. GA is not about fairness. If it were fair, you would be given more time with your grandchildren. If it were fair, you would be appreciated for the time, devotion, effort, and money spent on your child. If it were fair, they would be more understanding. If it were fair, they would discuss their feelings with you. Instead, our adult children use their own children as pawns in a game.

(Dr. Bone):

> I was recently asked the following question by a grandparent. "What should I do if I think my daughter's husband is trying to turn my daughter and their children - my grandchildren - away from me?" Unfortunately, this question, or others very similar to it, are questions that I get quite frequently. I believe the best way to answer this is to step back for a moment to discuss the basics of what happens when one tries to cause a child to turn away from a parent or grandparent with whom they have had a loving and close relationship. In other words, just what happens when the process of alienation is present?

> The first thing to understand is that parents who do this have a strong tendency to distort, exaggerate or even manufacture false claims about the target of their alienation. They lie. Sometimes

75

they do it intentionally and other times they believe their own distortions and technically become delusional. Sometimes they start out intentionally lying and then they begin to believe their own lies. Very often these parents have what we refer to as Personality Disorders which make them quite blind to seeing their own distortions and lies.

With this in mind, when we think about being a target of these lies and distortions, it is important to understand that the specific lies and distortions are, while unique to each situation, form patterns that are regular and therefore predictable. The most common patterns are distortions that falsely portray one are the following. They falsely portray one as being (1) self-centered, (2) unstable and untrustworthy, (3) angry and even dangerous, or (4) hopelessly inept to the point of being unreliable and therefore potentially dangerous. While there are other themes possible, I find these to be the most common.

When one is the target of this type of alienation, it is important to identify which of these labels is being applied to oneself. For example, in the case of the grandparent represented in the question above, how is this husband influencing the grandchild to be no longer close to the grandparent and to even mistrust them? What is he or she being told? Is the grandchild being told that the grandparent is angry and self-centered? Are they being told that the grandparent is unstable and therefore not reliable? I believe that it is important to develop as sense of just how one is being falsely badmouthed. Why is this important? It is important to know this so as to avoid falling into the trap of inadvertently coming across as somehow supporting the lies and distortions being told.

In order to get how this works, it is important to understand what is referred to as "Confirmatory Bias," or "Confirmation Bias." What these terms refer to is the absolutely innate human tendency for all of us to interpret information in ways that support what we have already been told about a given person. For example, if a grandparent is being falsely described as being angry and self-centered, and this is given as the reason the grandchild no longer wants to be with them, then it is important to not inadvertently act angrily or with angry frustration even when such reaction might be quite justified. The problem is that this understandable anger and frustration over being cut out of your grandchild's life, can be misinterpreted in ways that support the very lies and distortions that have been falsely leveled against you. Instead, it is best to react to these understandable provocations with patience and calm since this kind of reaction - patience and calm - flies in the face of the distortions being made about you. While this alone does not negate the alienation, it does not support it. My point is that it is helpful to know how you are being falsely accused so that you do not react in any way that can be misinterpreted to support these false claims.

The next point I would like to make is one that often strikes parents and grandparents as unbelievable. That is, alienated children are taught or caused to believe that the target of the alienation, the parent and grandparent do not or are incapable of loving them. This strikes most alienated parents and especially alienated grandparents as absurd. I often hear, "How is this possible for them to believe this?" Alienated parents and grandparents are predictably and reliably loving and unconditional in their love. If this was not the case, why would this organization even exist?

6

Parental Alienation
Syndrome (PAS)

AGA become a 501C3 Non Profit in 2012 in our quest to help grandparents nationally. Quickly, word spread worldwide. Wanting to find answers for grandparents who were begging and praying for some form of relief, AGA Headquarters reached out to the international experts in Parental Alienation Syndrome. AGA was the first organization to connect the dynamics of PAS to Grandparent Alienation (GA). Each leading specialist in the field of alienation we reached out to saw great potential on many levels, and looked forward to working with us. During that time a grandparent told us, "When you are doing God's work, the pathway opens." AGA's professional consultants agreed to collaborate on the complex dynamics and study of Grandparent Alienation. It is because of the dedication, passion, and availability of these AGA professional consultants that we have been able to provide suggestions to grandparents from the up-to-date advice of the experts. As you continue this chapter, you will come to recognize similarities between PAS and GA. The following information regarding PAS will offer insight and help grandparents gain a better understanding.

PAS occurs when one parent attempts to turn the couple's children against the other parent. A parent who is angry at the spouse or ex-spouse accomplishes this estrangement by painting a negative picture of the other parent via deprecating comments, blame, and false accusations shared with the children.

Most often, the mother has been the alienating parent turning the children against their father. Yet, in many families it has been the father who is the toxic parent poisoning the children against their mother. In general, the alienating parent is the least emotionally healthy, and often the wealthier since the legal challenges are quite costly. Parents who poison their children's natural affection for the other parent are doing serious, even abusive, damage.

Parental Alienation Syndrome is a term coined in the 1985 by child psychiatrist Dr. Richard A. Gardner. It describes a suite of distinctive behaviors that he argued were shown by children who have been psychologically manipulated into showing. Those behaviors include unwarranted fear, disrespect or hostility towards a parent, and/or other family members. Most children described in the paper were alleged to have been manipulated by the other parent and during child custody disputes.

(Dr. Bone):

> Richard Gardner noticed a very strange reaction in divorce, where a child will suddenly have a strange reaction to one parent. He studied this and defined it as Parental Alienation Syndrome. Custodial evaluations were part of his work at the time. A child would say something that wasn't true about their own parents. Illogically, some of these allegations ere of having been abused or neglected. He made a point that the children can be induced to lie. His statement was ground breaking back then. Because of this, he has, himself, become a target, as has his work.

> Parental Alienation and PAS are two of the most destructive and devastating phenomena that can affect parents, family, friends, and especially children. Cases involving these issues are perhaps the most vexing and difficult that exist in Family Court. They

require careful and painstaking preparation, analysis of voluminous documentation, preparation of experts and collateral witnesses. They can be difficult to demonstrate in court and include arduous steps that exceed the normal representation of a Family Law case without parental alienation. These cases exploit and wear down the system and do so in the service of alienation.

(Dr. Jill. D. Sanders 2012 AGA presentation) Alienation: When a child seriously resists and/or refuses contact with one parent. It involves severe distortion on the child's part of the previous parent-child relationship or of the rejected parent's weakness. Alienation within the family at any level is an unnatural family/human condition.

(Dr. Caddy 2012 AGA presentation):

> PAS is the resulting behavior and attitudes of a child who comes to believe a parent is unworthy of a relationship. Evidence of PAS dates back to the late 19th century. We've seen more than 150 years in the mental health literature. Historically PAS did not exist, because everyone in the village knew everyone else. In the 1940's, 84% of households included three generations.

> The alienated child displays an eagerness to tell anyone who will listen how terrible the rejected parent or grandparent is. He shows reflexive support for the alienating or favored parent. The child wants to convert you to the same agenda.

> The child exhibits irrational behavior such as rage. He can't think through the problem. Rage is evidence of love for the targeted parent. He wants to drive you to accepting the situation, in the crazy place where he is.

The diagnosis is delusional disorder, an abiding conviction that the formerly loved parent is now rejected, although unjustified. The child has a delusional system as a result of programming by the alienating parent. They believe something that is untrue and invalid. It is mind control which compromises the relationship with the targeted parent. We sometimes refer to it as a *parentectomy*. When a pathological parent drives this, it can get out of control.

In the beginning, if you begin to see the alienation process, become informed. Try to help the child gain access to the other healthy people or relatives. Talk to your child. Tell the child you are always there to talk and listen. Say, "I'm glad you are smart enough to see the difference between right and wrong. You strive to do the right thing." Say to the child, "I'm sorry you have to hear these things. I love you.

Do not confront the alienating parent directly. It builds the walls higher.

Dr. Bone explained that when a child has been abused, he typically doesn't reject the parent; abuse does not turn a child away from a parent. He indicates that even an abused child tends to stay fairly attached to the parent, and the child is protective of that parent. The child may feel responsible for what happened.

When a child has had an abusive childhood, then the child becomes an adult, the controlling parent still remains a very powerful person in his psychological life. Even if there was extreme abusive treatment toward the child, it does not cause the child to hate them… though they might have been fearful. Children who have been abused by a parent tend not to be critical of that parent. A child can be angry with a parent and still want to see them, or be disconnected and still want to see them. "The adequate abuse it would take to cause a child to become alienated from that parent would be in the extreme kind of abuse over a long period of time that involves police reports and trips to the ER."

The relationship is very strong. Dr. Bone describes PAS as a poisoning of a child toward the other parent, which is a very abusive act. He observes a constant theme, repeatedly revealing itself as a child trying to contort himself into the good graces of the parent. Dr. Bone declares Parental Alienation – PAS to be an extreme and bizarre state of affairs.

Dr. Bone points out that parental flaws themselves do not cause alienation. Being an inadequate parent doesn't cause alienation. Even if one parent is less competent, it does not cause alienation. When the parent has developed a deeply grounded relationship with the child, there is no alienation. A child does not hate that parent or have a terror reaction to that parent, though he might favor one parent.

Dr. Bone states, "In PAS, the kid is connected to one parent and totally disconnected with the other parent. It is a progressive kind of process, with reflexive support of the alienating parent. The child is completely aligned with one parent and misaligned or alienated from the other. There is an absence of guilt regarding the cruelty to that parent."

The targeted parent tends to be accommodating, and not in any way abusive. They tend to be more on the enabling side of the spectrum.

Dr. Baker states, "Alienating parents are obviously trying to damage the relationship with the other parent. This is in fact very abusive and causes damage to the child.

(Edward Kruk Ph.D. Parental Alienation as Child Abuse and Family Violence): Parental alienation is manifested through a child's reluctance or refusal to have a relationship with a parent for illogical, untrue or exaggerated reasons. It is the result of one parent engaging in the long-term use of a variety of aggressive behaviors that harm, damage and destroy the relationship between a child and the other parent. The target parent is demonized and undermined as a parent worthy of the child's love and attention.

(**Dr. Bone AGA presentation**) There is a fear-based reaction regarding the alienating parent. It's either my way or the highway. If the child is positive with the targeted parent; the alienating parent treats the child as if he had betrayed them. "What are you doing?' is the fear-based response that the child has to not following the party line that the alienating parent is putting out there. The dynamic that drives this behavior is fear.

Further explaining the dynamics of PAS, Dr. Bone stated that the child has been taught that he has already lost one parent. The child does not want to lose another. The experience that loss as one of abandonment and a loss. The message to the child about the other parent becomes, "If this child displeases the alienating parent, then he withdraws his love." It is a means to keep the enmeshment going. It is chilling to the child if love and affection are withheld. "This is an important dynamic that keeps the child operating in a fear-based kind of climate, a very enmeshed relationship (that child is really prohibited from thinking independently. He goes along with the party line). We see an unusual relationship with the child and the alienating parent. The child may be protective of the alienating parent, or in cowering fear of the alienating parent. They are a unit that is bonded together in an unhealthy way."

The negative interpretation transmitted to the child is that that parent does not really love him, thinking the parent is not capable of loving. This behavioral tactic used by the alienating parent, placing him in the middle, compels the child to choose. Putting the child in the middle is a way for the alienating parent to test the loyalty. It makes the child an active participant in the alienation process. That is a survival tactic. The alienating parent creates the impression that that targeted parent is dangerous.

Dr. Bone's experience spanning decades with PAS cases has shown that even imperfect parents manage to stay connected to their children as long as it's not interfered with by the other parent. He cites alienation equal to a distortion of reality. This is accomplished by distorting the history and the qualities of that other parent to the child.

The alienating parent says all sorts of things to make the child think that the other parent doesn't love them. Dr. Bone describes the child as operating under the weight of distortion, believing that their loving parent actually has become a source of fear and danger. The child comes to believe something that really isn't true. The child sees the things the alienating parent says, these distortions, as a valid perception. When a child is told all sorts of horror stories about the parent, it will produce a kind of anxious response on the part of the child. He internalizes this, having a neurological response.

Connecting PAS to a cult-like circumstance, Dr. Bone find many parallels between cult leaders and alienating parents. It starts with the influence of the alienating parent and not as a result of that child spending time with the targeted parent. For a child to survive a divorce in a positive manner, it is best for the child to have a good relationship with both parents. PAS creates dramatic internal conflicts, and is indeed abusive.

When the child is with the targeted parent, the alienating parent frequently calls asking, "Are you okay", implying there is something really bad about being with that parent. This causes the child to think he is in an unsafe or inferior environment. Should the child witness a problem, or even alcohol or drug use in the home of the targeted parent, the child is given the responsibility of repeating this information back to the alienating parent.

The child becomes a co-conspirator. It has the appearance that it is coming from the child and not the alienating parent. This transfer of information about the targeted parent bonds him to the alienating parent. It makes the alienating parent appear to be the victim of the targeted parent. Then the alienating parent forces the child to reject the targeted parent.

(Dr. Baker) There is a spread of animosity to the targeted parent's family. When the child had a good and close relationship with a set of grandparents, suddenly they no longer have any interest in seeing them, don't want to see them, and have a critical kind of response to those grandparents. These reactions are fundamentally unnatural. We don't see this when children develop strong attachments. These behavioral manifestations are inconsistent with what we know about children and attachment to adult figures. We don't see these in normal attachment to a parent.

Books authored by J. Michael Bone, PhD and Amy J.L. Baker, PhD provide further detailed information on this topic.

7

Does Your Child Rage at You?

"He scares me."

"My husband and I were in disbelief. How could a person you've loved your whole life can act that way?"

"I was walking in a parking lot when my son called me. We had spoken about an hour before. He had hung up the phone with his usual words, "By Mom, I love you." The next call was different.; so different that it changed my life forever. I heard shouting, cursing, and name calling. These profanities were being hurled at me. These words I had never heard my child speak before. The phone went dead....and so did our relationship. Just like that. Sixty years of history gone. I asked myself what could have transpired in the past hour that I would be attacked like this? I didn't know where to turn. I was in a state of shock, and too embarrassed and ashamed to tell even my best friend that my own child had done this to me. Who was this person? I didn't recognize him. To say I was shocked, frightened, and bewildered would not do it justice."

"A friend of our daughter told someone who then felt we should be told about the birth of our first grandchild. We knew nothing of the birth for two months. We later heard our daughter went ballistic with rage at the friend for sharing the information."

Outbursts of temper or rage are a common dynamic of Grandparent Alienation. As though it weren't difficult enough enduring a disconnect, the majority of grandparents have reported to AGA that their offspring have exhibited irrational behavior such as raging. This kind of raging crushes you to your very core; in turn, it allows them to feel powerful. When your son is not in power with his wife, he uses the power with the parent. (Dr. Coleman) The fact that your adult child has to yell at you shows you how fracturable a situation they are in at this time in their lives. When an adult child yells at you instead of simply talking with you about an issue, it is an indication of their fragility or immaturity.

Unfamiliar with the dynamics of Grandparent Alienation, grandparents do not know how respond from the shock, or how to fix it. They wonder how they are going to cope with this ongoing rejection from their own child, and the isolation from their treasured grandchildren. They have been given no explanation for the raging, and they don't know where to find answers.

When verbal abuse and outbursts of anger such as rage are used, grandparents feel shock, helplessness, and frightened. The parent does not recognize this person they raised and has known for decades. Things are being shouted to them that we could never have imagined saying to our elders. Offspring who rage hold more power over their parents than anyone else could. For parents who lovingly sacrificed for so many years their time, money, and attention; they are now deprived of their dreams of this love being returned. Additionally, their sense of self-worth lies in question. The life they always thought they would have at this point has been destroyed.

When they rage at you, is sounds like they have made the decision to reject you. It does not mean that they don't love you anymore. A raging son wants to drive you to accepting the situation in the crazy place where he is. Actually, he is thinking but not saying, "Can't you see this through my eyes? Don't you know what I am going through? Don't you know what it is like for me in there? When you come around or call, you make it worse for me!" At this point you can just respond with, "This is obviously not a good time for us to be together. I will come back when it is a better time for you." This is the time for you to take control of the situation. Move from fear to control. Walk away. Do not engage in any further dialogue. Attempting to engage in dialogue when blind-sided by a raging angry adult child, would only worsen the matters at hand. The best way to end a fight is often to refuse to engage in the first place. Be on guard against their abusive tactics. Recognize them. Avoid them. And refuse to succumb to their deception.

If your child is exhibiting disrespectful abusive behavior or raging at you, let your response show self-control. Grandparents need to role model self-control. Teach the right behavior so it sinks in without yelling, making threats, or other emotional fireworks. (Dr. Coleman) It is important to keep your cool. Your child probably thrives on getting a reaction out of you. If you do get angry, you're essentially letting them control the situation. If you child continues to engage in this type of behavior, walk away from their anger. Retreating from the battleground reinforces that you want to make peace.

(Dr. Coleman) Not wanting us to see the problems in their marriage, parents have been cursed at, ignored, and shamed by their adult children. They just cannot think through the problem. If they admit to themselves that they are wrong in their behavior, then they will feel the emotional pain. A narcissist does not want to allow this feeling. A narcissist does not want to admit that he/she has done this to their parent.

Remind yourself that the majority of these adult children do love their parents. There is a connection of the heart. Only through love will you get your child back; not through criticism, demands, or added guilt. Leave the door open for them, so they know that at a more vulnerable time in their lives they can come back to you. If reconciliation is your goal, show empathy and forgive. Forgiving is not forgetting. (Dr. Baker) The majority of adult children do not hate their estranged parents; they love them. At this time, they may not realize it, or behave in the appropriate manner.

Protect yourself by thinking of all the good you have done as a parent and grandparent. Remember all the positive roles you have played in their lives. Reflect upon the good memories you shared. Do not allow them to take this away from you. Remember who you are. Their false accusations are just that; false. You own the truth. If you did the best you could at the time you were raising your child, and continued to do your best for their behalf, then do not blame yourself for their behavior. It is time to place the blame on the other side. You are responsible for your behavior and your role modeling, not theirs.

8

Fear

"I could tell you story after story about how nasty my D-I-L has been just in the few years they have been married. I no longer want to be alone in a room with her for fear she might make up some nonsense about me, or my behavior with my grandson."

"I don't know how to respond to my D-I-L when she throws slings and arrow my way…which are completely uncalled for. She speaks to me in a tone I would never have done with my M-I-L. I am being accused of things I have never done."

"Purposely, I wait a significant amount of time before I call to ask for a visit. I always feel I am annoying her. The apprehension overwhelms me. She can be sweet, or so very hurtful and denigrating. She told me I must contact her, not my son if I have a question."

My very wealthy controlling S-I-L doesn't want me to have any contact with my daughter. We had such a close relationship till the babies arrived. She chose to stay with him, and I am afraid what he might do if I try to see her."

"I flew across country in hopes of seeing my daughter and grandson. My ex-wife happened to be there. The cops were called when they spotted me in the car outside their home. My grandson who loved me saw me, and ran quickly into the house. Obviously, her mom who has always brainwashed my daughter against me, did not want me to have a conversation with my daughter or *grandson. I know I always did so much for my daughter. Her mom just won't allow me to be a part of my family."*

"I make attempts to see grandchildren. I take a witness with me as you suggested. The fear that comes over me is almost crippling each time."

Grandparent Alienation is a fear-based phenomenon. It is a predominant dynamic that enables the mean-spirited behaviors of those who alienate, and it a powerful necessity in sustaining the control of others. When grandparents are left to feel that there is no relief in sight, that they cannot fix this, fear and stress replaces it causing some to give up the hope of ever reuniting.

(Dr. Bone 2012) Fear is an important aspect of this situation and relationship; and is necessary to sustain it. They manipulate their universe and they have control.

This emotional roller coaster journey leaves the grandparents afraid to say or do anything. They try over and over again to please, but the situation usually escalates. Should they say or do something wrong, they fear future visits will be denied. Because they do not want to jeopardize the marriage by telling their adult child the horrible ways in which their D-I-L or S-I-L has been behaving toward them, the controlling spouse continues to gain more power and control.

Countless numbers of AGA grandparents have revealed their fear to interact with their own child. This fear, if obvious to their son or daughter, will give the alienator more power than they deserve. It will enhance their feeling of control over the targeted parent, which is likely the desired result they want to achieve.

Grandparents frequently describe their position as "walking on eggshells." Take a look at all they have been putting your thru. Your family has been torn apart. Your reaction of being afraid of your own child, sadness, or even anger is therefore certainly normal. Try your best to shy away from those feelings of fear, and focus on a more positive attitude of moving toward possibilities.

You make the feeling of fear real to yourself, and it can keep you stuck. You are making it a determining factor in what you think you can do. When you have fear, wondering if you are the one doing something wrong, you are letting them control your feelings. Do not allow them to rule you by fear. Fear should never dictate your actions. (Jamieson, Esq. 2017) Do not allow fear to keep you from doing what you believe is the is right thing to do as a parent and a grandparent. You are still the parent and a role model. Persevere as best you can. Find the courage to forge ahead, because your grandchildren do not want you to give up on them. Do not give up because it's too tough. Persist through hardships to succeed.

This mean-spirited manipulation of Grandparent Alienation uses the grandkids as collateral as their parents play this cruel psychological game. The grandkids are being controlled. They cannot defy the alienating parents' wishes, or there will be a penalty to pay. They have to live with these alienators. Your grandkids have been placed in a position to witness how you have been removed from their lives. Even at a young age they fear that if they defy their alienating abusing parent, they too will be "cast aside".

When you are given an opportunity to be with your grandkids, or if by coincidence you see them; they may very well appear fearful or nervous in your presence, or behave in a negative manner. This is true especially if the alienating parent is also there. The fear response causes them to act unkindly toward you. They are afraid to defy the command of the parents with whom they live. If you witness this behavior, understand that these young ones have had no one to talk to about their feelings of loss and chaos in their lives. They have not had healthy minds guiding them. Babies are not born to hate; they have role models.

(Dr. Caddy 2012 AGA presentation) If they are given time alone with you, they will thaw. Let them experience your kind loving ways. Tell them you love them, and that YOU are a good person. They need to hear this, since they have not been allowed to develop their critical thinking skills. Do not say anything negative about their parents, it would be too difficult for them. Depending on their ages you can tell them that you are proud that they know the difference between right and wrong, and that you are trying to be with them to share in activities and to listen to them. If you have no contact with the grandkids, try to find a bridge person who can relate these statements to your grandchildren.

Fear is not exclusively felt by the young or old. It has a very powerful impact upon its victim. The targeted spouse fears from witnessing how the alienating spouse has effectively gotten rid of his/her parent. It exposes the frightening possibility of this happening to them should they seek a divorce. They may choose to stay in a bad relationship to oversee the well-being of their children, and to secure themselves to being part of their kids' lives. They fear PAS which results with the child being brainwashed against them by the alienating spouse. Even the smartest, most successful, and strongest adult children can fall victim to their powerful and controlling spouse.

Some things are more important than fear. Grandparents, conduct yourself with dignity and turn your fear into action. Face the fear by proceeding as if you are not afraid. Be only afraid of standing still; doing nothing does not move things forward. Believe in yourself; carry a can-*do* attitude with you. Be the actor if you must. Do what you think is the right thing to do as a caring loving parent and grandparent. Have confidence; just do it. By seeking out opportunities in situations, or creating an opportunity, you find out how much you can achieve. Make your opportunity as often as you can. The longer the alienators get away with their behavior the more control they gain, and the longer the game continues.

Jealousy

"My daughter needed my help when she had her two children. I watched them a lot, and my grandson spent a lot of time at my house. He became very attached to me. One day my daughter sent me a video of her son saying Grammie was her best friend. That was the last day I was allowed to see them."

"Our daughter has never been able to accept the fact that her children had fun with us, and were very excited and happy to be with us. She would even say to her son when he ran toward us, 'What about me, I am your mommy!' She was even jealous of her dog's affection toward my husband. I truly believe she could not deal with the competition, in her mind, of sharing her children with us."

"My son-in-law's parents became fiercely jealous of me and openly cruel. I saw signs before the baby was born. They were jealous of my successful career, and that they lived much further from our children. When my grandchild was born, I was told that the paternal grandparents could visit, but that I was forbidden to meet my grandchild."

'We cared for my son's babies for five years as the parents worded. We were devoted to them and love them. When our daughter had a baby, we then looked after that baby and the other two. It was hard, but I wanted to be there for my children. The jealousy began from the moment my daughter's daughter was born. An ultimatum from my son's partner soon followed. Either we limit the times with my daughter and her daughter, or we would not see my son or his children anymore. We couldn't choose, so they chose for us!

Amanda

"I could sense that my daughter was becoming jealous of my loving relationship with the new baby."

"I think that the reason she said it wasn't working was because she felt threatened that the boys wanted a relationship with me, and they loved me and missed me."

"Sometimes he ran behind the couch and then sometimes would cry when I left, occasionally reaching his hands out to come to me… not them. It was enough to be threatening for a jealous person, and also any type of guilt she might feel for working and not being a stay at home mom. Hard for any mom. But kids bond. This jealousy and need to control finally had been enough. She was over ripe for any excuse to get rid of me."

"Our daughter-in-law traveled for business weekdays, so we agreed to care for our granddaughter 24/7 weekdays. We basically raised her. When her mom came on weekends, the child began to reject her for me. We haven't seen them for two years."

"I figured out, after some time, that she was also extremely jealous of my relationship with our son that she actively worked to isolate him from us."

Envy is a reaction to lacking something and wanting what someone else has. Jealousy, on the other hand, is the feeling that someone might try to take what is yours. Jealousy and envy are closely tied together when relationships between family members have broken-down. They promote negative feelings that can be destructive to relationships.

Root causes of jealousy are typically symptoms of one or more of the following: insecurity, fear, low self-esteem, a hurtful experience of abandonment in the past, intense possessiveness, or a desire to control.

It is an emotion that everyone experiences to some degree, but becomes unhealthy when someone tries to control another because of it.

Jealousy is a common emotional reaction when a person is feeling threatened. It can lead to imagining things that aren't actually there. It is likely to cause a need for one partner to prove themselves and their loyalty over and over again. This can be exhausting and prevent a relationship from growing and establishing a solid foundation.

(Hibbert, PhD) Jealousy is another reason other people can be total jerks. Highly critical people are often not happy with themselves. When they see in someone else something they're lacking, or wish they had, they'll feel a need to criticize it. Their fault-finding may be a projection of how they're worried they'll fall short.

(Ni) Once you realize that what someone else is saying is really just about them, you'll find their words don't disempower you as much.

Getting past jealousy in a relationship requires building trust. One partner must trust the other enough to know that, regardless of the circumstance, the love and respect they share will prevent outside influences from threatening their relationship. This can be difficult if one partner is insecure and struggles with trusting.

(K. Smith PsyD) Smith writes that mild jealousy is considered an instinctual reaction that makes us want to protect what we feel is ours. Unlike simply being protective, jealous feelings can balloon quickly into destructive behavior, and cause us to act in ways that are selfish and controlling. She explains how it can even cause us to assume things are happening that are not. She relates how this jealous behavior can be extremely harmful to a relationship, and how the jealous partner is needy and constantly looking for reassurance that they are the only one, and that no one is a threat to replace them. Smith states how jealously can manifest in controlling and distrustful behavior, and even physical or emotional abuse. She tells how this jealous behavior sets up a pattern of distrust that is unhealthy and can eventually cause a relationship to collapse. She cites that the foundation of any healthy and happy relationship is trust and respect, and that a person struggling with jealousy is unable to trust the person they are with or show respect for them as an individual or their boundaries.

If the jealousy is caused by a close relationship between the grandparent and the adult son or daughter, it can cause a parent with a fragile personality to feel threatened. They believe that the love or time spent with their spouse's parents is being taken away from them. They view their spouse as their property.

A son who displays his love and praises his mom in front of his wife, can cause an insecure wife to develop a jealous attitude. The wife's hurt feelings are transferred to the son's mother, resulting in less attention given to the M-I-L.

An adult son and grandchild who love the paternal grandmother very much, may cause the fragile personality of the D-I-L to feel jealousy. Any attention, time, or love exhibited by her husband and children toward the M-I-L feels like attention taken away from the her. Feeling threatened, the undermining wife eventually attempts to get rid of her M-I-L. The paternal grandmother is punished, becoming the victim of another's insecurities. The grandchildren suffer from this loss. A healthier mind would realize the more love and attention their child receives from grandma and grandpa who love and care about them, the better it is for the well-being of their child.

(Dr. Bone) Daughters-in-law are jealous of this maternal love. The D-I-L may have a profound need of love and recognition and expect to be the most important woman in her husband's life. This results in the husband having to maintain two significant relationships; one as a son, the other as a husband. The D-I-L feels betrayed when she believes too much attention is given to his mother. She resents what her M-I-L gets.

(Dr. Caddy) When the son and the grandkids love the grandmother so much, the D-I-L becomes jealous of that love, time, and attention given to her M-I-L. When a wife feels this jealousy, she does not want her M-I-L bonding too closely with the grandchild. The M-I-L feels helpless, unable to stop what is happening, and unable to protect and keep her family from being destroyed.

When a child observes a parent's jealous reaction, it can cause the grandchild to be more withholding of their attention to the grandparent. Knowing they are being watched over by the insecure parent, they are careful not to defy "the rules".

A son should stand behind his wife, but he also needs to honor the emotional alliance with his parents. The son needs to realize that he can be loyal to his wife, and also be a good son. Ideally, the son should take a stand and assure his wife that he has enough love for both of these special relationships he wants to have in his life.

Should the husband one day show signs of strength by reaching out to his mom or dad who have been cut off, it may very well cause his alienating spouse to come down harder on him. The play for power and control is then stepped up a notch with a stronger cycle of denigration.

A jealous son-in-law who possesses a misguided sense of ownership of his spouse, needs to be recognized as the most important person in the lives of his wife and children. He does not want the love and attention of his wife and children to go to the maternal grandparents. This jealous or insecure spouse feels threatened that he may lose some control over your adult daughter.

When a separation or divorce occurs and a new husband or boyfriend (or a new wife or girlfriend) enters the picture, the same dynamic occurs. It is very common that the new member of the family will want to take over the role of most important and most loved. Additionally, as yet another set of grandparents enters the family picture, the new member may want his/her parents to play the dominate role as grandparents, or even replace the natural set of grandparents. The new person may not want share in the love and attention.

When there is competitiveness for the love in families, it creates a stressful situation which can lead to alienation. It also causes stress to the marriage. Grandparent Alienation is about a troubled marriage.

Other instances that spike feelings of jealousy include:

- The D-I-L's mother might envy any close relationship her daughter has with her M-I-L, thus creates a wedge between her daughter and the M-I-L.
- The D-I-L perceives M-I-L as favoring her daughter's children over her son's children.
- M-I-L who comes to her son's aid or assists him in his duty can upset the D-I-L. This is viewed by the D-I-L as interfering. Unaware of the feelings of her D-I-L, the M-I-L is punished.
- Feelings of envy and jealousy toward one set of grandparents when the other set of grandparents have more accessibility to the grandchildren.

Grandparents are not immune to feelings of jealousy. Feelings may spike if one set of grandparents live in the same town and see their grandkids every week, while the other set is further away and may only see their family once or twice a year. A closeness can develop between some grandkids and some grandparents, leaving the others feeling marginalized.

The ideal way for this to be handled would be for the middle generation to say that they and their children love all the grandparents very much, and that each relationship is special having its own unique and particular qualities.

Sometimes grandparents turn their envy and jealousy into a competition in order to try and keep up with the other grandparents (OGs). This competition can be even more pronounced during the holidays when gifts are exchanged. Grandparents who can afford to pay for an expensive vacation for their adult child, spouse, and grandkids can cause the other grandparents to feel some level of jealousy. Unable to afford to provide such luxurious opportunities and expensive gifts, this can place limits on opportunities to spend more quality time with the family.

When a grandparent is severely limited or isolated from contact with the grandchildren, and the other grandparents are allowed to see them, it is only natural that jealous emotions exist. Grandparents who have a difficult time getting permission to spend time with their grandkids may resent nannies, sitters, step grandparents, other family members, neighbors, and friends. Although one can have feelings of jealousy towards anyone, even someone they love, jealousy tends to be worse when they don't really like the other person.

Jealousy can show its face when there has been a death of a parent and then the surviving parent takes on a new love interest. Grandparents suffer the double loss from the death of their adult child, and from being cut off from their grandkids. They must work through the gatekeepers to find relief.

Amanda

When the surviving parent takes on a new partner, if may complicate the situation. That new person may be the cause of the disconnect. If the other set of grandparents are not helping your cause, it may be because their grandchildren visits may be in jeopardy as well. They too do not want to suffer the consequences of defying the gatekeeper.

Reach out to the new gatekeeper and the parent of your grandchildren from time to time with a brief, positive, and caring message. It is through this new couple that you will try to open the door. Show concern for them. Once again, it is through love, understanding, and your tenacity that your chances for a grandparent-grandchild relationship exist. Also try to contact past friends of your son or daughter. They might have been able to maintain a connection to the surviving S-I-L or D-I-L. Perhaps they can give you information about the children.

10

Siblings

"I listened to my sister cry when her son cut her out of his life. We were both lost for answers. We'd never heard of such a thing. I sympathized with her. I was thousands of miles away but I was "there". But when it happened to me, when our son cut us off, defamed us, slandered us, stripped the joy from our lives, she and her family remained in his life, but not in mine! This is unacceptable. This is betrayal. This rubs salt and vinegar on our thousand cuts. 'Sister-cide'

The death of my sister is a different kind of loss. I lost her several years before she died."

My ex's sister took my son "under her wing" unbeknown to me, and related his feelings and experiences with her own experiences of difficulty with communicating with her father. She added to his belief that the best thing to do was to get distance from me."

"My younger sister did not play a part in my alienation, but she continues the pattern in her own family. After her husband died, she alienated her own mother-in-law from her children's lives. Now her late husband's mother is a great-grandmother who has never met her great grand-child. My sister's daughters are now grown, and the oldest has also alienated her little daughter from the paternal side of the family."

"My sister has negatively affected my relationship with my daughter. As punishment to me, she told me that my daughter doesn't LOVE me. I have

been pulling away from my grandkids and daughter for the past two years. I miss my grandkids, but am afraid of my daughter.

"My daughter's daughter (my granddaughter) told my estranged son when he came to visit with his father, that if he did not visit me (the alienated grandmother), that she would no longer want to have anything to do with him (her uncle) and his family. She stated … If you can write-off my grandmother (your mother), then I will write you and your family off too."

"My older sister has told lies about me to my daughter. She tends to make a catastrophe about me to my daughter of anything that happens. I think my sister could be jealous because she has no grandchildren."

"We are denied access to our daughter's three grandchildren, but also our son is not allowed to speak to us or will be denied access as well. He lives down the street from us and has not spoken to us for three years. He just had to choose, and was influenced by his wife. The pain has changed the course of my life. Everything points to this being the way our lives will end."

"Amanda, great news! On Christmas day I got to spend several hours with my nephew. My grandmother and my dad got to be with him, too! Too bad my mom did not live to experience this. His other grandparents arranged it. My nephew had demanded to see his other grandparents! I was prepared for the possibility that my sister (who cut us off) had turned him against m. But my nephew hugged me and said that he loves me. It was important to me to tell him that I love him and I'm proud of him. I finally had a chance, and it gave me so much peace! Plus, I could see for myself that he's turned into a kind and smart teenager…my worst fears have NOT become a reality. It was wonderful. Proof that alienated children DO love their families and DO want them."

It is not unusual for the alienating adult child to cut off communications with siblings, other members of the family, or close friends. Those who do not follow in their line of thinking are cut off resulting in additional losses for the grandchildren, the cousins, aunts and uncles, and grandparents. If they have treated you this way, they are likely treating others this way as well.

When ties are severed between the parent and adult child, many times the relationship with the brothers and sisters remain intact. Other times siblings reject the one who causes so munch emotional pain in the family.

Siblings who become overstressed and outraged by the way their brother or sister is treating their parents, may decide to create a distance from their parents. The anger and emotional stress of witnessing and constantly hearing the stories of loss and cruel treatment can become too burdensome for them. With this heartbreak of witnessing the parent's emotional devastation, they may know of no other way than to disassociate themselves.

There are times when the sibling is close to the parent, but feels disloyal to their alienating brother or sister for being close to the parent. They may severe the ties with their parent and connect with the gatekeeper sibling. They may ban together against the parent forming bonds which bring them closer to each other, than to the parent. When the alienating sibling is in pursuit of negatively influencing their sibling to cut off their parents, the targeted sibling may align just to keep from being cut off themselves. Hence, all the young cousin relationships become the collateral damage for the grandparent, as the web continues to be spun.

Work on strengthening the bond between yourself and your children with whom you do have a relationship. Even if you believe that relationship is solid, never underestimate the power of those who alienate. It is best to let them know you do not want them to worry or take care of you. Try not to show them the extent of your sadness and anger. Tell them they do not have to reach out on your behalf, since that would place them in the middle of your conflict. They can still function as a bridge person to inform you of the well-being of your adult child and grandchildren.

(Dr. Coleman) If they have estranged their parents, they're never too far along to estrange themselves from their siblings or anyone else. Estranged children always feel ganged up on in this scenario. It will cause your estranged child to feel like your non-estranged child is taking your side. And they would feel hurt and misunderstood by that. Try to help them understand your situation without being overly critical or rejecting of their sibling. It will be easier to reintegrate the estranged adult child into the family once they are ready to reconcile, if they feel the family was compassionate about their need to estrange themselves rather than critical or judgmental.

Many grandparents have reported to AGA how the anger of the non-estranged sibling remains even after a reconciliation. With patience and good parent role-modeling, time will hopefully heal the wounds. AGA does hear stories of adult children eventually offering apologies to their parents, yet healing between the siblings may take much longer. Every situation is different.

(Dr. Baker) It is common for siblings to object to this opening of arms to the one who caused so much emotional pain in the family. Some remain angry and mistrustful. Caution is therefore a reasonable position to take. Let them know that you are willing to do whatever it takes for the family to come together again.

A great many AGA grandmothers have communicated their discovery that their own sister has joined this cult-like relationship. Sibling rivalry isn't always outgrown in childhood and may intensify as the decades pass. (Psychology Today 2016) Trying to "fix" a family problem by trying to fix a family member's attitude is seldom successful. Family roles are the product of years of practice. It is said that adulthood turns *rivalry* into *envy*: If someone is envious of what you have accomplished, that says a lot about their *own* self-esteem and sense of accomplishment.

The web of alienation continues to be spun as a once devoted adult child is successfully manipulated with lies and untruths by the grandmother's own sister. Being betrayed by one's own sister adds to number of those who have gone missing from what was once family. Unknowingly to you, the cult has been formed. You have been cut off, and the truth has been abandoned.

Dr. Joshua Coleman explains on his weekly webinars how grandparents left to feel they are no longer part of their own family. He speaks of the frequency of a sister of the grandparent selfishly using the situation to elevate herself to a more esteemed position with the gatekeepers. This may be due to long-standing sibling conflict or an underlying jealousy; some sisters use this to punish their sibling. The grandmother is then erased and replaced through the alienation process by a sister who attaches herself to the lies about her.

Having a sister assume your role with grandchildren and adult child can be terribly challenging. It makes it is extremely difficult to trust or continue a relationship with anyone who has told lies about you and tries to hurt you thru your child and grandchildren. What's even worse is that your own child has been brainwashed to believe the mother's sister, while not listening to their own mother.

Dr. Coleman suggests, "Should you decide, you may ask your sister why she is telling lies about you. Try to find out what your sister is saying to others about you. You can tell her how intensely betrayed her actions have caused you to feel. Let her know you feel you can no longer feel close to her or trust her, because she has chosen to hurt you through the people in your life whom you love the most. View this as a unique opportunity for resolution and reconciliation. Hopefully, your sister will empathize, and help you to break the unfortunate cycle affecting future generations in your family."

11

Support Groups

(Dr. Bone 2012) I recently had the honor of being asked to speak to a group called Alienated Grandparents Anonymous in Florida (AGA Headquarters). There must have been over 100 hundred present, all 100% attentive and all 100% trying to find solutions to re-connect with their grandchildren. As familiar as I think I am with Parental Alienation, that evening's talk was a clear and strong reminder of how grandparents are "tragic collateral damage" associated with parental alienation, as on person described it. The pain of the targeted parent is horrendous, and the pain of a grandparent who is equally cut off, but without any possible legal remedy is no less tragic. I believe that this group will replicate itself in many other areas and will be a strong voice of one of the most tragic, yet often forgotten, victims of parental alienation. I was struck by both their pain and their resolve. *Alienated parents and grandparents are predictably and reliably loving and unconditional in their love. If this was not the case, why would AGA even exist?"*

"I cannot thank you enough for all of your support this afternoon on our group conference call-in. Everyone had a brighter expression as they left the meeting! I'm going to support the grandmother you spoke with in court this week. She was so thankful to speak to you! The second grandmother you gave information and suggestions to, regarding her upcoming trip to see her son and hopefully her grandchildren, was bouncing around the room; how uplifting for all of us!

"Our daughter, with our granddaughter, opened the door. She looked startled to see us. Our brief meeting went well, and she accepted our gifts for our

grandchild. We wanted to thank AGA for all the suggestions, encouragement, and interest you have given us. HOPE has been restored! Thank you."

"AGA a lifesaver. We were kept from our grandchildren for five agonizing years. The strategies we learned from AGA made the difference for our reconciliation."

"AGA has shed a new light on what my wife and I have been going through for the past four years. We thought we were the only ones going through this, just as many on your website stated. We reached a very low point last week. We had just been left out of our grandchild's birthday and holiday celebration. We laid awake all night very distraught and trying to think of what if anything else we could try. The next day a very good friend who lives part time in Florida calls with the info on AGA. He just happened to be looking through the local paper, and saw some announcement of an AGA support group meeting. It was amazing how much of what we have personally gone through was exactly what so many others had experienced. I have renewed hope that now we understand what it is that has happened to us, and that there may be a reconciliation someday."

"I can't think of anything more important than to hear from others experiencing similar emotional hurt."

"Everyone's story is different, but the heartache of not seeing our grandchildren is the tie that binds us together and makes us strong! In a perfect world, our families would be together and we would all live happily ever after. Unfortunately, the world is not perfect so we have to do our best to maneuver through an imperfect world in hopes that we can reconnect with our offspring and enjoy our grandchildren. Reach out to AGA for knowledge and support."

"Helping others with their abandonment has helped us. We find comfort in sharing our stories and our feelings. We realize we are not alone. We find strength from each other in our support group."

"The significance of AGA meetings: We will be forever grateful for the many meetings we have attended. Without the professional & educational support, the heartfelt compassion and the only place in the world where we could honestly share our grief with people who really could say, 'I know how you feel'; we would not have survived the devastation of the Grandparent Alienation so cruelly imposed on us by our son. We are at the stage now where we believe that life does go on without our precious grandchildren in our lives. The pain never goes away; it just doesn't dominate our lives now. We've 'rejoined' the human race (after 3 years) thanks to the support of AGA; and we can actually feel joy at the many good things that do remain as constants in our lives. Thank you from our hearts and God bless you all for the critically important work that you do. We are so blessed for having known you. We pray that one day your work will be done because this insidious "disease" will be cured and no others will have to suffer. And, yes, our hope for the future is that our precious grandchildren will seek us out for the love that they've missed."

"My feeling of loss is very great. I feel confused because I have done nothing for this to be happening to me. When I am told I will spend time with my grandson, it does not happen. It is all very uncertain and unpredictable. I took care of him first four years of his life. Please guide me to a support group."

"Coming to AGA meetings contributes to our well-being, to our resilience, and to our healing."

"It was amazing of how much we have experienced was exactly what so many others had experienced. I have renewed hope that now that we understand what it is that has happened to us, and that there may be a reconciliation someday."

Amanda

"Thank you for making me feel that I really do matter."

"Thank you, Amanda, for the wisdom you share at just the right time. Thank you for knowing the right words to say in challenging times, and for your lessons and your listening ear."

"We are committed to not ever giving up in our quest to reconcile. We pray we can help others as well."

"I am such a 'fighter' and have been so miserable sitting in the "no grandchild limbo land", not wanting to flat out hate this mother who did this to my grandchild and to me - yet wanting to have some means of recourse to fight back. Your sharing your AGA dream and your AGA mission with me and so many thousand others all in the same boat has softened my anger and redirected it, putting it to good use. I will never be able to say thank you enough"

"Our alienation was extremely abrupt. Our daughter and son-in-law and their children were a major part of our lives, and us in theirs. We were always close doing all the usual grandparent duties. And then, we were accused of not caring about something going on outside the immediate family. To this day we still are unsure what we did. We were told we were never to see or come near them again. Our attempts to reconcile have failed. I just want you to know that your organization has educated us more in the past few days than in all the counseling and every other idea we have tried. Thank you for allowing me to tell my story, I needed to! It's funny, but I am ready to get involved in an organization that I never thought I would need."

(Rev. Dr. John Killinger) These are very powerful statements about the need for organizations like AGA to grow and help others, which they are trying to do. Thousands of grandparents, their children, and their grandchildren will eventually benefit from their efforts.

AGA is a Non-Profit 501c3 created for those who experience the excruciating emotional pain of being cut off from their grandchildren and great grandchildren. AGA is an organization which provides grands with information and support. AGA aims to educate, do research, and bring awareness in understanding of the global epidemic of Grandparent Alienation. Alienation affects millions worldwide.

AGA provides a forum, in a safe anonymous environment, for grandparents to openly vent and share their stories of inter-generational issues with those who "get it". No one knows how you truly feel more than those who are going through it. As grands get to vent their frustrations and sadness, they feel less isolated. At AGA support group meeting they can share their worst fears and thoughts, because they trust the other grandparents who are on the same journey. AGA aims to help our aging population become empowered and help to heal family relationships, while providing a vision of hope for those who have not yet achieved their desired outcome. There is one thing that cannot be taken away, HOPE.

When asked for the best advice he can give to a grandparent trying to cope, Joshua Coleman, PhD replied, "Support, support, support. Find people you can talk to. Social isolation is the worst part of any form of estrangement or alienation."

Carol Golly, PhD states, "What we know about peer-lead support groups: the most helpful support is between one another. Those who are living this awful situation are the best supports to one another. Their mutual experiences can validate, support, and encourage the members."

To help you process your strong and sometimes overwhelming feelings of heartbreak and to strengthen coping strategies, you might want to reach out for additional help from a licensed mental health provider. If you do, be sure to find someone who is well experienced in PAS, since the dynamics are similar to Grandparent Alienation. Otherwise, the advice offered may not benefit you.

The very first meeting for AGA was held in 2011 at AGA Headquarters in Florida. As the founders of this one and only start up support group, and new to the place that offered us a "home"; we wondered how we should assist all the people looking for their destination room. To our shock and surprise, they were all looking for us! As we listened to the 50 plus heartfelt stories being shared by distraught grandparents, I became so saddened that I couldn't even find my voice. I recall being so shaken from what I was hearing, that I actually had to sip water in order to respond between each and every word I spoke.

At the conclusion of that first meeting, the newly formed AGA professional Board of Directors told us that the only reason they came was because each thought no one would show up. They told us that they did not want my husband and I to be alone when that happened. We knew then that we had uncovered a new phenomenon. We know now such an epidemic exists worldwide. AGA has named this very sad circumstance Grandparent Alienation.

As Florida snowbirds returned to their home states, they expressed the need for continued support. They wanted a local safe place to vent and tell their own stories. In a time when a 501c3 was difficult to obtain in the United States, AGA was licensed in three months. Within a year and a half AGA had spread to all 50 states and was finding its own way into other countries. At this writing AGA has a presence in 22 countries. What we discovered was a worldwide epidemic; a mostly silent one at that.

A grandparent's love is said to be the most magical love of all – boundless, unconditional, and unbreakable – but not in every case. Believing there are millions going through this is indeed alarming, but at the same time in some ways very comforting. As each grandparent discovers they are not the only on going thru this, they find some relief. For years now, our website receives thousands of hits each month, and during the holiday season about 10,000 hits. The internet has provided an opportunity for grandparents trying to survive this emotional trauma a means to connect.

AGA Headquarters heard this cry loud and clear, then reached out to the leading experts in Parental Alienation Syndrome (PAS) who could provide assistance. AGA was the first organization to connect the dynamics of PAS to GA. Helping grandparents understand the psychology behind the many levels of alienation helps them feel less guilty, shameful, or defective.

AGA's Board of Directors and consultants are leading international experts in the field of Alienation. Our professional consultants are specialists in the fields of Mental Health, Law, Medicine, and Religion. They have joined Team AGA in our quest to examine this phenomenon from every angle. Our highly distinguished team of experts continually impart valuable information and advice, thus allowing AGA to offer suggestions. AGA Headquarters' suggestions are then coupled with the knowledge gained from communicating with many thousands of grandparents and the results of AGA professional surveys.

I dearly remember a grandparent once saying to me, "When you are doing God's work, a pathway is opened up for you." This held deep meaning for me, since every professional we asked along the way to join in our quest graciously accepted. For this we are grateful, as are all who have found us.

AGA firmly believes that a family's privacy is of utmost importance. Anonymity and confidentiality are essential components and a high priority. Our organization aims to protect those who attend meetings, conference call-ins, or communicate online from further intimidation and possibly a higher level of alienation.

A main focus of AGA is to cast light on intergenerational alienation. Contacting your local newspaper to run an article on this critical issue threatening our society will bring much awareness to our plight. We strongly recommend grandparents seriously consider not using actual names or allow any photos of themselves. Why create an opportunity for escalating effects?

As grands go through unexpected transitions in their later life, grieving 24/7 with symptoms of depression, it can be difficult for family and friends to provide the support needed. Studies show that the best form of help for complicated grief (grief without closure) is to attend a peer led support group. This is where they discover that they truly are not suffering alone. Many grands have a friend with whom they can confide, yet are cautious not to over-burden them with their unending sadness. Some do not share their ordeal even with their best friend, as they feel too embarrassed or ashamed that their own son or daughter has tossed them out of their lives. Friends try their best to console, yet there is just so much a friend can do to help. There are even some acquaintances who may condemn what they do not understand. They may wonder what terrible things you must have done for your own children not wanting to spend time with you.

When you feel like you have no control over what's going on in your life, your struggles become more manageable when you don't go it alone. AGA believes sharing feelings and empathizing with someone else's pain creates a sense of peace. Compassion from those who have experienced the same level of frustration and despair can counter the belief that one has been singled out for such suffering. With support, trauma is minimalized. Without a support system, the burden is even greater. Reach out for the support available to you. There are answers out there. AGA's goal is to help you find them, and to offer coping skills for those who have not yet achieved their desired outcome.

AGA recognizes that each situation is unique, though many commonalities are shared. AGA grandparents bring each other comfort. They listen, learn, and share suggestions with one another.

All experience this "living loss" of a child and grandchild. They want to share. Their stories are important. Each narrative provides valuable information, and each has something to teach.

The heartache of not seeing their grandchildren is the tie that binds grands in a support group setting. This is where they come to understand that they should not be embarrassed by this alienation, and that they can stop blaming themselves. Healthy minds want to fix things, while unhealthy minds do not. Thru AGA grandparents come to realize that if they did not cause this, then they alone cannot fix this campaign of denigration and domestic violence.

AGA grandparents identify with each other's heartache without placing judgment. They know the frustration of being a targeted parent/grandparent who is trying to deal with the rupture. Simply knowing they are not alone, helps them cope. Together they open their hearts, finding great comfort being with others who actually experience this human tragedy. Not having to defend or validate themselves while among their peers, being with grands who 'get it', and feeling safe to share their torment is the best form of help. In unity, there is strength. Sharing with others helps us gather wisdom and become empowered. Eventually, miracles multiply. The hundreds of AGA success stories is continually increasing, though even one would have made this entire project worthwhile.

Dr. Golly urges, "Anyone in this predicament to reach out to others who understand. You may not win each battle, but the goal is to win the war. Battles cannot be fought alone. You will need resources to navigate the difficult terrain that lies ahead; support, personal strength, a game plan, boundaries, and self-care skills will be needed for maneuvering through this emotional journey. If someone is manipulating you, as well as your adult child, the manipulation may reach a point where you feel as if you are unable to trust in your own reality.

Dr. Golly suggests, "Contact a licensed mental health provider with a deep understanding and experience in alienation and parenting strategies who can help you explore the best ways to deal with and cope with your situation. Additionally, having a friend or family member present when you need to have discussions may be a helpful way to stay grounded. It can also be helpful to join an AGA support group. Finding people who've experienced similar situations can offer helpful suggestions to develop a plan. The bottom line is, having supportive friends and family can help you get through this challenge. You need these people so you can process your feelings, receive good counsel, and develop a plan to move forward. These are the trusted friends and family members who can be with you when you attempt to see your grandchildren. This can be a good idea for your own well-being, but a witness may also be useful in the event of a legal battle."

(Rev. Dr. John Killinger) I have discovered the value of getting to know other parents and grandparents who have been or are in the same situation as mine. In one sense, it is consoling to know that this alienation problem is so widespread, and whatever the reasons for it, that we are not alone in being afflicted by it. This is true of whatever ails us – the loss of a loved one, the loss of a pet, the loss of a job, dealing with health issues, many other human problems. This is why AGA is such a powerful and wonderful organization.

View AGA's website: AlienatedGrandparentsAnonymous.com to find a location near to you. Our email address is: AGAInternationalHeadquarters@gmail.com

Knowledge is the first step for a plan. Understanding the complexities helps one to act accordingly. When you hear something, you can personally identify with, a light bulb goes off in your mind as a new piece of the puzzle comes together. If you take away even one bit of information from each section of our website, this book, the AGA newsletters, monthly national conference call-ins, Zoom meetings, or AGA in person self-help support group meetings; then process it and apply it to your adult children and grandchildren, you will come to see a clearer picture of the bewildering phenomena of our own children not wanting to have a place for us in their lives and in our grandchildren's lives. You may not be able to fix this right now, but you can educate yourselves to understand the varied dynamics behind the reality of alienation. Understanding is a helpful factor in developing coping skills.

Goals for AGA

- To educate the public about the growing problem of alienation of grandparents
- To raise awareness nationally and internationally of Grandparent Alienation and Parental Alienation Syndrome
- To offer support, understanding, and help validate the feelings of those dealing with the issues of alienation
- To provide information, strategies, and coping skills for grandparents
- To work toward reunification and healing relationships between parents, grandparents, and grandchildren
- To provide top qualified specialists to give the most updated information on the many dynamics of Grandparent Alienation
- To bring awareness and educate the public, legal, legislative, law enforcement, mental health, religious, and school communities about AGA

- To study and provide professional research on Grandparent Alienation
- To collect, coordinate, and disseminate information on the importance of grandparents in grandchildren's lives
- To study the global impact on the family
- To explore the impact of alienation on the grandchildren
- To consult, support, and advocate for Grandparents Rights Legislation in the State of Florida, nationally, and internationally
- To provide information for educating communities about Grandparent Alienation
- To manage and maintain a website which provides the most updated information on Grandparent Alienation
- To help other communities establish support groups – Strategic Alliance with AGA, Inc. Contact: AGAInternationalHeadquarters@gmail.com
- To seek grants to help achieve the Goals of AGA, Inc.
- To continue the Goals of AGA

AGA Headquarters provides assistance in setting up support groups globally. Those who have become coordinators are mostly grandparents, while some are mental health professionals, clergy, and occasionally other members of the affected family. Grandparent Alienation was not taught in universities. Therefore counselors, therapists, attorneys, and judges have not been trained to treat this phenomenon. AGA Headquarters offers professional trainings for attorneys and mental health professionals.

Grandparent Alienation is a phenomenon where the grandparents are truly victims of family law.

Being proactive by doing something positive about the situation is certainly better than just being the victim. When we help others, we are helping ourselves as well. Those who bring awareness to others have found passion in their mission. When you have the passion, you become a natural at what you do.

Conference call-ins with AGA Headquarters are available for individual support group meetings, as well as national and international call-ins for those in need support and guidance. This service is announced in the newsletter, and on our website.

So many are struggling silently around the world who would benefit from AGA support group meetings. Grandparents are in the dark not understanding what is really happening, or what to do about it. They are trying to make sense of this cruelty. We must try to find them. They are cut off from the family they raised, and are desperate for help.

Family is the foundation of society and civilization. The health and well-being of our adult children, innocent grandchildren, and families depends on each of us bringing awareness and knowledge of the horrible truth of this once hidden global epidemic. Bringing awareness is a form of hopeful prevention. If parents are made aware that this could happen to anyone, then they could prepare their sons and daughters at a younger age of such possibilities.

Initiate conversations with others and you will discover that almost everyone has some level of alienation in their extended families, or knows someone close to them who has been experiencing this. Consider forming a Strategic Alliance with AGA. Contact: AGAInternationalHeadquarters@gmail.com Whether you find one needy grandparent experiencing suicidal ideation, or 50 who think they are going through this alone, you will be changing their lives forever. Bring together those who suffer this unjust abandonment, and long for understanding. Our grandchildren and grandparents spend years living with feelings of hurt, shock, sadness, bewilderment, anger, betrayal, and helplessness as a victim of the injustice of Grandparent Alienation.

Help yourself as you help others. If you know what to do, then it is easier to figure out how to do it. AGA gives grands tools needed to navigate thru challenging times, as they yearn for their grandchildren and the adult child who "used to" love them. Knowledge is power, and luck favors those who are prepared. Anything worth having is worth working for, and nothing succeeds like persistence. Knowledge, passion, love, commitment, patience, and the tenacity of the grandparent are indicators of success.

We grandparents are treasure chests of talents, insights, and remarkable gifts. Together we can make a difference to serve the children we love so unconditionally. Team AGA has created The Grandparent Movement of action. Grandparents across America and around the world are joining hands and hearts, reaching and growing together to form a unity. They realize they do not have time to waste. Let us join together to draw on our collective wisdom as grandparents to chart a way forward.

All of them agreed: No, no, no, there is nothing you can do. Well, we saw more experts…. until we met Hope. Oh, Hope, she carries her name so well. She gave us the gift of…… a deep wide river. She pointed to it and said: Look on that side of the river, look, Your son is there, he is alive. Hold on to that thought… He is in much pain. He has put his thoughts, his feelings and his needs safely in a box They are of no use for him, if he wants to cope. And look, he is surrounded by fog. The fog is so dense that he cannot see you He cannot see his family waving at him on the other edge of the river. NOW <u>you</u> have a role: You must be the light So that one day, in maybe 10, 15 or 20 years, when the fog disappears, even for the time of 3 breaths, you ensure that the light is turned on. If the light is on, your son will recognize you and reach out for the help he needs, if he is ready to cross the river safely. I said: What? Me? Did you say the light? With my broken heart? Well, I had a purpose, a mission. I had a focus I looked around and found AGA… And we are here today… With you, my AGA friends You help me hold on to the light, you help the light shine *steadily and you give strength to the light and to me, Our son is still surrounded by fog, but the fog is less dense, less intense…*

Together, we carry the light, I am GRATEFUL to each of you. Rivka, AGA Support Group Coordinator Toronto, Canada

12

How to Form a Strategic Alliance with AGA

To register with AGA Headquarters, send an email to our headquarters: AGAInternationalHeadquarters@gmail.com

An AGA email address will be required. Use AGA and your location. Do not use your name as part the email address.

> Examples: AGA-MiamiFL@gmail.com
> AGA.OrangeCounty@yahoo.com

Find a location for your meetings.

How to Conduct an AGA Meeting

> Once a month 1 ½ hours
> Have a **sign-in** paper to notify grandparents of upcoming meetings.
> First Name Email Address

1. Sit in a circle.
2. Read the Open Welcome. (see below)
3. Select a chapter (or in part if the chapter is long) from this book to at each meeting.
4. Allow each grandparent time to tell a brief summary of their story. They want to share. Depending on time and number of grandparents in attendance, limit the amount of time allowed

for each person. You are the leader. This book will help you form strategies for communication with their adult children and grandchildren.

5. Announce details for the next meeting. Use only BCC when sending email announcements to your attendees.

Zoom meetings are being conducted as well.

Local coordinators' email addresses will be posted on our website: www.AlienatedGrandparentsAnonymous.com

Read the following **Opening Welcome** at the beginning of each meeting.

- Thank you very much for being here today.
- This is a support group for AGA and PAS.
- This is a self -help group, not a therapy group.
- We believe that with support, trauma can be minimized.
- We learn from each other in a support group.
- We hope our meeting is helpful, but ask you not to compare or judge.
- Because each of your situations is unique, we ask that you support one another on this painful journey.
- It is fine to share what you have learned, but we ask that you respect the confidentiality of others.
- We realize that each of you is experiencing some degree of cut off.
- Knowing we are not alone in this situation helps us cope with our heartbreaking situation.
- AGA offers suggestions from the advice of experts.
- IMPORTANT: Studies show the most effective help for the complicated grief, grief without closure, is to attend a peer led support group.
- If you decide to contact a licensed mental health professional, select a counselor who is licensed and familiar with PAS.

13

Divorce & Remarriage

"Divorce played a role in my alienation from my son and now my grandson. My divorce was high conflict, and my ex had an unhealthy coalition with my son."

"Most definitely divorce played a major role in my being alienated from the children who used to love me. I was the dedicated mom; he was the emotionally distant dad. After many years we divorced, and he assured me we could always be amicable and bonded with our *family. I eventually remarried, and my ex became vindictive. Never having been close to our children while they were growing up, his manipulation and material things won. My grandchildren had great allegiance to my adult children who had great allegiance to the father who lavished expensive gifts on them. I am no longer part of their family. I am* very hurt and disappointed.*"*

"Please help-I am emotionally sick. My daughter took the father's side in a divorce. She won't let me see my grandchild."

"I married a widower with a daughter and three grandchildren. We live about a 20 minutes' drive from them; however, we are basically excluded from their lives. We have no alone time with them. We cannot understand why we are treated this way as there was never any reason or anything that we did. My husband would rather have half a daughter than no daughter. He feels that any confrontation would be greeted with a complete cut off. We have suffered a severe sense of loss, and deal with constant feelings of sadness. His daughter has alienated her own mother, and most family members as well."

"My grandson's mother refuses us to have communication with him. She and our son never married. Although the relationship was a difficult one, until this past year she had allowed me visits. No one on our side of the family is allowed to see my grandchild any more. My son has since married and his child misses her half sibling. I know my grandchild must miss us very much. She is ignoring my son's visitation rights, too."

"Apparently my ex-wife has a vendetta against me. "I am the one not allowed to see my grandson anymore."

"Mom, it was those constant messages from you over the years that I knew, at the time of the divorce from my wife, that I could come back to you."

"Now that our son is divorced, we love hearing the words "Grammie and Grandpa" when we visit."

Currently, the United states has the sixth highest divorce rate in the world. Researchers estimates show over 40 percent of all first marriages in the United States end in divorce or separation. An estimated two-thirds of second marriages end in divorce. The divorce rate for third marriages is 73 percent. That second or third walk down the aisle promises to be an uphill climb, because remarrying comes packed with baggage. The major problems reported by remarried couples who get divorced are children from prior relationships and money. First marriages typically have time to solidify before children arrive, but second and third marriages often have to hit the ground running with children already there.

(Gentile, *Erasing Family Documentary*) Due to divorce in the USA, there are 22 million parents being cut out of their children's lives. 83 percent of divorces are sole custody. Imagine how many grandparents are the collateral damage of this aspect alone.

Divorce may severely compromise the grandparent-grandchild relationship. Although a divorce is the legal separation of two spouses and the dissolution of their marriage, in reality the families of both spouses can be severely impacted. Primarily the parents of the non-custodial divorced parent, usually the paternal grandparents, suffer the ill effects.

When divorce occurs, our grandchildren experience challenging life changes along with loss of love relationships. When the parents of our grandchildren divorce, they are free to abandon a relationship, but at what price? The meaningful bonds that a child has developed are frequently broken due to the selfishness exhibited to "get back at the other spouse". It creates an opening for one parent to underhandedly corrupt the relationship for the other grandparent. This toxic situation often closes the door to grandparents and extended family members, thereby significantly altering many grandparent–grandchild relationships.

When family upheavals occur, the welfare of children should be of utmost importance to everyone concerned. During these stressful times, children have a strong need for stability and continuing loving family relationships. It is the grandparents who can serve as this valuable source of security, balance, and support. Grandma and Grandpop can perform as excellent role models for behavior while there is chaos. Teaching the children how to properly channel their feelings and actions and being there to explain situations to them and to protect them, results in fewer adjustment problems. They will learn important life lessons that will serve them well for future challenges. We are all the results of our childhood experiences; therefore, having role-models of honesty and compassion during the difficult transition of divorce benefits the children.

Unfortunately for millions of children, the ability of grandparents having access to their grandchildren at this needy time can be compromised or terminated by an alienating parent. It is the grandparent who must keep striving to maintain the relationship. Since GP-GC relationships are usually determined by the parents, these children become the collateral damage in divorce. It is the child who is being punished, suffering from the removal of their support system. Spending time with Grandma and Grandpa takes on a whole new dynamic. This split-up leaves the grandparents and grandchildren feeling helpless over situations beyond their control. Severing ties to the other set of grandparents is not in the best interest of these children.

(Kornhaber, M.D. Foundation for Grandparenting) Hundreds of grandchildren entangled in these interfamily disputes told us they couldn't reveal their true feeling about their loves for their grandparents to their parents. They were forced to go emotionally underground. Many grandchildren dreamed of reuniting with their grandparents at a young age.

(Carol Hosmer Golly, 2016 Pruning the Family Tree: The Plight of Grandparents Who Are Alienated from Their Grandchildren): Eventually, when the middle generation remarries or takes on a new partner, the "blended family" faces many new challenges. Nowadays children are just as likely to live with a single parent, grandparents, stepparents, or non-relatives as they are to live in the traditional family. These family transitions are usually difficult for the young who may be torn by loyalty to the divorced or deceased parent. The third generation find themselves caught in the middle of the family chaos, changing things for them forever. There are things family members can do to make communication easier and help children adjust to their new reality. Once again, the focus should be on the best interest of the child.

(Dr. Coleman) In this era of "fictive family" where friends and others are presumed to serve as a solution to estranged or strained family relationships, grandparents can also be easily substituted out or replaced with stepparents or in-laws. Yet grandparents, especially those with a prior relationship to the grandchild, can't really be switched in and out like pieces in a Lego set. Children form powerful and important bonds to caring, loving and dedicated grandparents and therefore pay an emotional price when those important family members are removed.

When a couple stays together in a marriage or partnership where grandparents have been cut off, the grandparents ask themselves why their adult child remains with their toxic partner.

(Dr. Caddy 2013) explains:

> Your son or daughter has witnessed first-hand their spouse successfully getting rid of you, their own mother and or father. They fear seeking a divorce could very well lead to PAS for them. They fear their child being brainwashed against them. Power and control are at play here. Not wanting their own children to be turned against them, they chose to do the delusional dance of two, thus remain in the marriage. The targeted spouse aligns with the alienating spouse, and agrees to deny their parents access to the grandchildren as a means to keep peace in the home. (Stockholm Syndrome/Delusional Disorder).
>
> In second marriages, a spouse often complies because he or she does not want to be divorced again. Grandparents once again become the collateral damage of a couple remaining together and leaving the grandchildren as the true victims.

Dr. Coleman states the existence of divorce as a common dynamic putting one at a higher risk for alienation. He explains how resentments can be deep rooted, with some children never getting over it, no matter how it might appear to the parent. In many cases they may dislike or resent the people with whom their parents date or develop a relationship.

Divorce has become so commonplace that smaller numbers of adult children see themselves as part of an unbreakable family unit. When a divorce has taken place, it is easier for "the other parent" to brainwash a child against a parent. The child then sees the other parent in less than a positive light and has less empathy for the parent. This perception, encouraged by the ex-spouse and other family members who join the cult-like thinking, may endure well into the future. With distorted family values and clouded images occurring, the targeted parent falls victim. A frequent occurrence with Grandparent Alienation finds the mom who raised the child after divorce, to be the one who is now cut off.

Studies in the UK and Australia indicate that it is paternal grandparents who are most at risk of losing contact after parental separation or family conflict. Creating frivolous or unjustified reasons for not allowing GP-GC visits are common place in society. When a family with children is divided by divorce, unexpected complications may occur in the future. The link between the grandparents and the children becomes less certain, and their rights to visit the children will need to be clearly stated in the final agreement.

If there is to be a divorce be certain, at the time of the settlement, there is a provision stating specific visitation rights for the grandparents. Never trust verbal promises. Create a legal document which declares that you the grandparent, your name in writing, will have visitation rights. Be specific concerning the frequency and length of the visitations. The settlement MUST also state that there will be a "consequence to pay" should the parent deny these court ordered visits. This document can prevent later inter-generational conflict. The legal document will give you legal grounds to readdress the court. Document any visits denied. Notify the court each time your legal right to visit is denied.

In some states, post-divorce, you can apply to the court in the jurisdiction of the grandchild for the right to visit with an unmarried minor child. There may be challenges saying the constitutional rights of parents cannot be infringed by courts forcing them to grant grandparent visitation.

Research shows divorce increases the probability of alienation, thus making a reunification more of a challenge. However, divorce can also open the door for a reunification between you and your grown child. (Dr. Caddy) When a divorce occurs, it can be a positive for the grandparents. There can then be resolution to the relationship. The truth will eventually be found out.

AGA has been informed of numerous divorce cases where the grandparents finally have reconnected with their adult child and grandchildren. This is evidence of Dr. Caddy's presentation to AGA grandparents, "Divorce can result in a good situation for grandparents who have previously been cut off.

If you have not reconnected when a divorce has taken place, periodically keep in touch with the other grandparents. If their son or daughter is the custodial parent, the OGs may be another layer of gatekeepers. Send cards to them for special occasions. Include a friendly note. You might consider saying, "I have peace knowing you are loving and caring for our precious grandkids." Remember, this not about what is fair or what you might want to say, it is about doing what might work. The grandchildren would be the reward of your efforts.

When our adult children remarry and another set of grandparents are brought int to picture, it can compromise the time you have with your grandkids. It is only natural to feel some jealousy of the time being shared, or if location offers them more privileged time than you. When you do have your time together, it is important never to say anything bad about the parents or OGs. Do this because you are doing it for the good of the children.

New relationships are a possibility for divorced grandparents. Remarriage after late-in-life divorces do occur. When a remarriage takes place, parents want their grown kids to be okay with what is going on because they are so happy. However, they may fail to see what is happening in the minds of their children.

When older couples divorce and remarry, adult children and grandchildren are impacted. If the split-up is recent or poorly resolved, more ticklish emotions will be added to the mix. With the increase in healthy lifespans, there is a realization by grandparents that they have life left in them to live. Those who choose to marry again have their reasons, which include seeking companionship. They do not want to spend their remaining years feeling lonely, or being less involved. Those who are unhappy in their marriages sense that it is now or never. Retirement can highlight a couple's basic incompatibility, which may not have been so obvious when they were so busy with their careers and raising a family. These "gray divorces" and "silver separations" have doubled since 1990.

Some grandparents find themselves being granted little time with their adult child and grandchildren because their new partner has been brought into the mix. A lot of children from divorce don't want to have much contact with their parent's new spouse or significant other. As Dr. Coleman discusses, "Adult children may have to cope with vast feelings when their parent remarries. A jealousy may develop whether widowed or divorced. They may treat the new step parent with insulting and hurtful behavior and try to undermine the new relationship to bolster their standing. They often feel disloyal to the memory of the deceased parent or worry that they won't get as much attention. They may also feel that the new spouse will rob them of their inheritance."

(Psychology Today 2019 Kalish, Ph.D.) When men and women marry again late in life....adult children may live thousands of miles away and have their own spouses and children, but they are still able to interfere with their elder parent's second marriage. If mom or dad has remarried after the death of the other parent, even if the original marriage had been a happy one, the son or daughter may feel that, by remarrying, the surviving parent is obliterating the love for the deceased spouse, for their deceased parent.

When a remarriage or partnership of the grandparent takes place, there is no assurance that your adult child will like the new person you brought into their life. If your adult child appears not to like or respect the new step-grandparent in the family, they may have heightened feelings of disloyalty to the other parent. This new relationship may cause the adult child to feel the need to compete for their parent's love, attention.

Another source of conflict with respect to wealth often enters the scene. Your child may view this relationship as a warning that their financial resources will be limited. It would be helpful to let them know you are open to discussing their issues relating to ways they feel shortchanged by the divorce, or the remarriage. You may choose to discuss your estate with your child if you think it would be of benefit.

Do not to assume that your new spouse, the step grandparent, will be as attached to your children and grandchildren as you are. Best not to pressure your adult child to be closer to your partner than they want to be. In general, research shows that children of any age are often more upset by remarriage than by divorce. Grandparent remarriage would be best thought of as, "You don't have to like her or him, but you do have to be polite and respectful."

When grandparents remarry, they often become step-grandparents, bringing new children and grandchildren into the family circle. All of these changes will be easier for everyone involved if they are regarded not as losses, but as new possibilities. All involved should strive to handle the consequences with as much grace as possible. Unfortunately, we do not live in a perfect world.

Adult children should resist taking sides. When they chose to align themselves with one parent, they are allowing a pattern to develop which can be destructive to family cohesiveness. Having lived with their parents for many years, they may already have some ideas about where the fault may lie. Even if their instincts are correct, it is not about being right; it is about holding the family together.

Grandparents should not stay away from family gatherings just because it may involve some level of discomfort with a former spouse. Make an effort not to miss out on the joys of being a part of your grandchild's activities or milestones. Have a list of neutral topics for conversation in mind to avoid both awkward silences and sensitive subjects.

(Dr. Coleman) A divorce may also create a story in the child that there was a winner and loser after the divorce, and that one parent is in greater need of support than is the other. This can happen if one of the parents remarries and the other never does, or when the financial status of one of the parents worsens after the divorce while the other's either stays the same or improves.

(Dr. Bone) When the parents divorce, the adult child might side with one parent over the other, or they are upset with both parents. Some chose to separate themselves from you.

Remarriage after the death of a spouse may cause your adult child to feel disloyal to the memory of their parent. Watching their mom or dad love another, or even allowing themselves a closeness to their parent's new companion, can bring about a deep sense of betrayal.

To relieve their sense of burden, tell your adult child that their mom or dad would have wanted it this way. Examine the concept of being alone, and the right to happiness.

Dr. Kalish (2019) explores the dynamics of remarriage for the surviving grandparent. He brings to light the difficulty many widowed seniors have overcoming their feelings of loyalty when they remarry. He notes how the feelings of some grown children compound the emotions of these loyalty issues, while others are pleased that their surviving parent has the good fortune of comfort and joy in their golden years. He also brings attention to a feeling of relief that mom or dad is getting remarried and "the burden of caretaking" is off their shoulders. Some of the grown children think that mom or dad is making a mistake by choosing this person, causing the elder parent to feel hurt. An additional negative response to a remarriage may be one of abandonment if their parent moves away from the area to be with the new spouse. The concept of having mom or dad taken away, and possibly their baby-sitter, does not sit well with them. Dr. Kalish concludes that the best bond the older newlyweds can probably hope for would be a friendship between the grown children and the step-parent, stating this usually develops early on or not at all.

14

Reasons Why a Cut Off Might Occur

"I have never been given a reason why my grandchildren were ripped form me, and I receive no replies for request for a dialogue." To say I am distraught and frustrated, is an understatement."

"Although they lived only a few miles away., were have been barred from them. My daughter suffered from bipolar disorder and alcoholism for which she refused treatment. Her behavioral disorders caused many problems in her marriage and eventually visited emotional damage on her own child. Two months ago, she took her own life. Had I been able to see and interact with my grandchild and my daughter, I think this tragedy could have been avoided. As a former behavioral counselor, I would have been able to see her slow decent into despair prior to her ultimate solution. I would have seen the signs and been able to help her past the crisis. Mental illness cannot be detected from a distance. It's important that grandparents can assess the mental health of their children and grandchildren to prevent tragedies like this one. My grandchild is now without a mother, and I have lost a daughter. That opportunity was denied me as a result of the committee's decision and current Florida laws."

"The other grandparent, my ex, encouraged the alienators not to let me see my grandson."

"I believe our daughter's husband is the main factor and the reason she has not tried to reconcile. Her husband is from a dysfunctional family and doesn't have much contact with them, so he probably thinks that is normal."

Amanda

"I believe both my daughter and her husband have a mental illness, and they have bonded together to keep the grandkids away from me."

"Is has been a year since seeing my granddaughter. I raised her from birth. My daughter has a personality disorder, and is blaming me for everything that has gone wrong in her life. She took the little one from us. They have complete disregard for my grandchild's well-being and happiness. Her husband appears to be controlling the situation. He has taken the family and moved away from our entire family and her support system. I don't know how to protect her from her parents. The laws don't help us. We have no address or phone number for them. There are so many days I am not sure I can live through much more of this."

"My wife and I have four grandchildren, but only see one of them due to a family rift with the father of the other three."

"I was cut off from my son and grandchildren due a cult like behavior of the local LGBT community. It is an unusually bizarre situation. The day a message was sent to me, was the day I think of as the day my child and grandchildren passed away. It's the only way I can deal with this extreme loss."

"My son died in an accident leaving a wife and three children. I moved to their town to help be supportive. The OGs were unhappy with my presence. In time I was told I could only be with them when the others were present. The children came to appear nervous and won't speak to me when their mother is nearby. It hurts so much to see my grandchildren behave so differently in front of me now. The mom answers for them. Our side of the family no longer sees them. To lose your son is enough grief, but to lose his children as well is so painful."

Relationships are complicated matters. Basic conflicts, embellished misunderstandings, or false accusations may occur which can cause devastating consequences to the grandparents and great grandparents.

Grandparents with a history of mental and physical abuse, sexual offenses, substance abusers, or alcoholism, are among the reasons why adult children justifiably deny contact or have supervised visits with the grandchildren. Parents who flout the parents' rules about safety are also justified in denying contact with grandparents. If a grandparent poses a threat or serious risk to their grandchildren, absolute caution must follow. AGA however is an organization which focuses on the dynamics of unjustified reasons GP-GC relationships are severely limited or severed. These may include basic conflict misunderstandings.

The majority of grands report to AGA that they do not know what they did to cause the fracture in their family. They are left to endlessly question why this happened to them. Should a family conflict (one you probably don't even realize they have accused you of) warrant you not being allowed to meet, hold, or spend time with your grandbabies? What could possibly be so horrible that their own children would eliminate them from their lives? What would cause these parents to refuse their own children the right to have grandparents in their lives? Because grandkids are minors, they have no rights? Every child wants the unconditional love and attention of a grandma and a grandpop.

Behaving as though you no longer exist, you wonder how they could disregard all you have done for them in their lifetime. You tried to be the best parent you could at the time, protecting, guiding, and being supportive of them only to have them cruelly leave you. You wonder how they could just stop loving you. As the years torturously accumulate, having been heartlessly cast out of the lives of your son or daughter and your precious grandchildren, you question how you can love the child you don't like anymore.

(Dr. Coleman) No matter how good you thought your relationship had always been with your son or daughter, circumstances can change drastically. While some children exhibited problematic signs growing up, most were loving and caring children. The risk comes once a spouse enters the picture. Your child marries not only the psychology of their husband or wife, they also marry the psychological dynamic of the household in which their mate grew up.

You may observe signs during their dating stage and want to alert your child to a potential problem. From the wisdom of your years, you may want to bring this negative quality to their attention. If, however you say something negative about their choice in a partner, it may very well come back to haunt you someday. There is a real chance your comment will be heard by your child's choice of a partner at some point.

When a marriage takes place or a grandchild is born, one stands at risk of for an unexpected shift in the dynamics of the family. Some may have seen it coming, but most are blindsided by the cruel disassociation. It may be an abrupt rupture, or develop as future conflicts arise. A loving parent-child relationship which lasted for decades has ended at the hands of someone's adult child. It is the grandparent-grandchild relationship that results as the earthshattering causality. A grandparents' life changes forever.

(Dr. Coleman) In our present culture, their guiding light is simply whether or not the relationship makes them feel good. When you see signs early on that would cause you to want to tell your child to stay away, not marry that person, your child interprets it that the parent is questioning their worth and rebellious independence. If you interfere with their choice of a mate, they may embrace that person to reassure themselves that they got it right. So, if you don't like their choice, just try to understand it. The more you take a position against the spouse of your child, the more they will feel obligated to embrace them as a show of independence and autonomy.

Alienators with unresolved childhood issues, coming from homes of abuse, insecurity, or turmoil often repeat the chain. Focusing on their own needs, they create a world to make themselves feel safe and have more control. To accomplish their agenda, they must get rid of those whom they perceive challenge their control.

Targeted sons and daughters find themselves in the middle of this drama, inwardly feeling guilty and often unable to express their true feelings and love to their mom and dad. Parents who used to be there for them providing a sense of belonging and security, are now kept from participating in family experiences.

The targeted adult child does not want the grandparent observing the problems taking place in the marriage. Trying to keep peace in the marriage, they eventually align with the alienating spouse. Instead of finding the courage to stand up to the controlling partner, they decide to go along with the abuse toward the targeted grandparents. Thinking there is too much at stake to leave, or to leave their young children in the hands of the crazy-maker in the family, they decide to keep their nuclear family intact.

Dr. Coleman explains, "If the alienating spouse is a troubled person who has made your son or daughter cut off contact with you and others in the family, then your child probably feels like he/she has to make a devil's bargain: either be close to their spouse and have some version of peace, or insist on closeness with the rest of the family and be tortured by the alienating spouse all the time."

When a person chooses your child to marry, they are choosing the person you raised. They should be respectful, considerate, and polite to their M-I-L and F-I-L simply because they love their spouse. They do not have to like everything about their in-laws, but they should work on establishing a working relationship with them. Communication skills between a husband and wife need to be developed in order to find a comfort level for discussing problems which do arise. They should become a team and put each other first. However, putting their spouse first does not mean it is okay to eject parents from the family.

We remember the unconditional love and support we gave to our own children. We expected to be grandparents. We expected our grandchildren would know and feel the love and devotion of their grandparents. We lovingly invested much attention, time, and money for our children's well-being and happiness. We raised them to be self-assured and have self-confidence. We protected them from fears. Our baby boomer generation wanted them to like us, so we became friends with our kids. We formed a close attachment to them. The closer the attachment, the greater the hurt when a rejection shows its ugly face.

(Dr. Bone 2019 AGA International Conference) Baby Boomers had a more permissive form of parenting attitudes, and were less controlling than previous generations. The generation of our adult children now as parents leans toward the helicopter parenting style.

A helicopter parent is one who pays extremely close attention to a child's experiences and problems, particularly at educational institutions. Helicopter parents are so named because, like helicopters, they "hover overhead", overseeing every aspect of their child's life constantly. It means their involvement in a child's life is overcontrolling, overprotecting, and over perfecting.

At the 2019 AGA International Conference, Dr. Coleman discussed how in today's world of technology our younger generations have been captivated by electronics. They chose electronics, thus staying away from engaging in new relationships. They have not been focusing on developing the people skills of past generations. They don't put themselves out there to meet and form relationships as the grandparents' generation did. He spoke of how the recent younger generation never had to serve in the armed forces. Had they served, they would have learned to act differently. Serving in the armed forces would have taught them skills to take forward into their futures.

Our Baby Boomer generation wanted to do a better job than their parents did. (Sichel) We did not make the kinds of demands on our kids that our parents placed on us, and that fostered dependency and helplessness. So, our kids never learned to exercise autonomy in a healthy way.

Grandparents who now find themselves cut off from these same kids are suffering from the very thing they tried so hard to protect their child from all those years. The more you care about something, the greater the trauma of losing it. The more they gave, the more they have now lost. Each is now desperately trying to figure out how this could have happened to them (now, in hindsight, tracing the signs that were there early in the time of their dating or marriage); and, why our own adult children have decided to get rid of us and punish our grandchildren.

Many of this middle generation not only have a sense of entitlement and expectation, but they also fail to show the kind of appreciation that is the foundation of a healthy and loving relationship. It is more like, "Give me, give me, give me, and I owe you nothing in return". They want to be helped by their parents without any sense of obligation, but they fail to realize that we as their parents love them and want nothing but the best for them and their families. However, what we do want, at the very least, is to be respected. Sadly, this *give me* generation does not realize that there is a "quid pro quo" (something for something), and as parents and grandparents, we expect that our children should be able to understand that we have justifiable expectations to see and enjoy the joys of spending time with our grandchildren.

When this loving exchange with one's grandchildren is interrupted or corrupted, both the children and their grandparents suffer while they try to discern why things are not as they should be like other "normal" families.

So why does this alienation happen in the first place? Psychologist Joshua Coleman, PhD reflects upon our culture today as such that if a relationship doesn't make you feel good, then completely ending it is a reasonable decision. He affirms our society and culture as being more and more individualistic which means people are encouraged to define themselves on the basis of whether or not relationships (including parents) make them feel good, or good about themselves; and, whether or not those relationships are contributing to their self-esteem and personal development.

Dr. Coleman remarks, "Some adult children have become narcissists who care only about themselves. They have become people we don't like or recognize any more. This may be the result of a parent who did too good of a job raising their child, who are now heartless towards the parent who got the where they are today. This is a relatively new way of organizing family life and, from my perspective, weakens the ties between family members. Unfortunately, many parents fail to consider the loss they create in both their child and the grandparent. Both become victims."

(Carol Hosmer Golly 2016 *Pruning the Family Tree: The Plight of Grandparents Who Are Alienated from Their Grandchildren*): Limited research suggests that this phenomenon may occur as the result of a divorce or death in the middle generation, intergenerational family conflict, or through Parental Alienation Syndrome (PAS). Grandparents become collateral damage in PAS as their adult child is bad-mouthed and rejected along with their extended family. It would also seem apparent that grandparents could lose contact with grandchildren when they themselves become direct targets of bad-mouthing and rejection by adult children. For example, their adult child may unjustly deem an unwitting grandparent "bad" or "unsafe," and the adult child then denigrates the grandparent to the child, thus passing on the message.

A more intense relationship forms when a child is raised in a single parent household. Attaching to only one parent (usually the mother), increases the importance and strength of the connection to that one parent. It can also make it more difficult for that child to feel their own independence at some point.

Dr. Coleman, addressing this issue explains, "Because they didn't have others to attach to, the mother becomes too important to the child. They may become afraid of their own dependency, because they didn't have another parent to lean on. Because there isn't another parent to attach to, they may develop insufficient immunity to the mother's criticism and worries. Loving parenting can feel smothering or anxiety provoking to them because of the potential loss. The only way to feel protected from those emotions is to distance themselves. Children raised by only one parent, typically mom, often estrange themselves as a way to feel more separate. The children of divorce have little immunity tour pain and experience it very directly. They then feel burdened with those feelings, pulling away so that they don't feel so burdened.

AGA's team of professional experts in the field of alienation report the following reasons why adult children severely limit contact or severe the GP-GC relationship:

- They marry someone who is controlling, insecure, and jealous. For those with the need to control, everything is about their need to feel safe and secure in an unstable world. Anyone outside the realm of their control is very threatening.

- Family members may be jealous of another.
- The D-I-L or S-I-L may feel threatened by and jealous of your closeness to your grandchild.
- D-I-L is jealous of the close relationship you have with your son, how much your son loves you, and how much the grandchildren love you; thus, encouraging your son or daughter to stay away from you.
- S-I-L is jealous of the close relationship you have with your daughter, how much your daughter loves you, and how much the grandchildren love you; thus, encouraging your daughter to stay away from you.
- Family history is a strong indicator whether someone becomes an alienator. Your child marries the psychology of their spouse and the family relationships they experienced.
- If their background caused them to feel they were over-powered, rejected, devalued, or abandoned by their own parents; they may view their in-laws in the same manner. They engage in a campaign to brainwash your adult child to believe that you also are that way.
- If they were continually treated with disapproval from an overpowering parent, they may feel the need to separate themselves to feel their independence.
- They may think they did not get what they deserved growing up, and may view their failures or struggles as resulting from the parenting they experienced.
- Maternal grandparents who experienced conflict in their relationship with their daughter may also be at risk. This occurs even when grandparents had previously been highly involved in the lives of their grandchildren.

- Adult child feels that the grandparent will talk adversely to their children about them.

- Grandparent Alienation is a delusional dance of two, the targeted spouse may go along with the demands made by the controlling spouse.

- They are conflict avoidance. Not knowing how to handle the issue at hand causes them to avoid direct confrontation. As the resentment builds up, they withdrawal by cutting themselves off from you.

- The influence of an ex-husband often times contributes to the divide. Single moms report the bewilderment of their adult child gravitating closer to the ex-husband who had little to do with the rearing of their child. The grown child now has the long-awaited attention of the absentee father, placing the devoted mom in the losing position. Try reaching out to the ex-husband in hopes that he will eventually become an advocate for you to reconnect with your adult child and grandchildren.

- Although divorce and the negative influence of an ex-spouse is one of the most common reasons children estrange themselves from a parent, a difficult spouse that remains in the marriage can also alienate an adult child from the other parent.

- They may be trying to avoid a divorce, or possibly a second divorce.

- If they have cut off their parent, they may then cut off their sibling.

- If the other sibling decides to side with the parents, the alienating sibling may feel ganged up on, causing a cut off. Do not put your other children in the middle of your conflict with the alienating sibling.

- Your child's spouse or some other person may be powerfully motivated and successful in persuading your child to have a negative opinion of you. This may distort their view of you in the present, and may cause them to rewrite their history.

- They are unfairly influenced by an enabler: your son-in-law or daughter-in-law, an ex-spouse, or motivated extended family member.
- The daughter's-in-law mother may be jealous of the relationship between her daughter and the mother-in-law.
- When the middle generation remarries, the alienator decides to limit the new family excluding the grandparents from the prior marriage.
- Adult children of divorced parents may not want to have much contact with their parent's new spouse or significant other. They may feel disloyal to the other parent.
- The step-grandparent may have done something destructive.
- When an adult child passes away, the surviving spouse becomes a gatekeeper.
- The death of a son or daughter may eventually result in a future marriage of the D-I-L or S-I-L. The new spouse's desire to create their present-day family excludes the grandparents.
- Adult child may not approve of their parent's new spouse. They are jealous of the time and attention taken away from them, or the threat of the finances involved.
- The great-grandmother is at the root of the alienation of the grandmother.

Grandmothers have shared stories of their own mothers being psychologically abusive to them, now acting as agents to further the divisiveness between the following generations. The great-grandmother continues to transfer negativity, being critical of her daughter. She does not support her daughter, instead is supportive of the grandchild.

- The son or daughter is the alienator, and the targeted spouse likely joins in the severing of ties to the grandparents to keep peace in the marriage.
- Wealth, for varied reasons, is a common dynamic of alienation including:

When the adult child has been used to their parent paying for things, the relationship may be brought to a halt when the flow of money stops. When the parent decides their grown child should now pay their own way, they become angered and severe the ties. If no prior agreement was made clear and understood by the adult child regarding the financial support, it can lead to alienation.

Your son or daughter may have married into a wealthy family and lifestyle. Materialistic concerns and status become more important to them than being supportive of their parents.

- D-I-L or S-I-L fears the in-laws will interfere with their homelife, so they place your son or daughter in loyalty bond using the "them or me" ultimatum. The weaker targeted partner becomes abusive of their own mother or father to reassure their controlling spouse of their independence from the parent. For sons, it is a way to demonstrate their masculinity to a wife by "standing up to his mother."
- They just do not know any other way to feel separate from you than to reject you, especially for those who were once extremely close to the parent.
- When your adult child feels worried about you, deciding not to have contact with you is how they will choose to manage these feelings.
- The marriage has two different cultures which conflict. Certain cultures are very guarded and manipulative.

- Returning from military service, finds their spouse has taken on a new partner.
- LGBT Community: When a separation occurs, the grandparents become collateral damage.
- The adult child returns to the birth parent, cutting off the adopting parents.
- Shunning of a separated parent by a religious denomination, the grandparents become collateral damage.
- Focusing on their busy lives, they cast you aside.
- They are under the influence of an addiction to drugs or alcohol.
- They have an unresolved childhood issue.
- Alienators are master manipulators.
- Their actions may stem from a mental health concern. Their mental illness might interfere with their ability to regulate their thoughts or feelings.
- They may have some level of personality disorder at play.

The dictionary describes personality disorder as a deeply ingrained and maladaptive pattern of behavior of a specified kind, typically manifest by the time one reaches adolescence and causing long-term difficulties in personal relationships or in functioning in society.

The American Psychiatric Association, APA, defines personality as the way of thinking, feeling and behaving that makes a person different from other people. An individual's personality is influenced by experiences, environment (surroundings, life situations) and inherited characteristics. A person's personality typically stays the same over time. A personality disorder is a way of thinking, feeling and behaving that deviates from the expectations of the culture, causes distress or problems functioning, and lasts over time.

Types of Personality Disorders – APA

- o Antisocial personality disorder: a pattern of disregarding or violating the rights of others. A person with antisocial personality disorder may not conform to social norms, may repeatedly lie or deceive others, or may act impulsively.

- o Avoidant personality disorder: a pattern of extreme shyness, feelings of inadequacy and extreme sensitivity to criticism. People with avoidant personality disorder may be unwilling to get involved with people unless they are certain of being liked, be preoccupied with being criticized or rejected, or may view themselves as not being good enough or socially inept.

- o Borderline personality disorder: a pattern of instability in personal relationships, intense emotions, poor self-image and impulsivity. A person with borderline personality disorder may go to great lengths to avoid being abandoned, have repeated suicide attempts, display inappropriate intense anger or have ongoing feelings of emptiness.

- o Dependent personality disorder: a pattern of needing to be taken care of and submissive and clingy behavior. People with dependent personality disorder may have difficulty making daily decisions without reassurance from others or may feel uncomfortable or helpless when alone because of fear of inability to take care of themselves.

- o Histrionic personality disorder: a pattern of excessive emotion and attention seeking. People with histrionic personality disorder may be uncomfortable when they are not the center of attention, may use physical appearance to draw attention to themselves or have rapidly shifting or exaggerated emotions.

- o Obsessive-compulsive personality disorder: a pattern of preoccupation with orderliness, perfection and control. A person with obsessive-compulsive personality disorder may be overly focused on details or schedules, may work excessively not allowing time for leisure or friends, or may be inflexible in their morality and values. (*This is NOT the same as obsessive compulsive disorder.*)

o   Paranoid personality disorder: a pattern of being suspicious of others and seeing them as mean or spiteful. People with paranoid personality disorder often assume people will harm or deceive them and don't confide in others or become close to them.

o   Schizoid personality disorder: being detached from social relationships and expressing little emotion. A person with schizoid personality disorder typically does not seek close relationships, chooses to be alone and seems to not care about praise or criticism from others.

o   Schizotypal personality disorder: a pattern of being very uncomfortable in close relationships, having distorted thinking and eccentric behavior. A person with schizotypal personality disorder may have odd beliefs or odd or peculiar behavior or speech or may have excessive social anxiety.

o   Narcissistic personality disorder: a pattern of need for admiration and lack of empathy for others. A person with narcissistic personality disorder may have a grandiose sense of self-importance, a sense of entitlement, take advantage of others, or lack empathy. Diagnosis of a personality disorder requires a mental health professional looking at long-term patterns of functioning and symptoms.

Research shows it doesn't help to argue with a narcissist. There is no need to defend yourself because it is not about you. They see all fault as yours. You cannot change that. They do not see themselves as part of the problem. They insist they are the one telling the truth. A narcissist has to feel superior. They accomplish this by putting others down. Try not to engage in any emotional conversations with a narcissistic family member. They will just increase their defensiveness.

Dr. Bone presenting on the topic of Personality Disorders at the 2019 AGA International Conference stated the following: Those with personality disorders, which usually develop during adolescence, see things differently. It is clear to see why those with personality disorders cut off family members. Look at the situation from their point of view. Step into their world. Their reality is governed by emotion. Their happiness and contentment are based on everyone behaving the way they want them to behave. They have a tendency to make false abuse allegations. They may exhibit anger responses which is a protective layer. It keeps them away from feelings of loss. The alienating parent sees their child as an extension of them self, and expects the child to behave in such manner. If the child defies the parent's point of view, they view it as a betrayal. They feel it as an attack on them. Seeing their spouse as an extension of them creates an abusive relationship.

Addressing the issues of mental illness/personality disorders at the 2019 AGA International Conference, Dr. Coleman explained how it would cause an adult child to treat a parent in an abusive way. He remarked how it can interfere with their ability to balance their own their thoughts and feelings, or develop theories about how better parenting wouldn't have burdened them with the flaws they have, or the way their lives have turned out. He discussed why it may cause them to feel in some way defective or flawed, and need to blame the parent a way to feel less shameful. He furthered explained that it also can make them more vulnerable to manipulation from a more troubled spouse.

Dr. Coleman shared with the grandparents at the conference, "A person's reactions to events, either internal (memories, thoughts, or feelings) or external (conflict, stress, trauma) cause the person to react in ways that radically alter their view of themselves or others. It may also cause them to respond in consistently maladaptive ways. If your adult child is married to somebody who has borderline personality disorder, paranoid personality disorder, anti-social personality, or even if they have such severe depression or anxiety that they can't tolerate any disruption, they may force your child into an estrangement. It doesn't take a whole lot to trigger individuals who suffer with those forms of mental illness. Typically, they are not happy people. Happy people overall tend to be more tolerant, forgiving and loving."

He suggests when mental illness is involved to calmly state what you are willing to do or not do without blame, criticism, or guilt trips. Let your child know that when they talk to you in a highly provocative or disrespectful way, they make it hard for you to listen or pay attention; that you know they have something important to say and you want to hear it, but that you are unable to when they use a critical tone of voice. Don't let yourself be blackmailed. Don't criticize your child for trying. Simply say, "No, that won't work for me." Or, "No, I'm not willing to do that. But I am willing to_____." Empathize with what they are feeling or saying. Ask what they would like from you, specifically. Model being in control of your own emotions without acting like you are trying to control theirs.

15

The Enablers

"Their isolating us, the secrecy, and the apparent 'fear' among family members are enabling this to continue, which is why we need individuals and entities to reach out to help. My son's children should be respected all the time, by all of us, including family members, especially the Godparents, especially the Church, especially the School District, and the public. Silence is complicity. Their cousins just don't have the skills to talk to our son and D-I-L without feeling like they are taking sides. They are afraid to do or say anything. The children are totally innocent, and we have done nothing purposely or dreadfully harmful to anyone. The bottom line is that our grandchildren are hurting. Let's NEVER forget that."

"There are too many enablers watching, hoping, or ignoring; as we grandparents and our grandchildren are being emotionally devastated."

"My ex-husband, my daughter's father, helped her pay for a lawyer to fight me in court. He threatened me personally."

"My daughter-in-law is definitely a narcissist, and my son is one of her enablers. She has been the cause of great mental anguish for me. Our daughter-in-law has convinced our son it is best for him and their children to disconnect from us. The children are the real victims."

Enablers   Abettors   Cult Members

Alienators manipulate their world to cause the targeted grandparent, their spouse, other family members, and friends to believe that the reasons for their dismissal were all the grandparent's fault. The enablers come to believe the targeted grandparent is getting the treatment they deserve; that they did something to warrant an extreme reaction. These brainwashing tactics make it easier for the gatekeepers to rationalize their position. All those who do not fit their description as an enabler are eliminated.

They leave the grandparents surrounded by destroyed dreams of what they thought their futures would encompass. Their manipulation results in the targeted spouse's rejection, disdain, and lack of empathy toward the targeted grandparent. The alienating adult child and their enablers, manage to manipulate or damage the grandparent's sense of self in many ways. The more we know about these gatekeepers, the better we will be able to respond to their game plan.

Toxic people have an ability to triangulate third parties into an abusing victim. Those with narcissistic characteristics are dependent on others for their self-assurance. Narcissism does not exist in a vacuum. There are always enablers. Enablers reinforce a narcissist's behavior, and make the problem worse. Enablers support the behavior of their abusive controlling spouse. Narcissistic abusers surround themselves with these enablers, those who stand silently by, and rely upon them to be a backup against the targeted grandparent. Together they form an alliance in a campaign of hostility against the grandparent.

The narcissist doesn't care how they make you feel as long as they provoke an emotion from you. It makes them feel superior and powerful. Narcissists have no problem meeting their own needs first, before their children's or parents' needs, and feel completely justified in their action. They live with a chronic sense of entitlement to have life revolve around them. They see nothing wrong with their attitude or behavior.

To protect your happiness in response to the narcissist's tactics, identify the patterns they have, and learn to respond in ways that neutralize any power they have over you. The narcissist needs regular assurance that you are not competing, that you have no interest in proving who's better, who's right versus wrong, or who has more power. Do not compete to outdo them. Remind yourself to be centered and confident.

We question who the enablers are in our extended families. We are puzzled by who could possibly do such a horrendous thing. We are confused whether it is our own grown child doing this to us, or if our D-I-L or S-I-L is actually behind the cruelty. We are puzzled why our child allows this long term or life sentence to be cast upon us. How did they stop loving and caring about us? Do they ever think about us? Do they have guilt? Over and over we ask ourselves why have they chosen to effectively abandon us, or hardly acknowledge us. What could we possibly have done to receive such harsh treatment from the enablers who allow this to be effective?

If an ex-spouse (grandparent) is enabling the disconnect and the opportunity presents itself, ask your adult child how they felt hearing what was said about you. (Dr. Coleman 2019) If you have to refute something, do it calmly, lovingly, and briefly. Ideally, find neutral ways to defend yourself with statements like, "I'm not sure why your mother or father thinks that. But sometimes people have very different ideas about the past." Do not show your outrage and don't express anger at your ex, your adult child, or your son-in-law or daughter-in-law. It will just keep your child in the middle. Show your health and resilience by your affection, love, and dedication.

Grandparents tend to blame themselves and wonder how the decades of dedication, devotion, and love could have been destroyed. They feel like the person they themselves have struggled to become all these years has suddenly been taken away. They feel like they have had their identity stripped from them. The alienators and their web of enablers have simply taken it away from them. Grandparents question what kind of people could do such a thing, and what kind of people could support this human tragedy. Are they so vulnerable themselves that their adult children prey on their loving parents? As human beings who own the truth, grandparents have now been pushed to their emotional edge, and left to suffer this violent silence 24/7.

16

The Gatekeeper

"Not seeing my son for several years after he started dating her should have been all I needed to know about how they would handle things as a couple."

"She could be a very sweet and cordial person....until they got married."

"Our daughter has remarried, and there is now another child. We supported her in the new marriage, but she began to slip away again, as she did in her first marriage. Gradually, she drew her second husband into her feelings. They have both lied and use twisted aspects of truth to explain their withdrawal to others. They have convinced others to believe we are the ones who have alienated them, and that we do not approve of the new husband. These are false statements. We are a fun-loving and respectful family. We have no understanding why this has happened. Our attempts to reach out have been unsuccessful."

Gatekeepers prevent you from having contact with your grandchildren. The gatekeeper is the alienating person responsible for cutting the ties. Gatekeeping is the term used to describe the actions of a parent limiting, for appropriate or inappropriate purposes, the contact and relationship with the other parent or grandparent. Gatekeepers inflict abuse on their own parents, and therefore their own kids. The gatekeeper is the one with whom you should try to work things out.

(Dr. Coleman 2019 AGA International Conference) You can't go around them. You can only go thru them. Therefore, make sure to include them in most of your correspondence to your adult child. Make amends with them if you they feel wronged by you. Do not criticize your child's spouse. In general, do not challenge their boundaries.

If it is your goal to be with your grandchildren, then you must try to do what might bring positive results. Since resuming the once close relationship you had with your child and grandchildren is your goal, reach out to and strive toward making amends with the gatekeepers. Try to see the situation through their eyes. It is thru them that you will get your grandchildren back. Be the actor if you must. The prize is worth it. Do not give up on your grandchildren. They would not want you to give up on them.

It is extremely important to focus on your adult child. You are still the parent. Role model good parenting behaviors. Do not stop reaching out to your son or daughter. Let them know you love them and will always be there for them. This reassures them you will be there for them when the time comes. Do this without expectations of a response. Any response you do receive from your son or daughter is a good response, even if it is an unpleasant one.

Many paternal grandparents have been told by the D-I-L that they must make all communication directly thru her, not directly to their own son. This can be a testing of the waters to eventually take your grandkids away from you. Try asking her why she prefers this procedure, and if there is something she would like to have you understand so you can improve your relationship with her. Let her know you will be there to listen to her point of view. Try to settle this issue before she gains more control.

At times, you may feel like you want to say or do certain things, but focus on moving toward getting results. Do what you think will work, not what you think would be fair. Grandparent Alienation is not about fairness.

Continue to reach out and work on the relationship with the person who is the gatekeeper. Nothing succeeds like persistence. You never know when you will get lucky.

It is the gatekeepers who send that before mentioned list of demands to be satisfied before any attempts of reunification are to be considered. The list is constructed to look like you are the guilty party on many accounts. They try to make you think as though you have done something terribly wrong. Some items list of demands may contain an underlying statement allowing them to harbor less quilt for the role they have played. If you think some of the accusations hold merit, then by all means make amends.

Alienated grandparents interpret complying with their list of demands is a hopeful pathway for communication and a reconnect. Unconditionally loving parents will do almost whatever it takes. If some demands are out right false accusations, find a creative way to comply without compromising your integrity. By "asking" you to do this, they are putting you though a major trauma, and the results are unpredictable. Gatekeepers require all of this in order to gain more power and control. When grandparents make the effort to comply, there is no guarantee that the adult children will keep their end of the bargain. This doesn't mean you shouldn't try. As previously stated, many AGA grandparents have acquiesced to the alienators' demands. Unfortunately, once complied with, the gatekeepers up the ante. Lesson learned…healthy minds want to fix things, unhealthy minds do not.

17

The Other Grandparents OG's

"The details are in short supply because the other grandparents (OGs) cleared the decks for this to happen. It had been about 6 years since we were last together. Our grandson, now 14, demanded of his other grandparents, "I want to see my Grandpop and Grammie." The OGs brought him to our house. We spend the whole day with him. The OGs then took him to see his great-grandfather. We don't think his parents know this all took place, and we don't know if and when it will ever happen again. What we do know is that he loves us. You should be so proud of what your AGA organization does. The problems you've helped people solve, the tears you've helped to dry, and the happiness you've helped to create. The world is a better place because of AGA."*

"Our son and his family live about two hours from us. We are in our early 80's. Each time we arrive, our daughter-in-law offers coffee to my husband, but not to me. I sit at the dinner table while my husband and the others are being served, but nothing is brought to me. It's all just so obvious." When her parents are visiting along with us, they are both treated so well. Our son is very loving to us, but just accepts his wife's behavior toward me. I consider myself a very easy-going person, and have many good friendships. I just don't understand why she does this."

"Almost two years ago my son died in a fatal car accident, and his girlfriend (unknowing to my son or me) ended up pregnant. The other grandmother was granted full guardianship, and the state won't let us have any rights at all." For now, the OG does allow us to see the baby for limited visits."

"The other grandparents (D-I-L's parents) seem like the winners, and we are the booby prize. We know very well this does not define us. We can heal and rise above this, but we are human and it hurts big time."

"I felt suicidal for months when we learned from friends that we had a grandchild. My husband was very angry. Some details were shared with us by the other grandparents at first, but later they closed ranks, maintaining their need to keep their own close relationship and not wanting to put it into jeopardy by communicating with us."

"I know my daughter-in-law never has, not even a single overture, remotely tried to get to know me. I was actually shunned by her from the first day I met her 15 years ago, a red flag I ignored. I know they never encouraged the Smiths and the Jones to get to know one another. Perhaps if the other grandfather and I had had a few conversations, we might have 'pre-empted' some of this."

"I tried writing to the children's other grandparents and got a strong, 'Do not get my family involved in this; do not write to them again' from my son-in-law."

"The other grandparent encouraged, my ex., encouraged the alienation. He assured our daughter she should be "protected from me". I was the care-giving parent!"

"The other grandparent (ex-spouse) told lies that I was using drugs."

"I believe her mother-in-law was tired of hearing our granddaughter talk about her Mee-maw all the time. She expressed that to me at her third birthday party. I have not been allowed to see my granddaughter since."

"I have talked to our daughter-in-law's parents about all this only once in years. Of course, I had thought it must be just me who must have messed up along the way. Was I wrong! I learned for the first time that her parents, who are

decent, kind, and generous in every way; have been mistreated and alienated by their son-in-law and their daughter for almost ten years. They revealed that since the day they got married they have gotten to see them every two months, if they were lucky. The way our son has treated her parents is not the way he was raised, and it's a crying shame our daughter-in-law goes along, no matter her reasons."

"Our son's mother- in-law has been a beast from the beginning. She is in their business every day telling them what to do, say, and think. Our son put up with it, even encouraged it. We raised our kids with freedom, choice, responsibility. This mother makes rules, applies pressure and guilt, and plays them like a marionette. Her husband is weak."

"Sometimes it does bother me to see my grandchildren with the other grandparents." It's easier for them to get visiting time, so my grandbabies know them better."

A grandparent wanting to have a special bond with a grandchild is natural unless they want the grandchild to regard them as the most favored grandparent. This desire becomes questionable when competition, aiming to outdo the OG and an eagerness to be thought of as a more adored one, takes places. You may feel as though you have a special bond with your grandchildren, but the grandparents on the other side of the family feel the same way. Competing to be the most-loved only creates a problematic dynamic for the family.

Choosing to focus on just being the best grandparent one can possibly be, should include being supportive of the OG's. When the extended family gathers to celebrate special occasions, it serves everyone best if both sets of grandparents restrain from vying for the grandkids' love and attention.

The relationship with your grandchild is special, regardless of the other people in their life. Build up the best relationship possible, and let them know that you love them and will always be there for them, even if you are not around as much as you would like. Decide upon special activities that you could do together, or just hanging around with each other.

Grandparents who seem to be competing with each other, trying to buy their love or bribing them with their one-upmanship, makes for an uncomfortable family dynamic. When one set off grandparents realizes this and the OGs do not, it creates friction. The concept of more wealth and more stuff doesn't mean more love or personal worth. It is the way your grandchildren feel when they are with you that counts. The underlying jealousy and one-upmanship existing beneath the surface just divides grandparents.

The dictionary defines jealousy as resenting the person. Envy is defined as resenting the person's successes or possessions. These sometimes-overlapping emotions are factors in the OG relationship.

When the OGs have liberal visiting privileges (or if you think they do), and your visits are strictly limited; you are likely to feel resentful of the OGs. Oftentimes, one set of grandparents is not aware that the other set is also being withheld from seeing these grandchildren. This is most certainly a sign of the power and control of the alienator.

Many grandparents have shared with AGA how they always thought the OGs had a normal relationship with the couple, only to eventually discover that was not the case. If you have been marginalized from the family, try reaching out to the OG's. Start with special occasion cards, writing a pleasant note. Eventually, you might hear back from them. Attempt to develop an alliance with them. Perhaps they can serve as a bridge person for you to learn about the well-being of your family, especially if you are isolated.

When a couple choses to invite both sets of grandparents to spend time together, they can help to build a relationship between the grandparents which can ease any feelings of threat or competitiveness. On the other hand, when alienators work at keeping each set of parents from engaging with one another, it may be a sign that you are all being treated the same way.

Mainly, it is the maternal grandparents who have a more open-door advantage. The OGs want a relationship, so they agree to what is occurring to keep whatever they have intact. The M-I-L / D-I-L relationship is almost always going be complicated, magnifying the paternal grandparents' feelings of disconnect. Susan Adcox, author and grandmother states, "Possession, so to speak, of a treasured male, has been passed from mother to wife. A bit of jealousy and competitiveness is natural. Still, it may stand in the way of a close relationship, which may in turn stand in the way of closeness between grandparent and grandchild. Perhaps mothers-in-law are often unfairly criticized, but some tension is built into the role."

Daughters more commonly bring their husbands into their own family structure. When a son is pulled into the psychological makeup of his wife's family, it can produce a great deal of emotional pain and chaos for his parents. While the daughter-in-law's family may initially welcome a son-in-law into their family, sooner or later they may set up barriers for his parents. The son's parents suffer the consequences feeling devalued. When grandbabies enter the picture, the paternal grandparents are at risk.

AGA grandparents frequently report the negative influence of their D-I-L's mother. With insecurities of her own, the maternal grandmother adds to the stress of the family dynamics. Her intentions to lessen or cut off the bond between her daughter and the M-I-L often cause chaos as she takes on the role of an enabler in the alienation process. The paternal grandmother becomes her victim.

Parents have specific ways of doing things when it comes to raising their children. If the grandparent disagrees with their practices, it is wise not to offer opinions when not asked. Keep any criticisms to yourself. If there is something on your mind, take the time to assess what is bothering you. Don't immediately speak out as this could lead to upset. Be selective about what you allow your eyes to see and your ears to hear. The maternal grandparents have more privilege opening up to their daughter. The M-I-L who finds need to address a situation with her D-I-L should approach with caution, remaining calm and rational. It might be best to hold your tongue. Protect yourself.

Long-distance grandparents are especially likely to feel resentful of the OGs who are closer in distance to the grandchildren. Factors such as the health, employment, and financial status of the grandparents can limit travel. This is when computers and mobile phone technology come into play. Find out what form of technology your grandkids like to use, and learn how to do it. There's something available for all ages of grandkids. Having intergenerational technology visits is a great way to be closer to your growing grandchildren. Try negotiating for such visits with your gatekeeper. Stay interested and stay available any way that you can.

Some grandparents who experience a level of alienation have demonstrated a willingness to move (or move back) to live close to their grandchildren. Before you uproot your domicile, leave your job and the friends who have been your long-term support system, there are possible scenarios to consider. Some gatekeepers will try to persuade their parents to make this difficult and expensive move, only to continue denying them access to the grandkids once they arrive. If you have already experienced some level of alienation by the middle generation, moving closer does not guarantee positive results. If you have tried to move back before, and it didn't work out, there is no assurance it will work this time. If you have traveled to see your family and they still denied you reasonable or no visiting time with them, consider this a red alert. Do not allow yourself to fall victim to their alienating tactics. Protect your heart and your investment. Consider testing the waters by renting a place near them for a while. This may help you determine if there will actually be access to the grandchildren and a functioning relationship between the first and third generation.

Once you have arrived, welcome the OGs in hopes of forming a working relationship. Try to quiet any underlying natural jealousies or competitiveness simmering inside of you. Such thoughts will only cause you anxiety; they will not improve the situation. Enjoy the time given to you with the grandkids without keeping tally. Consciously avoid conflict with the middle generation regarding who gets more time. Try not to allow the emotional pain of being denied more time with your grandkids to interfere with how much time you dreamed of having. Acknowledge this feeling, but do not let yourself obsess over it. Being aware of and appreciating what we have, brings more serenity.

When the generation divorces, it sets the stage for fear and potential suffering regarding future GP-GC contact. The grandchildren become victims and suffer as the family divides. Combining divorce with the challenge of long distance, the chances for the OGs and the grandchildren to know and enjoy a growing and special relationship decreases drastically.

Since women still receive custody more often than men, it is the maternal grandparents who usually benefit. The paternal grands can easily become the collateral damage of the divorce. As more fathers win custody in the future, and with joint custody becoming more popular, perhaps divorce will not affect the GP-GC relationship as radically as it has up till now.

Many paternal grandparents and great grandparents find their contact glaringly reduced or completely cut off. Since the grandparents of the custodial parents usually play a more active role resulting in developing a closer relationship with the children, these hands-on grandparents can play an important role facilitating contact between the grandchildren and the OGs. Reach out to the grandparents who have an influence. Don't let any negative feelings affect your relationship with the custodial parent or OGs. Periodically, try to communicate with them. Send them a friendly note on holiday and birthday cards, leave an upbeat voicemail, or send a small gift for special occasions. Try to fit in to the best of your ability if you desire to be part of your grandchild's life. Eventually, the involved parties might agree on scheduling a specific day of the week or month for you to visit by cell phone video calls. More opportunities may lie ahead for actual overnights or vacation time. Being the OG can be a rocky road, but with the right attitude and creative thinking you might achieve great results.

18

Holidays and Special Occasions

"There's an empty spot on our counter every year for cards we never get or thank-you notes for presents we can't send."

"We totally understand your wanting to spend time with the other parents, but we'd like to spend some holidays with you too."

"I spoke of you and AGA today remembering how finding your group had saved my life those first years. It will be 5 years soon, and am sending this picture of our last Christmas together. I don't want to forget them, but it's so painful to think of them."

"I wanted to die. Even though I'm coping a little better each year, every birthday and holiday are torture to get through."

"We would certainly be lost without the help of AGA. We made it through Xmas without one gift or a card. We never ever believed this could happen."

"The package and letters I sent at Christmas and birthday seem to have mysteriously failed to be delivered."

"I physically hand deliver presents to my son at his office, because I am afraid a present dropped off or mailed to his residence would get confiscated and perhaps thrown away.'

"We decided to spend some of the money we planned to leave to our daughter. Another holiday was approaching. Knowing we wouldn't be with our

grandchild or daughter, we decided to take a cruise. On the crossing we spoke to most of the people onboard. When we mentioned that we could no longer see our granddaughter, we discovered that 90% of the people were not allowed to visit with their grandchildren either!"

"Since I've had no contact with my son and grandchildren, Christmas has become the most painful day of the year for me. It hurts to see my friends post pictures on Facebook of their families smiling around a Christmas tree. I can't do any of that, and that's what I had looked forward to at this age."

"As a father whose adult daughter refuses contact with me (due to influence of ex-spouse), I am heart-broken. I knew my grandson for six years; now he's told I am a bad person. I feel shame, grief, and frustrated. Not being involved as a grandfather is tough for me. *Today, Father's Day creates a platform for hope for me. I pray that today will be the day I hear something from my daughter.*"

"I was not invited to my daughter's wedding that we planned together for a year. After invitations were mailed out, she told me her dad (my ex) would not come if I was there. I was then told that I was not invited. She did not talk to me for four years. When she had two babies and needed my help, I got to bond with them for two years before I was cut off again."

"I have sent my grands Christmas gifts for 6 years now and have NEVER received a thank you. I am wondering if I should continue. My gifts are very generous. My daughter is brainwashed."

"When we want to get together for holidays, we hear… *Oh sorry, we won't have time to celebrate the holiday with you; we've already made plans.*"

"We are now seeing them at Christmas and for their birthdays. They came to our city for Easter to see their great-grandma. It was six years very long years. Things are going pretty well now."

"On birthdays and special occasions send balloons from a florist to the school or to be placed on their porch. Change florists each time you do this so the alienating parents cannot instruct the florists NOT to send things. Do this before the actual special occasion day to throw the alienators off the track. This has worked very well for me, and I have done this many times. I send gifts through UPS as they land right on the porch. I send very big boxes so they will be seen. It is essential to send them on a school day. Be sure NOT to put your return address. I change the return address each time. I explain the situation to the UPS people, and they are all very cooperative.'

"Leave holiday and birthday gifts at their doorstep. Timing is important. In Florida it is lawful to tie balloons to the mailbox POST. Use magic marker to write messages on the balloons. Knock on their door. Perhaps you'll get lucky. Tell the grandchildren you love them, and have been trying to see them."

Over the river and through the woods to grandma's house may not be the direction vast numbers of grandchildren will be heading for the holiday. December is supposed to be the most wonderful time of the year. Or, is it? Surviving the festive season has become a particularly challenging time for grandparents who wonder how they are going to survive yet another year without their sons, daughters, and grandchildren. These are supposed to be the times when families continue traditions. These are the stories that families are supposed to write together.

For those who have little or no contact with their kids and grandkids, intensified feelings of loss and loneliness are exacerbated by the holiday season. Traditional holidays such as Christmas, Hanukah, and Thanksgiving are filled with anxiety and a sense of dread. Thinking everyone around them is excited about sharing the special day with their loved ones, they know theirs won't be a holly jolly Christmas this year. They feel like they are the only person in the universe who's not laughing, eating, partying, and otherwise living life with the people who are supposed to love them the most. They have been shut out.

The sad reality is that most people are struggling with problems of some nature. It may not be alienation, but others have difficult issues in their lives as well. Even the happiest of families have their troubles. Odds are everyone is telling the good stuff while leaving out the conflicts. Across the world millions of people have different circumstances: some are seriously ill, some are feeling the heavy burden of grief from the death of a loved one, some are too far away, some are feuding with others, and some people don't have enough food. For many people, the reality of the holidays isn't so cheerful. Alienated grandparents in huge numbers are among those with extreme apprehension as holiday time approaches.

City sidewalks, busy sidewalks dressed in holiday style fill the air with images of love and joy. Hallmark specials and treasured holiday movies inundate the TV screens. Months of commercials and advertisements confront millions of shoppers. Surrounded by Christmas lights and Bing Crosby singing, "I'll be home for Christmas", for many it will be only in their dreams. No other day of the year is so thoroughly immersed in such high and mostly unattainable expectations for so many. Everywhere you turn is a reminder that you will not be doing what you used to do, or want to do at the time of the year customarily set aside for family connection.

Our cultures make such a big deal about holidays. They tell us how we should feel and celebrate when in fact there are so many who are quite sad on these days. In Western culture the Thanksgiving, Hanukah, and Christmas holidays are so ingrained that mothers who have been cut off begin worrying about them months in advance. What will they do to get through the season's message of peace, love, and togetherness? How will they protect themselves emotionally?

Amanda

The holiday season can be a particularly difficult time for those who are not in contact with family members. It is the time of year that makes us contemplate our existence, our relationships, and what really matters to us. Feelings of nostalgia surface bringing to mind happy childhood moments, traditions, and stories that families have been creating together. As alienated grandparents age, they hope to pass along some of their stories and traditions to the next generations. Being denied the opportunity to be part of their son's, daughter's, and grandchildren's family life is traumatizing. For vast numbers of grandparents who have been cut off from their close family, the holiday season does not feel so merry and bright. It is more like a private hell. They aren't able to celebrate in the manner they should. This creates a painful sense of loss and failing. For years, AGA's website has received about 10,000 hits during the holiday months. Millions of people are hurting deeply.

Since your adult child is choosing not to spend time with you, think about how you would like to spend your time. You deserve to have serenity, self-esteem, and to enjoy your life. Be kind to yourself. Realize that you are not alone in this situation, or the feelings that come with it. It takes a good deal of inner strength to be happy. Find the courage to make your happiness. It may be difficult to be happy when things are not going right, but it can be accomplished. Find others to share the day with, or plan an excursion.

(Sichel) It can be difficult to avoid comparing yourself with others around holiday time. If you have a less-than-perfect family, comparing your holiday experience with other peoples' is a recipe for increased sadness and isolation...People's basis for comparison is not based in reality, because most families have issues and most people do not have the perfect holiday that they would like to have, or that they'd like to remember from their childhood.

If you're in the midst of what researcher Kristina Scharp, PhD, calls "chaotic disassociation', meaning you have a volatile on-again off-again relationship, holidays present an unresolvable dilemma, one that's exacerbated by scrolling through social media posts of other people's amazing celebrations.

Alienated grandparents don't get to serve their family turkey dinner with all the trimmings. The grandkids are kept from learning how to make Grandma's hand-me-down recipe for stuffing. Grandpa doesn't get to make the annual last-minute run to the supermarket for the one ingredient they forgot to purchase. He doesn't get to watch the big football game with his grandson. Grandmas and grandpas are not invited for the baby's first Christmas. They won't be around the tree to witness the expressions on the faces of the grandchildren and marvel at the excitement of opening the presents they would have had so much fun shopping for during the year. They won't be standing by the menorah with the children as they recite the traditional Hebrew prayer and lighting the Hanukah candles. They won't partake in any of the eight nights' traditions of making potato latkas, gift-giving, or spinning the dreidel.

Millions of families will be without the grands at the family celebrations. The grandchildren miss out hearing stories of years gone by. As grands grow older in years, they are kept from passing along the stories of their families' heritage they so dearly want to share. They won't be at the gathering, and that's the way it will be for yet another holiday season. Hopefully, next year won't be too late for the miracle to happen.

A universal concern of grandparents is whether or not to send presents. Some don't even know where their family is living. If they do send the presents, it is likely that they won't know what the children like or want, or what sizes to buy. Plus, they have no way of knowing if the gifts are even being received by the children.

If you live in the vicinity, you could deliver the package to their doorstep. Be sure to take a witness with you, since false accusations are a dynamic of Grandparent Alienation. Find a large cardboard box, and decorate the outside with lots of holiday cheer. Attach balloons on top with their names in magic marker. Kids of all ages like to unwrap presents, so wrap each little item separately. With each item, leave a personal note of love. Include your address, phone number, and email address. Some day they may be able to reach out to you.

Just in case the presents do not reach the children, do not buy expensive items. It is the idea that you cared enough to do this for them that counts. Timing of placement is important. If you can get past any fear, knock on their door. You never know, you just might get lucky. Otherwise, when you think no one will be around, leave the gift package on the step for the grandchildren to see. Think of a time when the children are more likely to be the first out the door. If they live in a gated community, be creative. Another possibility is having a gift package mailed or delivered to them from the distributor. Be sure to request a card be placed inside the box to recognize you as the sender.

AGA consultant Charles D. Jamieson, Esq. suggested (considering an individual's circumstances) sending a card through the mail and via email for every birthday, holiday, or significant event. He encouraged grandparents to keep the cards light and not to badmouth the mom or dad. He suggested sending gifts for birthdays, holidays, graduation, and other special occasions. He encouraged the documentation of all your communications and your gifts.

Amplified by the sadness of being alone, how do such heart-broken grandparents cope with the turmoil of facing the holiday season? Grands who have been severely limited to or cut off from contact with the most important people in their lives can deal better with their emotional pain by focusing on things that will bring them some pleasure. If Plan A is not available to you, move on to Plan B. Create opportunities for your happiness.

Practical suggestions for enjoying more peace and happiness during the holiday season, even in the absence of your sons, daughters, and grandchildren include:

- If you are allowable limited contact, request a scheduled time for a special telephone call or mobile video call. The exact date does not matter, because any communication is good. If the OGs are celebrating the holiday with the grandchildren, waiting for your turn is better than nothing. Remember to do what you think might work, not what you think is fair.
- Make plans to celebrate with dear friends, co-workers, and family members you enjoy.

Call an old friend. Contact someone who is a positive influence in your life, who you know would be delighted to hear from you. You do not need a reason. Just say it's this time of year that got me thinking of you.

- Create traditions. Invite people who also have no family nearby to celebrate with this year. Plan to share the meal followed by a walk outside, or board games by the fire. You can offer to cook, share the chores, or prepare the food together.
- Bake your gifts. It will occupy your mind for days at end.
- Watch happy movies, or find a captivating book to help take your mind off being lonely.
- Get plenty of rest, exercise, go out-of-doors, and eat healthy. Some foods can trigger negative effects. When you take care of your body, you will feel better.

- Know that it is OK to feel sad or lonely. You don't have to try to fake it to live up to the expectations of others. Do things you want to do, not just the things you have to do.

- Indulge yourself. You deserve a gift, too. The best gifts are the ones you give yourself when you need them most. Treating yourself is an important act of self-care.

- Be mindful of what you *do* have to be thankful for in your life. Concentrate on those moments of goodness that so frequently become overshadowed by the disappointments. Reflect on what is going well in your life to develop an attitude of gratitude. No matter how troubled your year has been, you can find good when you look for it.

- Make a list of five things you have accomplished in your lifetime. Then write a list of things you can do to try to communicate with your adult child. Form a strategy; work your plan.

Figuring out what you need to get through those 24 hours, such as volunteering, going on vacation, visiting a shelter, or make plans with someone who is alone. The holiday season is about kindness; begin traditions that help the less fortunate. Taking your eyes off of yourself and focusing on those who have far less than you do, will help alleviate your sadness. When you start volunteering, you will likely become close with those you help or work alongside.

Do something nice for someone you know, or even someone you don't. Calling on a neighbor could be just the thing both of you need. Ask a local church or temple, hospice, hospital, community organization, or animal shelter how you can volunteer your time. Helping others helps you. With a bit of forethought and planning, holidays can leave you feeling up, not down. These emotionally high-risk days will be over as soon as they began. You will be back to the daily routine before you know it.

Attend AGA support group meetings where the support offered is from those who share similar experiences. Exchange contact information so you can call on them for support to minimize your emotional trauma. Plan a special holiday event with these grands. You will find comfort being among those with whom you share so many commonalities. Meet socially. It is good to have something special to look forward to during this trying time of the year.

Holiday time can be a more vulnerable time for the son or daughter who has severed the ties. This provides an opportunity for the grandparent to creatively reach out. AGA has always had many success stories during the holiday season - Thanksgiving thru New Year's. It is worth a shot. Take it!

It is the grandparents who must make the effort over and over again. Just sending annual holiday or birthday cards does not show you are thinking about their inner world, their feelings, or their point of view. You may think you acted in the best interests of your adult children, while they may feel that you failed to do just that. Try to deal with the distance they are keeping between you by offering opportunities for them communicate with you. Whether you prefer to send a card or post card, leave a voicemail, write an email, or send a text, do it more frequently. Consider a monthly message of unconditional love with brief information about your life.

If holidays cause you to think attending certain celebrations will upset you too much, don't feel obligated to say yes. Try to attend gatherings where you would feel more comfortable. Do not let your adult child take away from you what should be pleasurable opportunities.

While attending festivities, other grandparents are eager to talk about and show lots of pictures of their grandchildren. If you become ill at ease with a situation at hand, don't shy away from excusing yourself and moving on to others. Be prepared with short responses to what you think would be uncomfortable questions. If someone you are not close to asks you about your plans for the big day, just tell them your son or daughter and grandkids are traveling this holiday. If those you have a relationship with ask personal questions you can say, "We know all families have times when there are issues. This is not a good time for me to talk about this subject." Then STOP. You owe nothing more.

It is highly likely others will start talking about their grandchildren and showing pictures. If this is something that could upset you, say something like, "This is a topic I am having a difficult time with right now. We all know how family issues can pop up." You owe them no more of an explanation. It is time to set your personal boundaries and give yourself a break. It is time for you to do the very best you can to take care of YOU. Tell yourself you will get through it.

(Letchworth, AGA Elder Abuse Specialist) Just remember to take care of yourself. You do not have to answer any question you do not want to answer. Be prepared to change the topic. You are obligated to no one. Put a smile on your face, move on, and talk to others in the room.

You can always remove yourself from a given situation if the emotions are too much for you to handle. Politely excuse yourself from the table or gathering area to refill your drink or go to the restroom. Once there, take some deep breathes, text or call a friend, or put in earbuds and listen to calming music. If you arrive armed with these tips for dealing with stressful moments, you will do just fine.

Do not allow fear to stand in your way of role-modeling good parental and grandparental behavior. If you are invited to attend the family gathering, consider making a shorter appearance rather than staying for the entire time. If you have been invited to spend time with your family which requires overnight travel, it may be in your best interest to stay in a hotel.

You won't be interrupting their family routine, and you will limit the family drama, have a place to retreat to, and may very well be more welcome for return visits if you secure your own space.

If you are fortunate enough to have more than one child, direct your attention to making the holiday a happy one for them. The siblings and cousins have also suffered from loss. Do not let the ones who are missing overshadow the blessings you do have in your life. Focus your attention on making happy memories on the holiday.

Holiday season reminds us of the warm feeling of connections we have shared. Do not allow negative thoughts and the hurtful people in your life to keep you from indulging yourself of the good times and precious thoughts of your past. Reflect on treasured memories shared with your parents and grandparents. Share the good memories of holiday traditions past with those close to you. You own those stories, and no one can take them away from you. You also do not need to justify your day to anyone. "My holiday was nice and quiet," is typically a good response.

There is no right or wrong way to spend the day. It's just 24 hours. It will be over tomorrow, and all the focus will be on something else. Go shopping! Find or make a greeting card for each grandchild for every holiday or special occasion. Write a message of your love, and date it. Place a picture inside each card showing what Grandma and Grandpa looked like that year. Add whatever pictures depict the special adventures you enjoyed during the year. Tell them what you would have said if you were able to be with them. Place these into a memory box for the grandchildren's future.

Send a little gift to show you care. It is not the cost of the gift; it is the meaning behind it. It represents how much you care about them. Sending an age-appropriate book with your inscription at the beginning would mean a great deal to a child of any age. A book is a special gift that can last forever. Saving this collection of books with your thoughts inscribed, would mean a great deal to your grandchildren some day!

If you have no address for them, place the items into a memory box. Since there is no way of being certain they were handed your gifts, take pictures of what you do send. Keep a journal of your thoughts for each grandchild. Someday this will be the proof of how hard you tried to connect with them. This will be your chance for truth. Do this without expectations. Do this because it is the right thing to do. Do it to satisfy yourself that you tried your very best. Do it because you want your grandchildren to know that you never gave up on them. Do it because you want them to know how very much you love and care about them, and how hard you tried to be with them. Do it to give them a part of you. Do it to give back to them the other half of who they are.

Mother's Day and Father's Day are another of the hardest days of the year. Though every day has its challenges, these two days are especially difficult. There are silent expectations or hopes that this day in particular will be the day that their son or daughter will reach out to them and end the unbearable torment. Grands can't help but anticipate that on their special day love will surface, and they will once again hear the words "I love you Mom, or I love you Dad". They didn't call on the birthday, but maybe, just maybe, this symbolic day will soften their heart.

The questions remain unanswered. How many more days, weeks, months, or years will this torture continue? The closer it gets to the end, the faster it goes. Where is their heart? The youth of the grandchild cannot be revisited. How many milestones we will miss?

This was the son or daughter who once held their finger in their tiny little fist. This was the toddler who stood at their feet looking up. This was the child who followed your footsteps. This is the person who observed and learned from the wisdom of your experiences. Where did this person go? Where is the loving son or daughter you raised?

These are the two people who were there for them. They helped solve their problems, protected and nurtured them. These are the parents who were there for them the best they know how at the time. Now they live with anger and sadness having been tossed aside. They question if they will ever be able to get through another holiday and feel whole again?

It is most helpful to reach out to someone who can empathize with your emotional pain. You need someone to listen to you. Talking about this nightmare of a journey is best shared with someone who understands and has traveled the same path. Focus on all the ways you were and are a wonderful mother or father. Recall all of the efforts and sacrifices you lovingly and willingly made for the well-being of your child.

Holidays are special days; it is healthy for you to think about how you want to spend your time. Make a 24-hour plan in advance. Do not allow yourself to be tormented by unhappy thoughts. Be mindful of yourself; you decide with whom and what you would like to do. Be especially kind to yourself. Tell yourself that since your child is choosing not to spend time with you, that you still deserve to have peace, serenity, and to enjoy your life.

These days it is common that someone is cut off from those they love the most. Alienation has no boundaries. Remind yourself again that holidays can influence a person's thinking. Be good to yourself. You are not alone in this situation; your feelings are shared by millions.

19

Weddings and Births

"We received a call this morning from a close friend. He told us our son, who cut us off when he married, became a father today. How are we supposed to cope with this?"

"My sister and her family were invited to our son's wedding, but we were not. How do you think that made us feel!"

"Everything changed when he became engaged. I remember feeling for our son, wondering if he was hurting there without his mom, dad, and brothers at his wedding. It seemed too painful to even imagine, even if he chose this arrangement."

"I gave them a lump sum check for my daughter's wedding putting them on a $25,000 budget that I could afford. They exceeded that budget and then accused me of stinginess saying, "I guess you don't want your daughter to have a wedding dress!"

"The wedding took place in her grandparents' backyard. I wasn't allowed to come early enough to meet them before the wedding. None of her family mingled with my side. They avoided us at the wedding. Now I don't see my grandson."

"We were invited to our son's wedding. However, we were completely ignored by them, her family, and the entire wedding party. I wish I could have stopped

the wedding, but that was not possible. It was a very humiliating experience. We have been ignored for nine years."

"What was the saddest of all was my son's lack of participation in his sister's wedding recently. He sat there in a numb silence, as did his wife at his side the entire time. They left early."

Excluded from our own child's wedding or not being told about the birth of a grandchild would never have crossed our minds growing up a generation ago. In a more perfect scenario, parents would view the marriage of their child as a blessing, a happy milestone, and a significant sign that their children are on their way. But the fact is that many good caring parents are not invited to their child's wedding, and many do not receive a call from their sons or daughters telling them they have just become grandparents. Many may never know they have a grandchild, and some eventually find out through social media or a personal connection. Never having known such possible behavior existed, they are shocked when it happens to them.

Instead of fulfilled dreams of growing a larger family, becoming a grandparent has been replaced by a nightmarish scenario that may never end. Life has paused for them. They feel trapped with no way out. There they remain with broken hearts from love denied, and the destruction of the family unit. It hurts so bad because these are the ones who are most important in their lives, and who were supposed to be their future. That former conceptualization of bliss turns into a possibly of unending horror, leaving most feeling they cannot face life ahead without their adult child and precious grandchildren.

For most families, weddings are a highly challenging event. For parents who have experienced some level of disassociation or isolation, it is especially explosive or painful. If you have been invited to the wedding, let your child know that you would be happy to meet to talk about the upcoming event. Then, just be a good listener. Ask if there is some way in which you could be helpful. Try not to be defensive. Just listen and be supportive. Alienation is not about fairness.

Do not make or suggest any negative comments about the person your son or daughter is choosing to marry. Any less than agreeable statement or warning could someday be construed in a negative manner, only to be twisted and used against you. The very comments you felt necessary to bring up for consideration, can be the basis for cutting you off in the future. If you believe your son or daughter should consider some issues you have observed, perhaps you might mention them in the form of questions instead of statements. Be careful of your wording.

Watch your words. Our word is far more than what comes out of our mouths; it represents what we stand for. Sometimes we have a tendency to say things we do not really mean. That holds true for some of the less than loving things we might say to others in a heated moment of thoughtlessness.

If your son or daughter does not care to meet with you prior to the wedding, act glad to see them at the ceremony. Behave as nothing has happened. You are still the mom or dad. Exhibit good role-modeling.

Should you decide to attend the wedding ceremony to which you have not been invited, and if it is taking place in a public facility such as a church, temple, park, or beach; then choosing to sit in an area where you are not bringing a lot of attention to yourself is probably a good decision on your part. If you choose to find a way to get the attention of your child, and you feel somewhat comfortable doing so, that is your judgement call. Since the venue for the ceremony is in a public facility, taking a witness with you is always a good idea.

There will always be another event and another celebration: a birthday party, school play, athletic event, religious milestone, prom night, graduation, engagement, or a host of other special times. Because they have loved their children so much, they love their grandchildren. For loving caring grandparents, every day is special. Baby's first tooth, first steps, and first words all mean a lot to grandparents. If times were tough raising their own children, then becoming a grandparent would be their golden opportunity to give more time and attention to the next generation.

20

Money Matters

"Does my son really care about me, or is he just after my money? If I continue to lend him a hand, how can he learn to grow up and take responsibility?" If I don't continue to give him what he wants, then I risk losing him and my grandson."

"I feel as if they are just waiting for me to die to get my money. Perhaps they are giving me this silent treatment in order for me to die of a broken heart, or if they ignore me… I will just go away!"

"Our son's divorce was fraught with false accusations from his ex-wife to garner money and provide a framework where she could remove his children from his life as she did my life. He has fought against that and she challenges every visitation exchange with war words. It is awful for my grandsons and for him. The lies, deceit, and fabrication continue."

"When my son married, I let them use a second property I owned with no rental fee attached. Soon thereafter, his wife had her mother and sister relocate and move in with them. When my first grandbaby was born, I was cut off from 'his family'." He then decided to go for a graduate degree, and asked me to pay for the tuition. When I told him I would not pay for more graduate education unless I was granted visits my grandbaby, he declined the offer."

"My alienating daughter and her husband expected me to pay for their destination wedding; instead I gave them a large lump sum check, as best as I could afford. They exceeded that budget, then accused me of stinginess. Visiting

them prior to our alienation was a nightmare because they expected me to pay for everything while there, including our food, fancy restaurants they chose, entertainment, as well as paying for anything they chose while shopping. They relentlessly asked for loans which they never repaid. They never allowed me to see or to meet my granddaughter. My eventually setting strong boundaries and limitations on their expensive expectations became the key factor that contributed most strongly to their rage and my ultimate alienation."

"Nothing offered seems to be good enough– including the home I chose to give them as an early inheritance."

"Our D-I-L instructed our son, on more than one occasion, to ask grandma for money. This is something that we, as family, would never have done."

"My son-in-law's parents became fiercely jealous of me (my success) and openly cruel. The in-laws' jealousy was the second largest contributing factor to my alienation and never meeting my granddaughter."

"We made a decision to help our son get out from under the debt he accumulated since his brief marriage to the undermining daughter-in-law. Eventually, we found out this money was used to pay off her mother's debts instead of their own."

"I have experienced adult children being centered in monetary expectations of parents.

I was welcome to visit in my daughter's home until they used the inheritance from my parents to buy a home. I feel I was in their graces until the purchase was completed. I feel like there is some kind of connection between their finally using the money to purchase a home and my being dropped from their orbit."

Amanda

"*Our parents worked long and hard to provide for their family's future inheritance. We feel resentment now we are left with this rupture of their offspring's relationship.*"

"*My eventually setting strong boundaries and limitations on their very expensive expectations, became the key factor that contributed most strongly to their rage and my ultimate alienation.*"

I don't want to end my hopes of my grandchildren having a better quality of life because of their parents' financial comfort. I don't think is what my father would have wished."

"*We gave our daughter the wedding she wanted, and also loaned them the down payment to enable them to buy a beautiful home. Immediately afterwards she cut off ties with us, her siblings, and our extended family. I had always been very close to her previously.*

They have much contact with her in-laws who live several hours drive from them. I was advised by friends to be patient, that when she got pregnant, she would naturally come back to mom and Dad. She did not."

"*The alienation started from my son who felt entitled to me watching the grandbabies and borrowing large sums of money. When I put a halt to them taking advantage of me over and over while disrespecting me, that is when they cut me out of their lives. A year later at a family dinner at the home of my aging parents, we casually reunited. I still walk on eggshells waiting for other shoe to drop, and having my grandchild removed from my life again. I am careful with my words.*"

Money and wealth frequently play a dominant role in the dynamics of Grandparent Alienation. Money carries with it power, control, status, and opportunity. Financial issues add a whole new level of stress when alienation is a factor. Money becomes a rather difficult topic to talk about, since it is charged with such emotion.

Wealth can be an indicator of allegiance. It can lure your kids to that side of the fence. The one who possess a large net worth can afford to offer cash, possessions, and financial security. Money can influence the son or daughter you had a previously good relationship with to suddenly disrupt that relationship and align with the parent of greater wealth.

An adult child of divorced parents is often swayed by wealth. Many AGA grandmas, who often times alone devotedly raised and lovingly sacrificed for their child, have had this bond suddenly severed by an ex-husband who controls the greater wealth. Because the child has chosen to align with the dad and the money, the ex-husband begins a cycle of denigration regarding the mother. That once strong mother-child bond has turned into unfathomable heartbreak. This betrayal is a hurt like none other. The adult child seeks validation for their cruel actions by turning to their dad. AGA experts have spoken to this issue explaining how the alienating adult child doesn't want to feel more quilt than they already do. They don't want to look in the mirror and see what their unjust behavior has done to cause such pain to their mom. Therefore, when they feel a tinge of guilt, they turn to the dad for reinforcement of their treatment of their mom.

AGA professional consultant Dr. Coleman has discussed the topic of wealth extensively stating, "Money probably has more meaning than almost any material object. On the positive side, money can be used to express love, commitment, value, and security. On the negative side, it can be used to control, punish, manipulate, and express disappointment. In the parent-adult child environment, money may cause a child to want to be closer, to push away, to feel competitive with other siblings, to grow up, or to forever remain tied to the apron strings of the parent."

The decision of how to handle requests for money with an adult child is one that must be handled very carefully. Not wanting to say no to our kids, parents give. Baby boomers' pattern of giving and providing to the best of their means often times continues even after the kids marry and have their own children. Some adult children are not working as hard as they could to become more self-sufficient. They know their parents will continue to give financial support for their desired lifestyle. Parents with a pattern of paying for major expenses of their adult child can one day find themselves at risk of losing these relationships, if they stop giving.

If something becomes an entitlement over gratitude, perhaps it is time to rethink making your checkbook so readily available. When your child starts expecting your check to arrive, if you find them to be ungrateful, if you feel you are being taken advantage of, if you have a concern where the money is going, then consider a more intelligent way to give to your child. If your child attaches a request for money to a visit with the grandkids, you do have the right to say that you are not comfortable doing so.

If you do give money, but think it is being used for unimportant things, you might consider writing a check payable to their debtor instead. Pay only for things in your opinion are necessary. If money for food is what they need, delivering groceries instead of cash might be the better option.

Once you cut the money flow off, they may cut you out as well. Be prepared for the consequences. The grandkids are being used as the pawns. AGA communicates with grandparents stuck in this situation. You have to decide when to stop being the enabler. You decide when enough is enough. Things can go terribly wrong if you fail to set the rules down first. Be cautious not to make them feel guilt.

Since deciding to cut off funds may run you the risk of being cut off from the relationship, consider a loan. Should you decide to loan your child money for a down payment of a home or help pay off bills, draw up an official binding loan agreement. Using a formal document to outline the terms agreed upon, is a safer way to proceed. Be prepared if they cannot fulfill their obligation. You can write off the loan on your taxes if they do not make the payments.

There is also the option of giving a monetary gift with no strings attached. When you give an outright gift, you have no say over how the money will be spent. You are giving for the joy of it. For grandparents who have some visiting time with their grandchildren, it is a wonderful opportunity to help teach the grandkids to be grateful for things, their home, and their family.

Another option to assist may be an opportunity to invest with your child. This is where a partnership is involved. Legal documents should be drawn up. You then become a partner with a legal contract who has a right to a portion of the value of what you are investing in.

Do not just presume that by helping them out now, this generosity will be reciprocated in your future time of need. Come to an understanding before you hand over the cash. It is not in your best interest if you allow your soft heart as a parent to override logic. Be sure you can meet your own needs to take care of yourself first. Have your own emergency fund before you help others. It is okay to let your child know you are trying to take care of your own needs, are perhaps responsible for the caring of your aging parents, and diligently saving for your retirement. Nearly a third of all Americans age 55 to 64 have not retirement savings.

These can be overwhelming financial and emotional challenges. Have a discussion to help them understand your situation. Do not feel obligated to keep giving if you truly cannot afford it. Presuming they will help you in in the future because you have done so for them now, could become a real problem.

Keep in mind that if the undermining D-I-L, daughter, son, or S-I-L want a reason to cut you off they will find one. When the money is not be handed over, some may unfortunately no longer find it necessary to keep you around. It is cruel to think this way, but it happens.

Grandparents enjoy giving gifts to their grandkids. A recent survey shows spending by grandparents on their grandchildren is up an average of 7.6 percent per year since 2000. According to the survey, 42 percent of all consumer spending on gifts is by grandparents. This is not just about video games and the latest technology devices. The survey indicates that grandparents will spend $17 billion on education for their grandchildren this year, and more than $10 billion on clothing. Such expenditures have been rising for several years.

Some grandparents are wealthier and can afford extravagant gifts for their grandkids, while others are struggling on retirement pensions. This difference in income can create a tension as the lower income grandparents may be concerned that they cannot provide for their grandkids in the same way as their well-off counterparts.

The concept of more wealth and more stuff does not mean more love or personal worth for a grandbaby or a child. When the grandchild ages and their needs increase, grandparents like to help out. Grandparents who have experienced some level of alienation or isolation from the grandchildren should consider having dialogue with their grandchild before agreeing to pay for a big-ticket item. You may give without strings attached for repayment. Here lies your opportunity to role model appropriate behavior. Discourage the entitlement concept by explaining to them how important and proper it is to show appreciation for things. Discuss future communication and visitation with them. Offer them choices for scheduling your communication and the mode of communication.

A commonly voiced concern made to AGA is the decision regarding wills and estates. When there has been a cessation of communication, when their children have raged at them, shown no empathy, and used the grandchildren as pawns; grandparents look for alternative ways to disperse their assets. Presenting at the 2019 AGA International Conference, estate attorney James Karl explained how some states provide for a Generational Skipping Trust. This law protects an inheritance as it is independent of any influence by the alienating parent. Grands may prepare a Legacy Planning Trust, also known as a Dynasty Trust. The trustee takes care of distribution instead of the alienating parents. It also withholds monies from creditors and divorce situations. There is no probate and no judge involved. It can be revocable allowing for tweaking as you go forward. It is best to consult an attorney licensed in estate law regarding legal options available to you in your particular state.

Sometimes cutting your grown children out of your will, may not motivate them to think of their alienating spouse more negatively. It might cause your child to think more negatively of you. Your child might maintain that it is due to something that is not entirely their fault. If that is the case, you may be doing a long-term disservice to them as their parents, by cutting them out of your will.

Remarriage is another source of conflict regarding wealth. Research on failed second marriages has shown that the two issues most cited by divorced men and women as the causes of their marital breakup were money and children. Adult children may live thousands of miles away and have their own spouses and children, but they are still capable of interfering with their parent's remarriage.

AGA grandparents have reported how their adult kids resent monies being spent during their remarriage. Their grown children interfere with the scheme of things due to their fears of losing their inheritance. When seniors remarry, they may have a lifetime of savings, of retirement funds, profits from the sale of a home or a business, and money inherited from a spouse who has passed away. Their grown kids worry that the assets that would have been theirs, after the death of the surviving parent, will go to the new spouse instead. If your adult kids have these concerns, consider arrangements for a will and prenuptial agreement. This has become common practice for seniors who remarry but do not want to merge assets, preferring to pass their separate property to their children after death. Older people considering remarriage should consider the importance of getting legal advice before taking the leap. Family law attorneys who specialize in estates and wills can help you with your estate planning.

(Dr. Caddy) states:

> It is unfortunate but all too often true that when the parent of an adult child remarries, familial conflict in respect to aspects of that parent's Last Will and Testament may become an issue and even a point of conflict. Moreover, often the older the parent who remarries and especially if that parent is male and the new wife is substantially younger, the other family members who were in line to inherit upon the death of the parent may became very uncomfortable about the new circumstance.

Critically, it is how this situation is managed by all the parties, but especially how the father anticipates the possibility of the children's concerns and deals with them calmly, honestly, and openly that the best resolution to this problem can be sought and achieved. Sometimes the family as a whole is best served by having the father's attorney meet with them all together to explore their concerns and set out to openly search for a resolution with which the father is comfortable. If the situation is more sensitive and the circumstance brings about a heightened series of conflict, it may be best to bring on board an experienced psychologist to work with the father and consult also with his attorney, to achieve a solution that all can endorse as an equitable outcome.

21

Social Media

"We were aware of the first child, but had no idea about the second child. The only way I found out was that my other D-I-L saw the post on Facebook. Seeing the picture of my son's family posted, was like a knife through my heart!"

"I have to watch pictures of my grandson (that I didn't get) on my daughter's sister-in-law's page."

"There are no posts about the sleepless nights and awkward moments where I struggle to explain to people why I don't "have a family".

"My daughter blocked me from her Facebook page."

"I'm blocked from emailing, texting, and calling her."

"I had to stop searching, it was causing me too much pain."

"My daughter just had a child, and I didn't even know she was pregnant."

"It's like you're watching other people enjoying your daughter and the grandchild you're supposed to have, and you're left out in the cold."

"My daughter married her children's father while I had temporary custody of the children. I found out from a mutual friend that saw pictures on Facebook."

"We found out that our son and daughter-in-law were expecting when I looked up a baby registry online for one of my husband's relatives."

"One item I would like to see addressed is the effect of the internet when trying to communicate with grandchildren. We can try all we want, but if the parent has control of the phones, Instagram, etc.; there is no way to communicate. Internet manipulation – thoughts?"

"In a strange way, I feel I can make a connection even if it's through a computer screen. It's the last tie I have to holding on."

In the world of social networking, estrangement and alienation are being redefined with new complexity. Using technology does allow opportunities for grandparents to connect with grandchildren. As the world's first generation of digital grandparents, they can find pictures and videos of those they long to know. Through social media they can get a peek into the lives of their grandchildren and great grandchildren. It gives them comfort knowing of their well-being.

As humans, we are social by nature and crave bonding within relationships. Technology can be used to help keep families of separation connected. Cell phones, email, and texting help these families compensate by allowing them to communicate with family members when apart.

While social media outlets constitute excellent vehicles for fostering relationships; unfortunately, they can also be a continuing source of torment. All our lives we assumed we would be a part of things taking place in our family's future. Never did we imagine we would only hear about them on a very public platform. Grandparents who learn from Facebook that a new grandbaby has been born or a milestone has taken place, have deep feelings of hurt, humiliation, and grief from the exclusion. The online peeks are often painful reminders of the rejection and what they have lost. The peeks can bring to mind the cruelty placed upon them on a daily basis, exacerbate their loneliness caused by the fracture in the family, and decrease their self-esteem and well-being. They must decide when knowing thru social media is too painful, then to step back.

Social media allows alienators to reach out to anyone they chose. They can broadcast false information to humiliate the grandparent in a very public way. Grandparents are not responsible for the behavior of others; they are responsible only for their own behavior. Be careful how you react to someone else's behavior.

Social networking also adds a new dimension of gossip, hearsay, and visuals. Now that texts and emails are replacing face-to-face conversation, misunderstandings are easier to have. When you send an email, it can be altered and resent to others. Beware, if a troubled adult child or any of their enablers decide to forward your email, they can delete words or add new wording to your original message. A less than honest representation of you can now go viral throughout your entire extended family. Do not underestimate those who have joined the cult! Those who benefit from the rupture of your relationship with your adult child may exhibit these toxic behaviors.

If the parents do not stop you from reaching out to the children, then ask them which vehicle of technology the grandkids like to use. Otherwise, you might know someone who does have access and would be willing to share that with you.

Charles D. Jamieson, Esq., presenting to grandparents at the 2019 AGA International Conference stated that children are captives of the digital/electronic age. Everyone delights in receiving communications through the mail as well, even children of the digital age. He suggests you make the message light and singular such as, "Have a great day!", "Do your best!", "Hope that you enjoyed your soccer game last week!" He also mentioned sending cartoons, jokes, and other age-appropriate clippings that will tickle your grandchild's funny bone.

Attorney Jamieson discussed the use of phone contact or electronic contact through social media. This would allow for them to talk about or "virtually" enjoy together, books or a series of books, play games, discuss television shows, watch movies, sports, academic subjects, extracurricular activities, and other issues in the grandchild's life.

If Grandma and Grandpa want to build a good relationship with their grandchildren, they can find ways the grandkids would best like to connect. There are many types of social media available to help you keep in touch. If you want to connect with your grandkids, you have to learn what is out there and how to use it. All the choices can quickly become overwhelming for grands, so let's break them down into categories. Knowing about these categories of social media and understanding why people use them, can open new ideas and channels for engaging with your grandchildren more effectively. By b*ecoming a Virtual Grandma or a Virtual Grandpa, you could even* enjoy coordinated family meals where grandparents and parents cook the same food and Grandma and Grandpa join the family table via an iPhone, iPad, or tablet.

Social Networks: Connect people online
Media Sharing Networks: Share photos, videos, and other media
Blogging: Publish content online

The following are examples of widely-used social connections from which to choose.

Facebook updates, Microblogging, Twitter feeds, Tumbir, Picture Sharing, Instagram, Snapchat, Video sharing, YouTube, Facebook Live, Periscope, and Vimeo are popular. In cases where an adult child disassociates, these can allow you to view pictures of a new grandbaby, birthday party, team sports events and school identity, vacation, or graduation ceremony.

Facebook is a highly popular utility for relationship sharing. It provides a way for you to build connections and share information with those you choose to interact with online. It is likely that someday your grandchild will have a Facebook page. If you create a Facebook page of your own, they can find you; or you can find them. If you do not know how to do this, be sure to ask a techie acquaintance to help you set up your Facebook page.

If you have been blocked on Facebook, try sending a "friend" request to the child's acquaintances.

Twitter is for short text content. You can share your thoughts and keep up with your grandchildren via this real-time information network.

Follow them on Twitter or do internet searches to find out where your grandchildren attend school.

Instagram, Snapchat, and YouTube are media sharing networks. You can use these to share photos, video, and live video online. These start with an image or video to which users may decide to add content line captions, mentions of other users, or filters.

YouTube and Vimeo use video as the mode of communication.

Snapchat gives you a more spontaneous glimpse of each other's lives. It offers the opportunity to film video and shoot photos on the fly, and share them immediately. Then, once your recipient opens and views the Snap: Poof, it disappears! Snapchat is not intended to be a broadcast social media where *all* of your followers see *everything* you post.

Mobile Phone Applications are free of charge anytime and anywhere. These apps are wonderful tools for communicating with family overseas. Locate the icon for Apps on your cell phone. Start chatting once your family request has been accepted.

The following are suggestions for popularly used vehicles of communication through technology:

WhatsApp You can send pictures and videos, and make calls and video calls.

Messenger This Facebook chat is available as a stand-alone app for your mobile phone. Code named Facebook Messenger, this app allows you to get in touch with your Facebook contacts without signing-in to your Facebook account. Facebook Messenger allows you to make free instant messages and international calls, share your location with you contacts, send photos to your contacts, and send voice messages.

WeChat Whether you want to send messages or share photos and videos, you can freely chat. Where ever you go, you can get in touch with your family. WeChat offers a sticker gallery to make your chats more fun with your grandkids. On Moments, you can share your photos and video with your family, and see their Moments at any time. Get face-to-face with you family instantly.

SKYPE Skype allows registered users to communicate through both instant messaging and voice chat. Voice chat allows telephone calls between pairs of users and conference calling. Skype supports conference calls, video chats, and screen sharing between 25 people at a time for free. You actually get to see one another's face!

FaceTime *FaceTime* is Apple's service app that supports video and audio calls between compatible devices. Think of it as a phone that uses your

Wi-Fi or cellular data connection instead of traditional phone lines. You can use it from any iPhone, iPad, iPod touch or Mac, to call anyone else using any one of those devices.

Freeconference.com Free of charge. Sign up online. You will be given the dial in number, access code, and host pin number. This allows you to place a call, and have others call in. No limit on number of callers at one time. International calling dial-in numbers are available for many countries.

Touchnote.com It is very important to reach out periodically to your son or daughter. Do this without immediate expectations. Sending a post card is more likely to be glanced a then your letter in a sealed envelope. Touchnote sends a picture post card for you. Just follow the simple instructions on their website. Send a happy memory photo of you and your child that will trigger positive thoughts.

Online Games: No matter where children are in the world, grandparents can keep up with their goings-on, and vice versa. Many online games are user-friendly and benign, appealing to players of any age. Use online games and activities to connect with your grandchildren. For some grandparents it can be a barrier for communication, a foreign language that seems too daunting to learn and understand. But for those willing to take the leap, technology can be a bridge between grandparents and grandchildren, allowing them to forge a routine connection that was impossible in previous generations.

Whether your grandchild is around the corner or around the world, being apart does not mean you cannot be a part of their lives if you can connect thru technology. Video and voice connections give you one-on-one bonding time together. Making memories and interacting is what counts. Exciting animations, pictures, and videos engage even the youngest grandchild. You can also bond over instructive apps or play educational games. Infants through early grade school children learn by playing with you. Do an online search for grandparent games. Many apps and games are designed to bring people together. On the internet, kids get to be the experts, teaching an older generation how to behave in a strange new environment. The bottom line is that loving grandparents want to find a way to bridge distance. Making memories and interacting is what counts, and if you are creative, you can find a way!

Another of the most popular reasons so many people use the internet is to conduct research on one's favorite projects or topics of interest related to personal hobbies. When grandparents find a website based on their favorite hobby, they discover a whole community of people from around the world who share the same passion for those interests. This is what lies at the heart of what makes social networks work, and this is why social networks that are focused on hobbies are some of the most popular.

There are many opportunities to engage in dialog via social media websites. The fact that there are so many ways to connect with like-minded individuals online can be very exciting and beneficial, but it is essential to proceed with caution. Keep in mind that not everyone who shows up on a social media website is who he or she claims to be. Exercise caution and closely guard your personal information any time you engage in social networking activities, regardless of what kind of social utility you are using.

AGA provides a vehicle for future hopeful communication with grandchildren, along with informative AGA YouTubes. The AGA support group in Maricopa County Arizona has created two channels in YouTube: "To Our Alienated Grandchildren, With Love" - Hopefully alienated grandchildren will someday find this channel and leave messages for their grandparents. "Alienated Grandparents in Arizona" - Alienated grandparents nationwide frequently leave messages for their grandchildren in the "comments" area right below the videos. Both channels are regularly updated with new videos using information from AGA grandparents.

There have been complaints about our widely-used social media platforms for some time now, therefore the AGA Coordinator for Maricopa County decided to do a little research to find out what complaints were being said about them on the internet. Her conclusion, "I suspect that if these unfair practices continue, other choices of social media will become available as many people close out their accounts on the current platforms. If and when this does happen, it would be wise for our grandparent generation to keep up with the new trends to know what the youth is tapping into, and to have accounts on the new platforms so that they can find us. Many of us hope for the day that we can resume communications again on social media, without any interference from our alienators."

22

Heath Issues

"I have fourth stage cancer. I have called my son several times, but received no response. I explained my illness to him via voicemail. I have asked him to please let me see him and my little grandchildren before it's too late. I never heard back from him."

"We have not seen our grandchildren in three years and six months. And, of course, we are heartsick. They were suddenly without notice or any known reason 'taken' from us at the worst time in my life, days after brain surgery from which I have thankfully fully recovered. I felt like my grandchildren had been kidnapped, and I just felt helpless. We didn't know why, and we still don't know why, so we're left after all this time to grieve and guess. No father should ever have to hear or bear this sort of treatment from the son he loves. I do not believe my son would be behaving this harshly for this long without being 'encouraged' by someone in some way or another to do so. Not my son. I just don't believe it."

"I try hard to focus on my health: this has been physically and emotionally draining. But I know I have to stay as healthy as possible. I continue to send cards for birthdays and Christmas to my youngest daughter and her children. I don't share this place I'm in. My stencil on my craft room wall reads "Hope is the Anchor to my Soul"."

"With some serious medical issues looming, life itself may be fragile and fleeting, making the urgency of relationship repair even more pressing. I don't know what to say or do to make things better."

"I have serious issues with my blood pressure. I have no doubt this is from the long-term anxiety this cut off has created. It has taken its toll on my health for sure."

"Prior to a complete cut-off there were years of bullying behavior, including a carefully executed campaign of character assassination. They portrayed me as suicidal to my family and friends and tried to use that as justification to cut me off from the kids. But my sibling, recipient of some of their damaging letters, said that what they were doing seemed better geared toward provoking a suicide than preventing one."

"It's killing me. I feel like I'm dying of grief, and think about suicide a lot. I lost my other child in an accident recently, and now I am cut off from my only other child."

"This situation has made me clinically depressed, robbed me of seeing a future of enjoyment. Every birthday, Mother's Day, and holiday is filled with sadness and self-loathing because I feel useless. What sort of mother loses her child and grandchildren?"

"Restricted contact with my beloved grandchildren has taken a measurable toll on my emotional and physical health. Other than the death of my husband, I have never experienced such depths of anguish as I do over this inexplicable loss of relationship."

"This aching loss is taking a huge toll on both emotional and physical health and sleep quality. I have never in my 70 years experienced anything quite so devastating."

"During my wife's illness, I believe that our son's absence began to prove that his wife was already beginning to dominate him. Though he seemed happy to see us in short bursts, he became more aloof and got even worse about not returning calls or texts. After she died, I think he just put it out of his mind *and moved on with his new wife. Perhaps seeing my daughter and I reminded him too much of his inner pain. I am not sure."*

"When my granddaughter was born, her mother was rude to me when no one was around. The following months were chaotic. My son was diagnosed with stage four terminal cancer, and she wouldn't let me visit with him."

"My daughter and I were close before the marriage. We were therefore devasted to find out they already had a 10-month-old girl. A mutual friend and our other daughter were sworn to secrecy. We heard that our daughter raged when she learned the friend had told us about the birth of our granddaughter. I felt suicidal for months; my husband reacted with anger. The OGs were hesitant to give us any more than a few initial details, in order to maintain their need to keep their own relationship. My life has been on hold, and I have been physically ill with no diagnosis. How can human beings be so cruel to each other?"

"I asked him if he received my phone calls regarding my diagnosis of cancer. He simply said yes, offering no words of comfort."

"My life has been on hold, since we found out through the grapevine that our first grandbaby had been born. I have been physically very ill, and have had several medical evaluations without a diagnosis. How can human beings be so cruel to each other?"

"The pain and loss are something that I can't describe. Life is sad and pointless. All I feel is loss. I am clinically depressed and have just started a course of anti-depressants. I hope it will help me to get some sanity back. My life is full of pain and I can't feel any joy, although we do have grandchildren from our other daughter. The pain of my daughter and the grandkids missing from my life haunts me every minute I am awake, and in my dreams. This situation has been called a living bereavement, and it is like that. You are alone with

this loss and pain because it's yesterday's news for friends and family. This has taken away the peace from the retirement we should have had and hoped for. I don't know if people who use their kids as weapons know the harm they cause, but I know that I don't wish this family tragedy on my worst enemy, not even on the woman who has ripped my heart in two."

"I know I should be taking better care of myself. But I keep thinking 'Why bother'? When I don't feel loved by my children, it's hard to love myself very much."

"One of most sad and concerning factors for us as grandparents to face is realizing that the dementia and other symptoms that come with my wife's disease, is that the disease may not allow for the time it may take for reconciliation. She has told me that if we cannot be with our children, their spouses, and our grandchildren while we are on this earth, then we'll see them in heaven."

As we age, we encounter a host of physically challenging problems. Nothing compares though with the relentless sorrow we can carry in our hearts. The overwhelming consequence of being cut off from our cherished grandchildren is the feeling of helplessness and worthlessness. Grandparents are trying to make sense out of no sense. They think of themselves as problem solvers because they are rational people, but suffer because they cannot fix the seemingly unfixable. The answers are locked away somewhere in the cold hearts of their adult children, where they will probably remain until it is too late. This knowledge is the frustration turned inward, and is what makes the suffering so profound.

Carol Golly, PhD explains how alienated grandparents are suffer and experience profound emotional and physical health problems in grieving the loss of contact with grandchildren. It can be intense chronic grief leading to lowered life satisfaction, numbness, shock and denial and post-traumatic stress disorder. Grandparents also suffer serious consequences including depression, anxiety, and suicidal ideation. Golly suggests, "Grandparents may be helped through mutual aid and advocacy groups such as Alienated Grandparents Anonymous (AGA)."

A study conducted in the United Kingdom shows loss of intimacy and intimate connection with grandchildren, subsequent new physical and emotional health problems, worry about the well-being of their grandchildren, and profound sadness and depression were some of the reported consequences of cessation of contact.

Some people do not see the harm that Grandparent Alienation does to families. It is an invisible abuse, because no one sees the anxiety or the broken heart. Grandparents feel this, and it can make them ill. Countless cases of stress-related illnesses may be the root cause of those illnesses which may include migraine headaches, high blood pressure, gastrointestinal disorders, sleep disorders, obesity, TMJ, acute anxiety, PTSD, and depression. Health effects of abuse include traumatic injury and pain, as well as depression and stress and anxiety. Elder abuse can lead to an increased risk of nursing home placement, use of emergency services, hospitalization, and death. We must reach out to enlist the help of physicians in identifying the symptoms of alienation as a possible underlying cause of illnesses in their adult population. We must also reach out to pediatricians so they can consider alienation a possibility when a child's behavior is questioned.

(Hyman, M.D.) I personally have seen a lot of trauma from family dynamics manifest into physical illness, especially the relationship between child and parent.

Many older patients have not shared the trauma or embarrassment as most are too ashamed to confess their circumstances, even to their doctors or clergy. They often blame themselves for having failed, perhaps believing they are at fault, when in actuality there is no rational explanation for the treatment they must endure. In their hearts they know that they have been good, loving, and giving parents. They cannot accept the catastrophe that has befallen them. Because they have done nothing to deserve such wrath, or are unaware of something they may have said or done unintentionally, they should place the blame on the other side.

Evidence confirms that good quality relationships are a key part of a good fulfilling life, and equally important in all stages of life. These strong relationships are central to our happiness and well-being, and are a critical element later in life. The first generation has invested in their family relationships. Family ties have a positive influence, and help people through the transition in later life. Not surprisingly, studies show a breakdown of these relationships affects grandparents with changes to their mental, emotional, and physical health. Not knowing about the well-being of their grandchildren or the lives of their children is excruciating, negatively affecting their own well-being.

(Golly 2016) As we age, we encounter a host of physically challenging debilitating problems. Though, nothing compares to the grief without closure - the unmitigated sorrow that alienated grandparents carry in their hearts. The solutions are in the hands of their adult children who show no empathy. The acute, progressive, and overwhelming consequence of being cut off from cherished grandchildren is the feeling of helplessness, and a feeling that it may be too late in their years to fix for them.

As we transition into our older years, relationships become a critical element alongside of health and finance. During our golden years we especially appreciate the partners, family, friends, and neighbors who care about us. It is during these years that grandparents are enthusiastic about their grandchildren, and the majority see them as "the reason to be". This close relationship can cause great pain when it is forcibly removed due to family relationship disruption. Lack of this relationship is associated with a range of negative impact from depression and loneliness. When grandparent relationships fail, they present complications for their care and future support. Grandparents expected they would remain of key interest to their adult child. Not prepared for the onset of the emotional family bond being severed, they are left with worry and a lack of understanding why this has happened to them.

With a decline of this support system, it becomes harder to maintain as the stresses of aging take their toll. In the later years of their lives, it becomes even more important for grandparents to teach and nurture the third and fourth generation. Yet for the majority of these grandparents, not enough time remains to change this.

(Psychology Today June 2017) states, "Having positive relationships with family members, especially with adult children, can be critical to good health."

As we age, social support is beneficial. Those who feel unloved by their adult children and very much alone may be less likely to have a healthy lifestyle including warm connections with others.

A study published in the *Journal of Alzheimer's Disease* on May 2, 2017, found that those who have loving relationships with their adult children are less likely to develop dementia later on than those who have negative relationships.

AGA has communicated with many grandparents suffering serious health issues, including life-threatening illnesses. They tried reaching out for comfort from the child who has cut them off, only to be denied. This is severe emotional abuse.

Dr. Coleman has offered grandparents explanations of the common behavior of many alienating adult children ignoring the health issues of their parents. He has discussed how our grown children may not have much tolerance for our sufferings or health issues. It may be their defense against worrying about us, or feeling overly responsible for us. He cites their non-caring attitude is due to grandparents using these illnesses only to bring them back into the family before they are ready. Some may not want to feel any more guilt than they already do. They basically remain focused on themselves and their nuclear family.

Experiencing this family relationship rupture, even when it has continued for years or decades, many people say the emotional pain persists or re-occurs at particular times. Triggers such as birthdays, holiday season, Mother's Day and Father's Day, and anniversaries are especially difficult. An unexpected sighting or hearing about them from others sets off deep-rooted emotions. Triggers can cause a person to re-live and re-experience the initial grief, the loss and trauma responses, while at other times they can be managed.

(Carol Hosmer Golly, Barry University) Golly's peer reviewed publication *Pruning the Family Tree: The Plight of Grandparents Who Are Alienated from Their Grandchildren* sites research studies in such situations. Alienated grandparents are suffering and experiencing profound emotional and physical health problems in grieving the loss of contact with grandchildren. It can be intense chronic grief leading to lowered life satisfaction, numbness, shock and denial and post-traumatic stress disorder. Alienated grandparents suffer serious consequences, including depression, anxiety, grief, suicidal ideation, and physical health problems. Grandparents may be helped through mutual aid and advocacy groups such as Alienated Grandparents Anonymous (AGA). Given the potentially serious deleterious consequences of Grandparent Alienation to both grandparents and grandchildren, social work interventions are needed that address feelings of grief and loss of grandparents when they lose contact with grandchildren. Family bonds are considered to be sacred. When they fray or break permanently, it can cause profound and grievous pain for those involved.

AGA has direct witness to our grandparent population sufferings. Grandparents Alienation is a form of complicated grief, a grief without closure. There is continued hope for reunification, which results in ongoing stress for the grandparent and makes it difficult to achieve closure in the grieving process. Grandparents start each day yearning for of the grandchildren they miss so much. They hold a belief that life is meaningless as a result of their loss, and how severe a price they are paying for the middle generation's arbitrary decisions. They fear never seeing their grandchildren again, and worry about the safety and well-being of the children at the hands of such cold-hearted parents. There is a constant underlying feeling of sadness knowing they are missing out on the precious formative years, being shut out of family gatherings and events, and unable to pass on family history and traditions.

Being a grandmother or a grandfather, and then in a flash it's gone, causes them long term stress. Stress is a common theme expressed by AGA grandparents. There is long term and ongoing stress of not knowing if or when the adult child will come back into their lives, how long this will continue, or if it will ever be fixed is overwhelming. Our grands wonder if the child "who used to love them so much" feels any emotional pain. Questioning there is no relief in sight, they are consumed by fear. They are afraid to say or do anything. The grandparenting role is always in doubt. They never know if they will be allowed to babysit their grandchildren, or if they will be invited to family celebrations. As a result, they suffer from anxiety and untold stress.

At night, these same thoughts keep them from a peaceful sleep. Many have shared with AGA their feelings of neglect, blame, ridicule, chronic grief and symptoms of post-traumatic stress. They find themselves is a state of shock, denial, shame, rejection, betrayal, and despair. The older grandparents feel there is not enough time to change anything. The thought that as parents they are in any way directly responsible for our adult children not wanting us in their lives, causes such emotional pain that it elicits depression, anxiety, rage, and suicidal ideation. AGA has been informed of 11 grandparent suicides who were cut off from their adult child and grandchildren. None of these grandparents attended AGA support group meetings. As cited in an AARP magazine survey report, nearly one in three parents estranged from their children (PAS) reported have contemplated suicide. That's almost 10 times the annual average rate for suicidal thoughts, according to the Center for Disease Control and Prevention.

When grandparents find themselves in the position of being denied what they believed was their God given right to love, hold, and spend quality time with their grandchildren; it sets their lives into complete turmoil. Because our identifies are closely tied to our perceptions of ourselves as parents, a high percentage of alienated parents become depressed, some even suicidal, as a result of the cut off. Grandparents reveal the emotional pain as a torture too heavy to carry. They wonder how they are going to make it through another day. Their sorrow keeps them in limbo where they are unable to fix the problem, yet unable to get on with their lives. If only they had known they were not alone on this journey, had support from those going this tragedy, and that there is hope.

Suicidal ideation, which an AGA survey showed is experienced by the majority of grandmothers, must shout out a message loud and clear, "It is time to focus on the grandchild!' YOU must be there for THEM! Do not allow your thoughts to be so cruelly unfair to your grandchildren who are anxiously awaiting a reconnection with you, too! Grandchildren who knew and bonded with you as young as age three to five will remember how they felt when they were with you. A grandparent in such despair needs to consider how their grandchild would feel if Grandma or Grandpa are not there for them when they are old enough to find them on their own. Will you help AGA bring awareness of Grandparent Alienation so those who suffer will learn they are not suffering alone?

Grandparents who have been so sad for so long may need to take a healthy break when no change in sight. If you have tried and been repeatedly crushed by a son or daughter who wants no contact, if you have been caught up in an endless loop of recharged grief, or if your health is being affected, it is time to say enough is enough; take a break. If you have been stuck with the idea that a relationship, even one that causes such pain is better than none, it may be time to take a break. Continually walking on eggshells to maintain an abusive or one-sided contact, or yearning for the son or daughter and grandkids you used to know, may reach a point for you to say to yourself "enough is enough".

Taking a break for a few months or more is not giving up. Each day of your life is a precious gift. It is okay to give yourself permission to take care of yourself. Do not let these cold-hearted people hold you back from a healthier more fulfilling life. It is possible to reclaim your self-esteem and confidence. Know that you must keep yourself healthy mentally and physically for a very special reason. There is HOPE. Your grandkids have missed you, too! Whether a grandparent has had the most precious opportunity to bond or not, grandchildren want grandparents. Just as you look forward to the time when your grandchildren may come looking for you, you must honor them by being here for them when they do.

Move beyond the pain. Make a pact with yourself to visit these feelings only once a day for a brief specific amount of time. Be prepared to switch to a follow up activity. Become proactive, not reactive. Stay active in the community. Your grandchildren would not want you to waste opportunities; they would want you to have a meaningful life.

Share your situation with your physician and clergy since studies show that family disassociations are associated with later physical and emotional problems. Enlist their help to consider the link between the patients' illnesses and the possible contributor of Grandparent Alienation. Provide them information and the AGA website: www.AGA-FL.org. Enable them to help and bring awareness to others.

Awareness about elder abuse, though widely unmentioned, has started to increase across the world. It is defined as actions or lack of appropriate action which can cause harm or distress to an older person, occurring within any relationship where there is an expectation of trust. All types of elder abuse can have an impact on the health and well-being of the older person.

A recent report from the World Health Organization on *Rise of Elder Abuse* stated: "Little by little, the world is beginning to see that psychological abuse is the most pervasive and includes behaviors that harm an older person's self-worth or wellbeing such as name calling, scaring, embarrassing, destroying property or preventing them from seeing friends and family'. Psychological and emotional abuse can include a range of controlling behaviors."

The report also focused on financial abuse, and the failure to meet an older person's basic needs. Health effects of abuse included depression, stress and anxiety; finding that elder abuse can lead to an increased risk of nursing home placement, use of emergency services, hospitalization, and death.

A study, supported by WHO, showed that almost 16% of people aged 60 years and older were subjected to either psychological abuse (11.6%), financial abuse (6.8%), neglect (4.2%), physical abuse (2.6%) or sexual abuse (0.9%). The study found that the abuse of older people is on the rise, and that we must do much more to prevent and respond to the increasing frequency of different forms of abuse.

The report revealed that by 2050 the number of people aged 60 and over will double to reach two billion globally. If the proportion of elder abuse victims remains constant, the number of people affected will increase rapidly due to population ageing, growing to 320 million victims by 2050.

Elder abuse is seldom discussed in policy circles, less prioritized for research, and addressed by only a small number of organizations. The report stated, "Governments must protect all people from violence. We must work to shed light on this important societal challenge, understand how best to prevent it, and help put in place the measures needed."

The United Nations General Assembly, resolution 66/127, designated June 15 as World Elder Abuse Awareness Day. It represents the one day in the year when the whole world voices its opposition to the abuse and suffering inflicted to some of our older generations.

This is Abuse

"My husband had not been doing good and passed away a month ago from a massive heart attack. I texted and begged my son to come to the memorial many many times, but he did not show up. It is tremendously heartbreaking to lose a husband of 50 years, and to continue to be alienated by my son."

"I happened to see my son-in-law and granddaughter a few days ago. We were in a parking lot and within several feet of each other. He had my granddaughter turn around to face the opposite direction until I passed by. She wasn't allowed to say hello to me. Very cruel. My grandchild is being taught to hate."

Grandparent Alienation is considered by the experts in the field of Alienation to be a severe form of elder abuse and a severe form of child abuse.

Amy J.L. Baker, PhD

Alienation is emotional abuse of children.

J. Michael Bone, PhD AGA Consultant

If there is any tragedy that has befallen life in the modern world, it is the loss of the extended family. In the mid 1940's an excess of 85% of families were extended families, meaning that there were three generations of a family living under one roof or very nearby. As we fast forward to as long ago as the mid 1970's this number falls to only 11%, meaning that grandparents are only an everyday part of children's lives in very small numbers. While I do not know the exact statistic of the disappearance of the extended family in 2014, I would guess that it must be less than 3%. What does this mean? Unfortunately, this means a great loss of sharing of life experience as well as a loss of wisdom that only this experience can yield. When we add to this the fact that marriages are as likely to end in divorce as they are to survive into the senior years, one can easily see how the fragmentation of the family has led to an overall loss to our young people.

It is well accepted and understood that grandparents provide a perspective and balance that only experience can yield. While the world has changed and continues to change at unprecedented speed, it is the wisdom of experience that can best provide balance to this change. Therefore, when parents divorce and children find themselves suddenly in two households, very often the resources that grandparents bring to grandchildren are diminished; or in the case of parental alienation, destroyed altogether. I am a strong supporter of Alienated Grandparents Anonymous (AGA) for this very reason. AGA has committed itself to addressing this tragic loss directly. I believe that the State of Florida can potentially lead the rest of the country in addressing this problem by seeking to restore the rightful and important role that grandparents can play in a child's life. I am proud to be associated with AGA.

Glenn Ross Caddy Ph.D., A.B.P.P., F.A.P.A. AGA Consultant

There is no question but that unless there is legitimate reason to prevent the grandparents and children from enjoying a complete family life together (such justification may be the true psychological pathology or physical abuse of the children by the grandparents), that the alienation of children from their loving parents by one or both parents is pathological and constitutes child abuse. This is simply because grandparents play an important role for the children in defining the depth and family and the support system of love inherent in the family just as uncles and aunts and cousins contribute to the breadth of the family surrounding the support, love, and well-being of the children. These people are far more than friends, they are blood and they are love.

Tragically, it is common with alienation that when one set of grandparents or both sets are the victims of alienation the entire family on at least one side is estranged and splintered. The children who suffer this alienation have no context of cohesiveness or normalcy in of extended family life. They do not learn or know normalcy and they suffer profound emotional consequences therefrom. I have treated people in their 30's and 40's who came to realize in the context of the therapy that they were the victims of parental [and grandparent] alienation and their suffering has ranged between confusion and unimaginable psychic pain and psychopathology.

Joshua Coleman, Ph.D. AGA Consultant

I think the long-term effects of these estrangements are generally harmful for grandchildren. They learn that attachments are temporary and that families that were once loving and close can quickly become distant and angry. They're also presented with the model that estrangement is a reasonable way to manage family conflict.

I'm hopeful that as there is greater awareness of the impact of estrangement and alienation that less families have to be faced with it.

Small children often form attachments to their grandparents that are as significant, if not more significant than those they form with their own parents. In many cases, grandparents—even those who were an intimate and involved part of their grandchildren's lives—are suddenly denied contact because of a conflict between the parent and the adult child or the spouse of the adult child.

Currently in the US there are few ways to successfully remediate this situation once it occurs. This is because parents in the US have complete authority over determining whether or not a grandchild can have contact with a grandparent.

Children, from this perspective, are viewed as a kind of property over which the rights of the individual parent are ascendant over the rights of the grandparent. While most people would be sympathetic to a parent's decision to restrict or deny contact with an abusive grandparent, my clinical experience shows that most grandparents are denied contact, not because of their abusive behavior, but because of a recent or longstanding conflict between the parent and adult child or the adult child's spouse.

However unfortunate and painful those conflicts, the decision to end an attachment to an otherwise loving and involved grandparent is something that should be considered in a far broader context than the rights of the parent. If parental neglect can and should be considered a form of child abuse, certainly a parent's decision to end a loving and attached relationship between a grandchild and grandparent should also be considered a form of abuse.

Grands perform a really important role in the life of a grandchild. Studies regarding this relationship show the importance to a child's social and cognitive development, and for their safety and security in the world. Depriving a child of this suddenly taking this away from a child is a form of severe child abuse. These grands have been a positive powerful attachment figure to the child. If this attachment is taken away, it is traumatizing to the child, and makes their world a mush less safe place.

Carol Golly, PhD, P.L., MSW, LCSW, RPTS   AGA Board of Directors

Doctoral Dissertation: Intergenerational Conflicts- Grandparent Alienation

When you erase family from children's lives, you pay for it. The attachment of a grandparent when broken by these parents is a very sick thing. It is considered by experts a very severe form of child abuse.

PAS is considered a severe form of child abuse. Children are deprived of protective and vital relationships, sometimes permanently. Alienated children suffer may problems later in life., often becoming depressed, anxious, and self-injurious they are at high risk of drug and alcohol abuse, suffer from mood disorders, have low self-esteem, and have trust issues and unsuccessful relationships. There is growing evidence that PAS is inter-generational.

Charles D. Jamieson, Esq. AGA Consultant

Alienation is a form of emotional abuse, harms the child in the short term, but it can also have long-term effects including but not limited to: depression, alcohol/drug abuse, low self-esteem, problems with trusting, and a cycle of alienation that extends to their own children when they are parents.

Rev. Dr. John Killinger AGA Consultant

I agree that Grandparent Alienation is BOTH child abuse AND elder abuse.

CHILD ABUSE

The parents of this country would rise up en masse if they suddenly learned that the government had passed rules limiting the amount of vitamins and nutriments children can receive in their food or the number of books they can read in school. Yet parents who keep their children away from the grandparents are limiting by 50% the amount of grandparent love, knowledge, and interest those children are going to receive in the most formative years of their lives.

ELDER ABUSE

Citizens would be angry with a neighbor they learned was keeping an elderly person locked up in a room in their home and limiting the food, water, and company that person received. Yet parents who prevent grandparents from seeing their own grandchildren, their flesh and blood, are seriously delimiting the joy, happiness, and well-being of those grandparents.

My wife of 63 years, Annie, has died. My life would be vastly different — I would be comforted — if I had regular access to my grandchildren and could SEE with my eyes the future of our progeny. But alas… Anne Killinger authored, "A Son is a Son Till He Gets a Wife… How Toxic Daughters-in-Law Destroy Families.

Pascal J. La Ruffa, M.D., FSAHM Fellow-Society for Adolescent Health & Medicine

Over many years as medical director of two boarding schools, an inpatient treatment center for addicted youth, two universities, and all the public schools in our suburban community, I was often faced with the responsibility of guiding many teenagers and young adults through their emotional pain. Most of those frustrated and depressed students were faced with the monumental task of dealing with their education and the demands of everyday life. It was upsetting to realize that the majority of their problems centered around the perceived lack of love and encouragement from home. This fomented their feeling of helplessness to cope - without the armamentarium needed to survive in our complex world. Many had turned to alcohol or drug abuse to ease the pain, or sexual promiscuity to feel wanted, physically and emotionally. This behavior did not cure the problems, but intensified them. Often, the situation would escalate to the point of self-abuse.

I saw many cases where grandparents blamed the son-in-law (or daughter-in-law), and the other set of grandparents laid the blame in reverse. Sometimes, it was the adult parent(s) who blamed one or more grandparents. Try to imagine the feelings and confusion in the child (or children). Now, they had to deal with arguments and attitudes from one set of parents - two sets if divorced - and four grandparents - maybe six. How can the child be expected to deal with all this, and try to make the best of life on his own? This is abuse of the worst kind: mental, emotional, and social. That's where I would work with the children, as their coach and mentor. The adults - I referred to family therapy. It was crucial for the son or daughter to have someone on their side, who would be non-judgmental and keep everything strictly confidential.

J. Singer, M.D.

We all recognize child abuse? Or, do we?

When pain is inflicted willfully, we call this child abuse. Society sometimes goes so far as to view corporal punishment or spanking as abuse. So, we can safely say that intentionally causing a child pain is abuse.

Not all abuse is so obvious. Emotional abuse is not captured on a physical examination or x-ray. When a close loving grandparent is removed from a child's world, the child feels emotional pain. We all age, and we all die. Grandparents die every day. If their grandchild was close, we see the emotional pain this causes. We can try to explain death to a child. We can tell them about the "cycle of life".

When the loving close grandparent is still alive and purposely extracted from the child's world, and this separation is intentional, in inflicts pain. Why isn't this a form of child abuse? It intentionally inflicts pain on a child.

We must protect our children and respect parents' rights. But we must also recognize child abuse in all of its many forms.

Vickijo Letchworth   AGA Board Member

Elder Abuse Response Advocate-Instructor Florida Coalition Against Domestic Violence

Grandparent relationships are vital for a healthy childhood. Grandparent Alienation is abuse. No one, including grandparents deserve the abuse caused by alienation. You cannot change anyone, but you can change how you react to them, and how you let them effect you. Abusers don't change, they just go on to the next victim.

Richard Warshak, PhD

Warshak (2010)… Isolating the child from the grandparents makes a child more vulnerable to the negative influence of the alienating parent, as well as downplaying and ignoring the significant contributions made by the grandparents to the children.

Grandparental alienation can have the same or even greater negative effects and consequences on a child as to parental alienation. When one considers the impact on children of having been the victim of intentional direct and indirect attacks on the grandparents, the children are exposed to a combination of psychological and emotional abuse. The effects may be less pronounced than the effects of parental alienation although they suffer many of the same symptoms if the children have been exceptionally close to the grandparents on a very frequent and, to some extent as well as, on an intermittent basis.

Abe Worenklein, PhD AGA Consultant

Visits with a grandparent are often an important part of a child's experience, and there are benefits from the relationship with the grandparents which the child cannot derive from any other relationship. There is little dispute that grandparents can play a very significant and enriching role in the development of their grandchildren. Grandparents who have continually been positively involved with their grandchildren can compensate for the children's emotional turmoil as a result of the parents being emotionally less available to them during ongoing litigation between the parents.

There may be serious developmental and detrimental emotional concerns for the child if grandchildren are denied access to grandparents.

The American Psychological Association

The grandchildren of Parental Alienation Syndrome, those being manipulated by one parent into rejecting the other parent is considered abusive.

A Family Unfriendly Plan United Kingdom

The child without grandparents can suffer profound genealogical confusion, as well as serious emotional deprivation. Every child has an inalienable right to know his or her family. It's a serious thing to deprive a child of this, and it will inevitably have repercussions.

Grandparents can play an enormously significant role in children's lives, and can provide a sense of history and family continuity that encourages a child's sense of belonging and security. I doubt there would be many health professionals who would disagree that a child cannot have too many people around to love and nurture him or her. The love of grandparents is unique, and the life of a child bereft of this love is the poorer for it.

This is especially so when the separation is deliberately instigated by the child's mother. In these situations, the loss of the grandparents' love is further exacerbated for the child by maternal hostility towards people the child would like to love, if he or she had a choice. This causes confusion, anxiety and fear in children, who are too immature to deal with the complexities of adult emotions.

Kruk 2019 Psychology Today: *Parental Alienating Behaviors: An Unacknowledged Form of Family Violence* (Harman, Kruk, & Hines, 2018), appearing in *Psychological Bulletin*, and *Parental Alienation as a Form of Emotional Child Abuse: Current State of Knowledge and Future Directions for Research* (Kruk, 2018), appearing in the *Family Science Review*—have sought to shed light on the latest research pertaining to parental alienation as child abuse and family violence, and as a form of human emotional aggression.

The research shows that for violence and abuse to occur, two criteria must be met. Kruk reports, "There must be a significant human injury, and it must be the result of human action. PAS fits this definition in relation to both child and partner abuse. The two aspects fundamental to parental alienation as a form of emotional human aggression and abuse are the behaviors of the alienator and the effects of these behaviors on the targeted victims."

Amanda

This research examines alienating behaviors and the impact of such behavior. They are measured by current public health and legal definitions of child abuse and family violence, with the articles providing an index of parental alienating behaviors (a classification of the abusive behaviors of perpetrators) and a categorization of parental alienation effects on victim children and target parents.

Formerly unaccepted as a distinct form of abuse, these two articles signal a shift in psychological science toward identifying and categorizing PAS as a form of both child abuse and family violence. Kruk declares this a powerful response to the scientific discovery that parental alienation is more commonplace and damaging than is generally assumed, which affects millions of children and parents worldwide. Given the previous lack of acknowledgement of alienation and denial of the phenomenon by many legal and mental health professionals, the two above mentioned articles now provide a call to action toward the development and testing of effective educational, mental health, and legal interventions to prevent and mitigate the effects of parental alienation as a form of intimate terrorism.

24

Coping When Cut Off from Access to Your Grandchildren

"Someone called my wife and I this morning to inform us that our first grandchild had been born. This call did not come from our son or any member of the family. How do you expect us to cope with this?"

"There were several moments that I have scared myself by not wanting to live. I honestly cannot think of anything that has hurt me so deeply in my life. I have cried more in the last six months than I have in the last six years. I have watched my husband cry from a broken heart over this more than anything in our 30 years. I have had some medical problems with all of this. My self-esteem has plummeted as I second guess myself constantly. I had this huge amount of time on my schedule that I was not used to, because that time was filled with my grandson for the previous six years when they were sometimes incapable of caring for him. I have bitterness and anger that I'm still dealing with for my grandson's parents. I don't like feeling this way about my daughter who I thought I was close to, but obviously was very fooled. I also wonder about how my grandson is coping. I know that children can be resilient, but I can't help but wonder what kind of long-term affect this will leave on him. Does he think we abandoned him? Does he believe all the bad things he has been told about us? There are more feelings than I can ever write about this. It is a tragedy and it has been a deep level of grief that is worse than losing a loved one to death. The unfairness and cruelty are more than can be written- for both the grandparent and the grandchild(ren)."

Amanda

"I have had a difficult time not feeling like trash, or feeling that I deserve the punishment for whatever I did. I'm coming to believe I did something so horrendous I earned this.

"Heartbroken, my expectations about my involvement in her life were turned upside down."

"My help comes from God, and if I didn't have him, I would end it."

"The shock has turned to sadness because we don't know how our grandchildren are doing; in school, at home, job wise, health wise or if their parents treat them well. They could be being abused and we would never know. We wonder if they are happy, do they have friends, do they have dreams, do they even know we exist? I guess the unknown is the hardest aspect to cope with given that it seems to be the black hole of hope."

"My grandmother worried every day of her life about my welfare. She wanted to die. The only hope she had to keep her going was that she'd see me again."… a granddaughter

"I had thoughts yesterday that helped me and may help others, too. Instead of the intense hurt I seem to live with, I forced myself to see the pathos of the situation. What kind of world has this poor girl created for herself to live in? How confined and lonely must be a world where every day you are hurting the people that love you? How grey must be the cell created where the doors are locked to love and kindness and family? I feel pity in place of anger."

"It is so hard to believe that this can actually happen to someone from a happy, healthy, normal family…but it can and it does. AGA has been a lifesaving organization for me."

"We have no choice but to bifurcate our lives. Certainly, my grandchildren are with me 24/7. Yet, I have been able to live and enjoyable life alongside

all of this grief. We are blessed with so many good friends that love and care about us. They are our family now. I don't get over the emotion, the desire to be with my grandchildren, or the essence of alienation; but we cannot waste our remaining years. We've made the choice to go forth despite all of this. We've educated ourselves, and set our boundaries. We could not have done this alone. Our AGA family is there for us in spirit, and when we need them. Just knowing you are all out there in spirit means the world to us."

"It's been eight years now since I saw my daughter. I have accepted my fate. I am thankful for what I DO have and do not dwell on what I have lost. The brainwashing has done a good job on my daughter. I am taking good care of myself."

"Life goes on without our precious grandchildren in our lives. The pain hasn't gone away; it just doesn't dominate our lives. We've rejoined the human race thanks to the support of AGA."

Knowing grandsons and granddaughters are out there somewhere, and wondering what kind of life they have been left with; eyes fill with tears, and hearts are laden with sorrow. Grandmothers hold in their heats the value of the relationships lost, even when they are being invalidated. Yearning for an adult child does not dissipate with time. Disconnected grandparents have been wounded emotionally, psychologically, and may experience stress related physical illnesses. Not only are the grandparents trying to cope, but the grandchildren are suffering as well. Wondering how to cope with this loss, it is important at this time to step back and give value to the relationships we do have.

(Dr. Baker) Grandparents who experience exceptionally limited visitation or have been cut off from access to their grandchildren suffer unending anxiety. Not knowing what awful things they are being accused of doing, not knowing the lies or distortions of the truth are being told about them, whether this sentence placed upon them by their own son or daughter will ever be resolved, or how long it might take to fix this is a source of constant stress.

(Golly 2016) Given the potentially serious and deleterious consequences of grandparent alienation to both grandparents and grandchildren, social work interventions are needed that address feelings of grief and loss of grandparents when they lose contact with grandchildren.

National author Anne Kathryn Killinger, *A Son is a Son Till He Gets a Wife...How Toxic Daughters-in -Law Destroy Families* stated, "I applaud the work of AGA. Only other grandparents who are not allowed to spend time with their grandchildren have any conception of the unnatural stress this place on our lives. My husband and I have four grandchildren we can't visit, two of them whom we have never once laid eyes upon. To a mother's heart, this is one of the most unbearable psychological burdens imaginable."

(Rev. Dr. John Killinger) Religion is always useful in helping us to reset our minds in a larger framework, freeing us from our limited focus on ourselves and our own problems. As painful as my alienation experience has always been, something inside my brain changes when I shift to thinking about God and the world and the suffering of others. My pain isn't gone, but it suddenly becomes muted or bearable when I realize how much other people are hurting and how much pain there is in the world.

(Fr. John J. Ludden, Pastor 2012) The ability to forgive brings freedom. Be free within yourself. What you do with your pain is what you are in control of now. Write a note to your grandchild each month; try your best. You know in your heart what you are doing is good, loving, and pure. The way she/he treats you is out of your control. You are in control of the present moment, and that is what saves your destiny.

Numerous AGA grandparents have been told by their alienating adult children to see a therapist. Unfortunately, they refuse to look in a mirror. Instead, they build a case against you among those who have joined their cult. It is the middle generation who need the therapy, but the grands end up going just to cope. A therapist may not be able to help you fix the situation, but an experienced counselor in PAS will at least understand the dynamics of alienation.

If you feel the need, contact your county mental health association. Tell them that you are looking for a counselor who can help you with managing your stress and anxiety, and can give you guidance for improving family relationships. Request counselors specifically familiar with alienation issues. An inexperienced and uninformed therapist can possibly adversely affect your situation. The same holds true when an adult child seeks therapy. A therapist without a full understanding of the complex dynamics of alienation can worsen a disruption of family ties.

The dynamics of Grandparent Alienation are similar to Parental Alienation. Higher institutes of education have provided studies in PAS, but GA was not taught. AGA has held trainings for mental health providers and attorneys.

Life is too short not to create your own happiness aside from your difficult situation. Find ways to lessen your grief and make your own happiness. Do not allow yourself to shy away from the people and activities that could bring back your identity and self-worth. Claim your own worth as a person and a loving parent, and for your sacrifices and achievements over the decades.

Gain strength by spending time with those who make you feel good about yourself, and open the door to new adventures. Focus your attention away from the stressing thoughts. Ask yourself what would you suggest if your friends were going through their own personal grief.

Do not let this situation define who you truly are as a person. You get to claim your own value as a parent. Your child can say whatever he/she wants, and obviously does, but you should value all the precious years of love and sacrifice. Your mind which controls whether you live in agony or in peace. When your mind wanders to those sad thoughts, bring it back. Set boundaries and limits for yourself. Gaining freedom from those constant negative thoughts is your objective. Making assumptions can cause unnecessary stress for you. In fact, when making an assumption we are really passing judgment without knowing all the details.

Communication plays such a vital role in all healthy relationships. When sons and daughters deny a platform for you to express your thoughts, it often results in misplaced anger, sadness, or resentment. Realize that anger is your worst enemy, as it may cause you to do something to worsen the rupture.

Learning to cope with the stress requires practice. It doesn't mean that you approve, like, or find it easy to accept what is happening to you. It is accepting life on its own terms regardless of your feelings about it, and finding effective strategies to cope.

Limit the amount of time thinking about the things that worry you. Designate a specific amount of time each day to reflect upon your grief. Sit in a quiet comfortable position and begin to take some deep breaths. Pay attention to your thoughts. For every negative thought, counteract it with a positive thought. If it makes you feel better to cry or let out your hurt, anger, or frustration, use these moments to do so. After the allotted time for the grief, channel your thoughts to the good times you shared with your children and grandchildren. Be prepared to switch to a pleasurable activity. Occupy yourself with a great book, happy TV show, a hobby, computer game, listen to your favorite music, bake cookies for a friend, or take a walk in the fresh air.

Tell yourself you did the best you could at the time, that no parent is perfect, and that their memory of you is incorrect. Be kind to yourself, and trust that nothing is permanent except change. Embrace who you truly are. Do not allow the alienation to be your only focus. Think of what you would be doing now if it were not for this anguish. What if your grandkids were all grown up, and you had to occupy your time? What would you be doing with your time?

Alienation is certainly a roller coaster of devastating emotions. The person whose opinion you care most about, your child, is willfully putting you though this agony. Unsuccessful attempts to work out the conflict with the parents of your grandchildren, for months or years, causes one to face stress on a daily basis. As pioneers in alienation, grands are stuck in a predicament they are not prepared to solve.

Talk about your feelings to a support group, friend, counselor, pastor, rabbi, or spiritual counselors. They are appropriate confidantes with whom you can talk to about family disconnect. Provide those who can help with AGA's website to validate your feelings and emotions. For women, friends are essential to a healthy life. Having a trusted friend to share your troubles with is helpful. They won't know how to fix the situation, but they offer a compassionate listening ear. Before we created AGA, my BFF was my personal daily lifeline.

Support and comfort surround a parent due to the death of their child, but is absent for targeted grandparents. Isolated grandparents are left to feel they must constantly validate themselves to others; that their own behavior must have caused such horrible punishment.

AGA continually hears from grandparents whose adult children have sadly passed away. Then, twice the victim of tragedy, are severed from any relationship with the grandchildren when a new partner or spouse enters the scene to influence the cut off.

Numerous cases have been brought to the attention of AGA whereby a daughter has fallen victim to the deadly evilness of their spouse or boyfriend. Because no body for evidence has been found, he remains the prime suspect. With no proof for a felony conviction, the children remain with the birth father, leaving horrified, distraught, worried grandparents cut off from access to their grandchildren. Tragically, we live in a time in this country where individual states do not protect these children.

While no caring grandparent gives up instantly, after suffering with no change in sight, they often feel alone, misunderstood, and have a profound feeling of loss or anger. Grandparents are distressed imagining what their grandchildren are being told. These little ones are left wondering why grandma and grandpa don't come to visit them anymore. This causes heartache and serious concern for the first and third generations.

These children will not forget the love and security they felt from their grandparents. Continue to make all possible reasonable attempts to connect with them. Tenacity is an indicator of success. Do this to know you have tried everything you could. Set your emotional boundaries, and guard your heart.

Grandparents live with guarded behavior for the future of the relationship. Abandonment of varied degree by their own children has resulted in fear, more rejection, and insecurity. They express the anxiety from being afraid of their son or daughter. Grandmothers in particular find that this fear and anxiety have become characteristic features of their lives. With their own child engaging in such hurtful behavior, they question their failure, wondering where their own parenting went wrong. The ending of constant fears and the search for peace of mind are objectives of each grandparent.

Recognize that an adult child will usually favor their spouse over the parent when conflict arises. Spouses should be devoted to their partner, but that does not mean they have to get rid of their parents. At the AGA International Conference 2019 Dr. Bone stated, "Your adult child wants to be connected." Dr. Caddy remarked, "They either drank the Kool aid, or are too afraid to pretend they didn't. There are different rules today."

You cannot change someone's behavior, but you can change how you react to it. Knowing you are not the only one going through this helps you cope better. You need not suffer in silence any longer. Now you can share your problems with those who "get it" at an AGA support group meeting, or on an AGA national or international support group conference call. Many books and articles are available on the topic. Learn what you need to know. The acquisition of knowledge empowers you. Educating yourself in the varied dynamics involved in the complex reality of Grandparent Alienation allows you to form a strategy and work your plan for a hopeful reunification.

Having been cut off from your child and grandkids is an intensely difficult situation to deal with for anyone, especially for grandmas; traditionally the nurturing parent. Embrace who you truly are. (Dr. Coleman 2019) Try not to personalize their rejection. They're being controlled by a powerful person or dynamic. It isn't their fault."

In discussions with AGA grandparents, it is not uncommon that the alienating child will have some communication with the dad, but not the mom. The bond with the mom would stir deep set emotions, causing them to feel more guilt. It would force them to look at what they have done. It is easier for the child to communicate with the dad, then walk away without such guilt.

What you are being put through can take months or years to hopefully change. Dealing with those who have a different moral compass or some level of personality disorder is challenging. This is harshly cruel and unfair treatment. Protect yourself. Remember that if you did the best you could at the time raising your child, and that no parent is perfect; start channeling your thoughts in a positive direction to be kind to yourself. It is not your behavior in question here.

Grandparents, reflect on your life. You really are the master of resilience and survival. You have survived tough times and challenges, over and over. If you have done it in the past, you can certainly do so now. You are an experienced problem solver. You overcome; you don't give up. While you may feel overwhelmed by the intensity of the current situation, try to take each day one at a time. Unfortunately, life doesn't serve our every wish on our timeline.

Memory a is very powerful mechanism. Suddenly, something triggers a moment from the past; a flashback of a special hug, smile, statement, or gesture you once shared with your grandchild. Recalling this joy brings a smile to your face, and a warm feeling fills your heart. On the other hand, you may recall a troubling event when you were treated unjustly. This triggers sadness, and the loss of a once loving healthy relationship. These emotional triggers around us cause a sense of helplessness and hopelessness. The journey of alienation is an ongoing drama of devastating hurts, disappointments, and bewilderment. Always *expecting* the unexpected, it feels almost impossible to find peace. This kind of hurt demands for a means for coping.

With the sudden extreme changeableness of this journey of alienation, targeted grandparents must remember to guard their minds. The daily hurts and disappointments of loss require that they be careful as to what they allow into their thoughts each day. Try hard not to believe the negativity of everything you are thinking.

Research has shown that the mind will naturally gravitate toward the negative thoughts. Positive and negative thoughts are handled by different parts of the brain. Negative memory has a greater impact taking up more space in the brain, because there is more to process. As the bad takes up more space than the good, it causes us to more frequently feel the sad emotions. As we remember negative events more than positive events, it is only human nature to replay the negative thoughts in your mind.

We naturally remember the bad, but it is also important to take the time to remember the good. Understanding that pondering the wrong memories makes us sad and that dwelling on the right memories makes us happy, we must try hard to be proactive. Train your mind to stop focusing on the bad. When negative memories come back, we relive them over and over again. These are depressing emotions. Stop replaying the negative things that have happened. Learn to switch your thinking to healthy and happy thoughts. Think of all the things that went right for you, and the accomplishments of your lifetime. Practice focusing on the good memories instead of worried thoughts. Counteracting your negative thoughts with positive ones creates new brain cells in becoming the new you.

Remaining in a state of high or chronic stress, you will continue to feel overwhelmed and stretched to your limits. There is much research pointing out how unrelieved stress exacerbates emotional and physical problems. Learn coping skills to manage your stress. Pain and fear must not define your days, or who you truly are. Consciously take notice of the things you should be grateful for having. Every morning when you wake up, make a choice for happiness. Be thankful for the relationships you have been given. Appreciate your spouse, partner, and friends, and acquaintances. What would it be like for you without these special people? Tough times and falling down are part of everyone's life. Let the kind people help you get yourself back up to living. You do not want to look back some year, only to find that you wasted life.

Help friends with their problems to take away focus on your own. Helping others helps us. Make a list of things you would like to do with those people.

Remember who you are, and that you own the truth. Think of what you would be doing if you were not going thru this. Go to those places and people that feel good to you. Spend your energy in a positive direction. Think positive thoughts.

Being afraid is a terrible feeling. Coping with such feelings is particularly difficult for grandparents when it is considered that in the United States statistics show that 72 % of grandparents state that being a grandparent is the most important and satisfying part of thing in their lives. (American Grandparents Assoc. 2014)

At anxious moments, when the feelings of anxiety and panic occur, practicing breathing techniques can be a therapeutic means to calming yourself. You can practice deep diaphragmatic breathing when you need a tool to help you calm down. Take a long, slow breath in through your nose. Hold your breath to the count of three. Exhale slowly through your mouth, while you relax the muscles of your face, jaw, shoulders, and stomach. Your stomach looks as though it is expanding when you breathe in, and then contracting with each breath.

If your mind wanders, bring it back to focus on your breath. If you need to, count each breath slowly to help you focus. As thoughts and feelings arise, acknowledge them. Continue your dep breathing several times. As you build your mindfulness practice and concentration, you may shake off anxiety, quiet your mind, and feel more serene. The good news is that by changing your breathing, you can reverse the symptom, resulting in a calming response. Learn how to change your fearful thinking and your negative imagery, because each time you frighten yourself with those thoughts or images you re-stimulate your body's emergency response.

Since our breathing is dictated in part by our current thoughts, make sure you also work on changing your negative thoughts as well as your breathing during panic. If you can let time pass without such intense focus on your fearful thoughts, you will have a better chance at controlling those thoughts. Practicing relaxing breathing techniques when you feel anxiety building, will work to the degree you are willing to concentrate on them. Put most of your effort into not thinking about anything else; not your worried thoughts, or what you will do after your finish the breathing skill.

Imagine a peaceful place. As you create this image in your mind, think of what it looks like: the aromas, sights, sounds, landscape, and people or animals.

Transcendental Meditation techniques are also helpful in reducing fear and anxiety because it cultivates a deeper sense of blissful self and well-being that anchors the person in all the ups and downs of relationships.

Post-Traumatic Stress may develop in some who have had the shocking experience of Grandparent Alienation. Most people experience a range of reactions after such trauma. Those who do not recover from the initial symptoms may be diagnosed with PTS. Several grandmothers have reported this diagnosis by their physicians. The Anxiety and Depression

Association of America website states that women are twice as likely to develop PTS as men. A UCSF study of individuals with PTS symptoms, published in the October 26,2012 issue of Journal of Psychiatric Research, found that women were more likely than men "to develop a stronger fear response, and - once conditioned to respond fearfully - were more likely to have stronger responses to fear-inducing stimuli."

Alienators are master manipulators; therefore, you may not be aware you are being manipulated as it is happening. You may understand their actions stem from a mental health concern, but regardless of how you think of the situation it can be helpful to remain calm when dealing with it. Try to contain your emotions and feelings instead of giving them the reaction they may be seeking; since in time, as they gain more control, the manipulating partner becomes more powerful. Do not allow them to take away from you a meaningful daily life, as they have already taken away your grandchildren. Keep in mind that the controlling parents cannot remove how the grandchildren felt when they were with you.

You would not want your grandchildren to be upset 24/7 because they cannot visit with you. You also do not want them to spend their youth in a constant state of sadness. Likewise, they would not want you to live your remaining years in that manner. We would like to think that our grandchildren are making positive choices. We want them to remember the happy and meaningful times shared. We want them to enjoy their lives, and keep a happy place in their minds for us. We want them to be peaceful, and enjoy opportunities to develop their talents and interests, make good choices in developing new friendships, make the best of their days, and aspire toward their goals. What we want for our grandchildren is what we should be doing for ourselves.

Live life. Leading a productive life under such circumstances is no easy task. It does not mean that you have to approve, like, or find it easy to accept what is happening to you. It can be a challenge to fully live in the present moment without reverting to what has happened to you. Our minds are driven to the what if's: "I should have said or done this, or I shouldn't have said or don't that." You must try to work hard to keep your mind and body healthy. A kind, happy, loving, and mentally healthy person is what you must be for your grandchildren when the time comes that they are able to find you; whether you have previously met them or not.

(Dr. Baker) It is essential for you as the targeted parent to be able to take pleasure where you can. Take in and be present and awake to the pleasures that do exist." There is no rule that says that a targeted parent should or must be miserable every second of every day. There is no need to feel ashamed or guilty for enjoying a good movie, having a laugh with a friend, or forgetting the alienation drama for a while. Notice what is good and right in your lives.

Dr. Baker encourages parents to achieve this is through living a mindful life, being emotionally present to the moment-by-moment experiences that life has to offer. She recommends developing an attitude of gratitude for what is good and what is working – even in the face of enormous struggle and suffering.

Know that the alienating adult child is still your child, and that in the vast majority of cases they still do love the targeted parent. They may not behave in such a manner or think they do at this time, but they do love you. There is a connection of the heart. Start thinking positive thoughts instead of negative ones. Only through love will you get your child back. Through your child, you will get your grandchildren back.

It may feel like your adult child hates you, but it doesn't mean that they do. There remains the connection of the heart. They may not behave as such since they may not always know it themselves at this time, but they do love you. Understanding this makes copying less burdensome.

Grandparents who have been cut out of the lives of their adult children whom they have loved so much for so long, often question a loss of love for this person they no longer recognize. AGA commonly hears the words, "How do I love the child I don't like anymore?" Don't punish yourself if you have had these thoughts. Should you be blessed one day with a reconciliation, you will feel the love you once felt just as your daughter or son will. You may not forget how you suffered, but you will move on together from that present time toward a better future.

Periodically sending those messages of love to your alienating child, will let them know you will be available to them when they are ready. If you stop communicating, they will likely interpret that to mean you do not love them anymore. With Grandparent Alienation, it is the grandparents who must try harder. The tenacity of the grandparent is an indicator of success.

There may come a time in your life when you need to take a break, or walk away from all the drama and the people who create it. Taking a break is not giving up. As in all relationships, you are entitled to set boundaries for the way people treat you. Set your boundaries to protect yourself when needed. Boundaries are the lines you draw that teach people how far they can push a situation before you will no longer take it. If they are making you angry, upset, or sick right now, then you have not drawn any boundaries and they will push you to your limits and beyond. Realize that it is out of your control for now. Turn it over to a higher power if you believe in one.

You may be one of the lucky ones for whom a miracle occurs. To date, AGA has participated in well over 200 success stories. This is proof that there really is hope. You may be one of them! Think of this as having a real chance of reconciling. With an educated strategy, you can increase the odds in your favor. What we have learned is working for many. In the past eight years since our founding of AGA, Inc., all of our efforts would have been worth it had only one family been saved from another day of destruction.

Finding self-compassion is necessary for moving forward. Forgive yourself if you have made any mistakes along the way. Since nuclear family relationships have broken down, you will need a support system in place. Turn acquaintances into friendship, and encourage new relationships. Spend your time and energy in a positive direction with positive thinking people. Feel vibrant again. Create a wider base of social relationships from colleagues, organizational groups, community centers, sports events, health clubs, theater groups, writing clubs, local conservancies, animal shelters, and a wide variety of hobbies and interests. You will find listings of activities in your local newspaper. Try some of these opportunities until you find what you truly enjoy. Talk about the good things in your life with others. It is your choice whether to mention your personal situation. You do not have to answer any questions you do not want to answer.

View each day as a gift to do something enjoyable; returning to activities once enjoyed, or exploring new opportunities of interest. Revitalize yourself, and the quality of your life. Do not isolate yourself. Changing routines helps. Reach out to the ones who can help you enjoy and find more peace in your days. Take actions to deal with your unhappiness, and maintain hope. Really trying is the best you can do. You can face these challenges. Think positive. Make a decision to move forward with confidence. The difficulties you have encountered can be used as the tools to prepare yourself for personal growth. It takes inner strength, but it can be accomplished.

There are community services specifically designed to empower and enrich seniors while enhancing the quality of their everyday life. Do the research for your location to find exercise, body conditioning, and chair exercise classes for those with activity restrictions. Try Tai Chi, Yoga, Arthritis/ Balance, table tennis, pickle ball, golf, swimming, biking, arts and crafts, nutrition, or other activities that spark your interest.

- Make use of the good and happy memories you have stored away.
- Rest, eat healthy, and exercise.
- Journal your thoughts. Writing about them is a form of healing.
- Make a list of five goals you would like to achieve to improve your daily life. Focus on areas that would create a healthier and more peaceful existence. What are the necessary steps to take in order to achieve these goals?
- Volunteer to help others less fortunate. Channel your energies into positive activities that will make a difference in someone's life, even if they will not solve your problem. We are what we do and who we help. Make a difference in someone's life; contribute to society. Helping others helps you.
- Start living your later years more fully.

Alienation is a battle. You will win the war. Validate your identity as a parent and grandparent. It is through this that you will find the strength for this journey. Focus on all the ways you were and are a wonderful mother or father. Think of the effort and sacrifices you lovingly and willingly made over the decades for the well-being of your child. Develop a mantra to find inner peace.

Nobody has it all. There will always appear to be people who have it better than you, but no one has it all. Each person you meet experiences problems, trials, and weaknesses. This is what makes us human.

Regulate your emotions so you may then approach your situation with a clarity. It is through knowing that your children are still your children, and that they need you, even though they cannot tell you and may not always know it themselves at this time, that you will find the courage to forge ahead. You are deserving of happiness.

25

Religion and Faith

Grandparents provide psychological, religious, cultural, historical, financial, and physical support for their grandchildren. When reared in a delusional cultish environment, they are robbed of normal loving extended family relationships. They are at risk of suffering from a variety of psychological distresses.

The Torah discusses *obligations* not *rights*. Parents do not *own* their children. The *Shulchan Aruch* (Compendium of Jewish Law) rules that determinations of visitation and custody are to be based on an assessment of whatever is most beneficial for the children. However, just as there is a commandment to "honor your parents", so too there are "*halochos*" (Torah-derived obligatory behaviors) to honor grandparents. Parents are commanded to show respect and honor to *their* parents by allowing them access to their children. Nay, relating to one's grandparents (barring the possibility of abuse or ill mental health) is deemed an honor and privilege. Preventing ones's parents from seeing their grandchildren is a transgression of the commandment '*kibud av v'eim*' —honoring one's parents.

(Steve Hayes, Baptist Minister of Counseling, 2014 AGA Ecumenical Panel): The scripture is full of dysfunctional families and strained relationships between siblings and also between parents and children. It is part of the fallen human condition. According to the scriptures it will only get worse as we race toward end times and society drifts further away from God.

Pastor Hayes, citing passages from the bible, advised grandparents to make sure they nurture and protect their original relationship, the marriage. He encouraged asking God for wisdom to understand what your adult children and their spouses can tolerate; saying that usually less is more. He inspired grands to demonstrate self-control over their emotions and speech. He advised keeping the circle of involvement as small as possible: resisting the urge to have family choose sides, keeping the children out of the middle, and being careful how you defend yourself when you feel misrepresented or attacked. The pastor recommended taking the high and humble road enduring injustice while trusting God and leaving Him room to work.

(Rio de Janerio, Brazil, July 2013): Pope Francis took the opportunity to impart special greetings for Grandparents Day in Brazil. "How important grandparents are for family life, for passing on the human and religious heritage which is so essential for each and every society!" the Pope exclaimed.

"How important it is to have intergenerational exchanges and dialogue, especially within the context of the family." Citing the Aparecida Document, the Holy Father expressed the themes highlighting the important role that the youth and the elderly have in society. "This relationship and this dialogue between generations is a treasure to be preserved and strengthened! …young people wish to acknowledge and honor their grandparents. They salute them with great affection, and they thank them for the ongoing witness of their wisdom."

(Pope Francis, Cuba, 2015) The issue of how to bring families in conflict together was addressed. You may imply your own interpretation included in his words…It is the grandfather's responsibility. The grandfather has lived long enough to give advice. It is the grandfather who is responsible for the growth and development of his children and grandchildren.

(Pope Francis, Philadelphia) The Pope spoke of the extreme importance of grandparents in society, to the family unit, and to the grandchildren. He spoke of how they help to create moral, religion, and ethics into the family unit.

(Rabbi Adam Miller, 2014 AGA Ecumenical Panel) Rosh Hashanah is the day of judgment. Books containing the deeds of all humanity are opened to review, and each person passes in front of Him for evaluation of his or her deeds. During the ten days of respite, Jews are supposed to

begin self-examination and repentance. The Divine Book of Judgements that in in the balance for ten days, waiting for repent, will be "sealed" on Yum Kippur. Grandparents, let us work together to find peace in our lives and with our families. Communication, reunification, and peace are our goals. Consult your clergy regarding Grandparent Alienation. Bring awareness that AGA exists.

Pastor Robert Winn

AGA Consultant   AGA Coordinator

Mid.Nebraska.AGA@gmail.com

Dear Ministry Professional:

There is a silent killer lurking within the lives of a significant segment of people to whom you minister. The impact of this killer is widespread and is growing exponentially. You may be aware of its existence, but you may have never identified it, observed its methodology or understood its motivation.

"Grandparent Alienation" (GA) is a fairly recent designation for this attack upon people you know and love. As an attack on the family and on the family of God, it has crossed cultural, socio-economic, and religious boundaries with abandon.

Amanda

"Grandparent Alienation" refers to two different acts of alienation. First, adult children choose to erect boundaries, which limit or eliminate their relationship with their parents. The cruelty of this unforeseen alienation is devastating to parents, who have given life to, nurtured, loved and protected their children since they were born. Second, those same adult children commonly choose to extend those boundaries to include the alienation of their parents from their own children, leaving loving grandparents, who patiently waited for years to enjoy their grandchildren, in a disoriented state of bewilderment and heartbreak. By their choices, these adult children have unknowingly shattered their own lives, the lives of their parents, and the young lives of their children. This is why the leading international experts in the field of alienation are now identifying "Grandparent Alienation" as a severe form of both elder abuse and child abuse.

Without intending to do so and without realizing the long-range consequences of their decisions, thousands of adult children are also quickly and effectively dismantling their entire extended family, which took generations to build. Furthermore, these young adults are establishing a very poor foundation for the future of their own families by modeling for their children that conflict resolution is best achieved by casting unwanted people from their lives. To justify this action, they are, out of necessity, forced to alter the truth about their parents and rewrite the history of their growing up years.

From a theological perspective, the origin of "Grandparent Alienation" lies within the sinful heart of man and has been with us since the beginning. From a contemporary perspective, its meteoric rise in recent decades can be attributed to many of the same factors which have more recently driven lawlessness and hatred onto streets across our nation and around the world. But, sadly, it may also exist unnoticed in the pews of your fellowship. Built into the fabric of this phenomenon is an insidious self-protective mechanism, which protects the anonymity of its perpetrators and demands silence from its victims. The most vulnerable victims are the grandchildren, because they have no voice. Not only are they kept from the knowledge of the truth, but they are unknowingly used by their parents to play a punitive role in the lives of their grandparents. Even normally perceptive ministry professionals don't often realize all of the many complexities of a particular alienation story.

Observing "Grandparent Alienation" is far more difficult than defining it. You may have observed it without knowing that you have done so. You might have momentarily wondered why the Smiths, a couple in their sixties who attend your Bible study, never show anyone pictures of their grandchildren. The Johnsons, whenever asked about their grown children (who were well known in your community for academic and athletic achievements in high school but have not been seen for years in church), explain their absence by remarking about how *"Young people these days are just too busy for old Mom and Dad."* You might have seen Alice Roberts' eyes watering just a bit as she received the rose that your church provided for each smiling mother on Mother's Day. What you may not have seen, and were probably not told, is that the Fullers received a letter from their son four years ago on his wedding anniversary. He announced that he was breaking off all contact with them, and that any cards or gifts sent to him, to his wife or to his children would either be returned or discarded unopened. He also declared that any attempts to communicate with them would be ignored. What you may not have realized was that Bill and Mary Ferguson's daughter was married last summer. Although all of her siblings and their children were in attendance at her wedding, her parents were not informed about the wedding until two days after it was over. Sadly, you may not have noticed any of these things. Although these grandparents in your congregation desperately need to share their burden with you, they are often too ashamed to do so. Fearing that they may be met with a lack of understanding or with biblically uninformed judgment, they choose to suffer in silence.

Careful observers will understand the severity of that suffering. Alienated grandparents grieve every time they see their fellow "golden agers" enjoying a burger or an ice cream cone with their grandchildren at a local fast-food restaurant. These "senior saints" may prefer to avoid church activities they once enjoyed, especially those at which families with multiple generations will be in attendance. For the alienated grandparent, the simple joys of life have been replaced with depression and, at times, suicidal thoughts. The pain of alienation runs that deep.

Nearly every alienated grandparent who has dared to bare his or her soul to someone else has been faced with a series of common questions: *"Why are your children doing this?" "What do your children say the issues are?"* Some grandparents have endured questions asking them to identify the things they must have done to provoke their children to erect such seemingly impenetrable boundaries. Sadly, many people of faith, including some clergy members, start with the assumption that these young adults must have good reasons to take such drastic and hurtful measures against their aging parents. Alienated grandparents are all too familiar with the reactions of their friends and extended family members: the body language, the skeptical questions, and the subtle but perceptible change in relationships. All of these reactions broadcast, in less than subtle ways, that judgment has been passed against them, and that a quest for the truth is not forthcoming.

Therefore, a once proud mother, who has unconditionally loved and sacrificed for her children from the time of their birth, silently endures the angry defiance of her son. A loving father, who would still willingly give his life for the "apple of his eye," repeatedly faces the sting of humiliation from the cruelty of his daughter's words. Alienated grandparents constantly live with the memory of those terrible words and actions, which are replayed over and over again in their thoughts.

These beleaguered grandparents are faced with the realization that the love and concern that their children once had for them have been completely withdrawn. These same adult children have intentionally removed the joy of grandchildren from their lives as well. They receive no phone calls which inquire about their welfare or which express interest in their lives. Special days in their lives (birthdays, anniversaries, Mother's Day and Father's Day) are ignored, and the invitations they send to their adult children proposing family gatherings and holiday celebrations (Easter, the Fourth of July, Thanksgiving and Christmas) are met with silence. They are neither informed of nor invited to the special events in the lives of their children and grandchildren. With one fell swoop, these adult children have destroyed the family life that their parents have painstakingly crafted for decades. Met with an impenetrable silence, these parents are usually offered no reasons for this alienation and are given no opportunity for dialogue. Reconciliation is impossible without communication. Even though these seniors need physical and emotional support in their elderly years, they are instead met with the immeasurable suffering of dishonor, neglect and loneliness by those who, according to God's design, should be offering them loving support. This destruction of an elderly couple's future at the hands of their adult children seems incomprehensible.

Therein lies the plea of this letter. Many alienated grandparents have turned to clergy for help. But, for a variety of reasons, many ministry professionals have chosen not to become involved in any way. Some, while seeking help, have even had the validity of their relationship with God called into question by members of the clergy. Those who study the truth of God in the pages of the Scriptures must provide care for these hurting souls. These alienated grandparents are reluctant and afraid, and they do not know where to turn for help. But way too often, spiritual leaders have also been reluctant and afraid, choosing not to reach out to these hurting believers and their family members. Those who are tasked with speaking boldly on behalf of God must not allow their fears, whatever they may be, to silence Paul's challenge in 2 Timothy 4:2 to *"... be ready, in season and out of season, to reprove, rebuke, and exhort, with great patience and instruction.'"* The need is great for men and women of faith to speak on God's behalf to those (grandparents, adult children and grandchildren alike) who need to hear His voice.

"Alienated Grandparents Anonymous (AGA)" is prepared to assist your ministry in several ways:

- to help you identify the tell-tale signs of either partial or total "Grandparent Alienation" in your congregation;
- to help you observe the patterns which adult children often follow to denounce their parents;
- to explain how those adult children seek to win the approval of their siblings and extended family members and how they attempt to turn their hearts against their parents as well;
- to help you understand a biblical explanation for the widespread acceptance of this destructive delusion; and
- to provide you with tools which will enable you to offer the comfort of God's sufficiency and the hope of His promises to those who find themselves in the midst of what seems to be a never ending and horrific storm - a storm generated by their deeply loved but prodigal adult children.

"AGA" can direct you to ministry professionals who themselves are weathering the storm of alienation. They want to share with you the comfort they have experienced - a comfort promised by King David in Psalm 34:18-19 (NASB):

"The Lord is near to the brokenhearted and saves those who are crushed in spirit. Many are the afflictions of the righteous, but the Lord delivers him out of them all."

You can contact AGA at the following email address: AGAInternational Headquarters@gmail.com

26

Strategies for A Hopeful Reconnect

"What I did, but was once afraid of trying, was to send a post card every day to my son until I finally heard from him. I only said things like what I had for lunch, where I went that day, and always that I love him. Nothing personal or asking questions. Four months later he called me like nothing had happened."

"After seven years, my son came back to me. He was getting a divorce from the wife who broke us apart and kept my grandsons from me. He told me it was the messages I kept sending to him that he knew he was welcome to come back to me."

"The strategies we learned from AGA made the difference."

"It's never too late to try again to make this work for us."

"I followed your advice and shared it with my husband. He agreed with it as he was previously strongly going to take the route of ignoring them and allow them to find out they finally missed us on many fronts, and would invite us back into their life. Wrong. So, we learned from you. We practiced what you shared and our son started to come around, despite what awful things she was likely saying about us behind our backs."

"Alienated Grandparents Anonymous (AGA), which is a rich educational resource and international advocate, has encouraged us to "never give up". This is the best and most enduring advice we have received to date. In our case, it is especially applicable since it seems we're fighting this battle almost

alone sometimes. There are too many enablers, watching, hoping or ignoring, as we grandparents and our grandchildren are being emotionally devastated."

"It's like a miracle each time there is a success! What seemed impossible can happen!"

"Your suggestion of a once-a-month email is something I can do, and perhaps something I can do under my DIL's radar screen. When trust drops to zero, your mind goes a big crazy on you."

"My daughters have not spoken to me in eight years. When they all married, I decided it was time for me to find happiness in my life. I divorced their dad. They aligned with my ex. I took your suggestion and sent emails to my daughters. That day I heard back from the one of them. It was a very promising letter."

"Thank you for taking the time to schedule a phone call with me. I hadn't seen my daughter or grandson in two years. During our conversation, I mentioned to you that my daughter's father was in ICU. I had not informed her, because I didn't think it would matter to her. But you wisely advised me to let her know, because it might be an opportunity for us to possibly reconnect. I left a voicemail with the message. I got a call from her thanking me. She wants me to come to my granddaughter's birthday party in two weeks. And, she wants me to come to a school play in June!"

"I left a voicemail for my daughter. It's been five long years since her husband has been keeping her and my granddaughter from seeing me. My daughter called me that day! I couldn't believe it. It was a voicemail. She said, thanks for reaching out to me, Mom. I love you, too." Thank you, AGA, for the suggestion and encouragement. I am sooooo excited."

"After not seeing my little granddaughter for over two years, and never having met my new grandchild, I finally got to see them! I just showed up at their

house with a witness (as you suggested). They let us in. We stayed for an hour. We got together a few more times on the trip. They acted as though nothing had ever occurred. I didn't say a word about it either. Thanks for your help."

"There was such turmoil going on in my family last year. My heart was terrified, consulted with friends, and prayed a lot. It was a very difficult road. Recently, and with much prayer, a change of heart took over and the situation has improved 100%. I am in awe of this, and incredibly grateful. I think AGA is much needed. Please don't disappear. There will always be someone out there that needs help. Thank you - peace."

"My son has been divorced for years, and the children were adopted by the new husband. I tried many many ways over 10 years, but the parents did not want me in their life; I think because my religious beliefs are vastly different. I hired a private investigator as your organization suggested. Since then I have had emails, phone conversations, and photos. I believe the parents do not want us to meet. However, I am very relieved that they are healthy, sound, and happy. It is difficult to recover the easy relationship between us. However, I am blessed that I now have contact. Thank you for your help."

"Following one of your suggestions a few weeks ago, I told my daughter in a text that I love her and will always be there for her. Since then, she has been less angry and less rude. That's progress. Thank you."

"I just had to let you know that thanks to our conversation this week, and to your invaluable recommendations for me-which I took- I now have my daughter and my grandchildren back in my life for the first time in two years. You were my "divine intervention!"

"Send postcards or lovely cards made into postcards to the school. When the office staff sees the cards and the positive and loving notes, they are quite likely to give them to the grandkids. Perhaps the teacher does NOT KNOW about

their alienating parents, and this is OK. Many alienating parents try to keep
their secrets and lies out of the school system. Be sure NOT to overdo the cards,
but to make the words meaningful and full of love. These cards could make
the parent rage and will want it to stop, because he has lost some control. If
you are lucky enough to get the enraged e-mail, be sure and save it, laminate
it, and include it in all your documentation."

Trying to repair your relationship with your adult child and feeling the situation is impossible to fix is not an indicator of getting your child and grandchildren back. Each of the hundreds of success stories AGA has been a part of has been an unexpected miracle in the eyes of the reunited grandparents. If seeking reconciliation is your goal, then remember that Grandparent Alienation is not about fairness, it is about doing what might work. The best reason to reach out yet again is that it just might work this time!

Think not as a victim, but as an earnest proactive person. Do not let fear be your guide. Approach this with understanding. You are still the parent. Face the challenges of this disconnect with confidence. Be a positive role model for doing the right thing. It is passion which makes good things happen. Remarkable achievements begin with your thoughts. Decide to be extraordinary, and do what you need to do. See these problems as opportunities for growth. When we step out of our comfort zone to test ourselves, we grow. It is the difficulties we have been confronted with that are the tools we can use to prepare us for improving future situations.

Parents who want to reconnect with their sons and daughters need to question the pain of their adult child. Empathize with what your grown child might be going through, and consider possible reasons why they have been a part of the disassociation. Consider unresolved childhood issue which you may not have properly dealt with at the time. Perhaps your child lived with deep-run feelings and heartbreak of their own, which they did not share with you. It is never too late to try to heal an injured relationship. At least you will have the satisfaction knowing you tried your very best.

Success can usually only be achieved when the grandparent continues to make continuing and ongoing efforts to reach out to the parent/gatekeeper in a non-threatening and loving manner. Although success can never be assured, time, persistence, and patience are the keys to the possibility of an eventual reunion. The tenacity of the targeted grandparents' efforts directed toward the children, is also a predictor of the grandchildren reaching out to them in the future. Recognize your grandchildren's birthdays and special occasions, and keep documentation of each of your efforts.

Move to action. Work toward a hopeful reconciliation. In the words of Edmund Burke, "The only thing necessary for the triumph of evil is for good men to do nothing". Ignoring a problem is neither smart nor sensible. Even a failed attempt at solving the problem is better than not doing anything. Think of this as developing and testing a formula. Just like science, it may eventually bring results to benefit so many. Consider it the constructing of a bridge between the generations of the family, helping each of you to get to the other side.

Dwelling on your past disappointments of reaching out to your kids assures no future growth. See these problems as opportunities for your preparedness. Achieving even limited contact is better than complete isolation, so examine your ability to work toward a reconciliation. Make a concentrated effort because your grandkids want you in their lives. (Dr. Caddy 2013) There are many problems which can be solved. This is a dilemma. We have to work thru dilemmas. Learn about them.

C. Paul, Foundation for Religious Diplomacy states that the techniques used to bring warring nations and religious rivals together can help families with seemingly unresolvable conflicts – including religious, philosophical, or lifestyle differences where people believe they cannot with integrity compromise. He suggests focusing on a respectful and even friendly relationship with someone who is your opponent, your rival. He encourages the parties to forge rapport; someone must make an overture. You can meet in a public place for a meal, as it provides social and physical safety and a psychological boost from eating together.

Paul cites how honesty and emotion in sharing can usually crumble part of the wall separating people. The possibility for healing is in sharing and feeling listened to, confided in, and trusted. The desire is not to debate this issue, but to witness, share experiences, and be open to letting each other do the same. He notes that you cannot influence somebody unless they feel you are open to their influence.

"Let your adult child know that it is important to reconnect for the well-being of their child." (James Karl, Esq. 2014)

Prepare yourself for when your chance may come to do what is in the best interest of the child. Develop your strategy, and carry out your plans. Timing is important. If you know they are experiencing a more vulnerable time in their life, this can work to your benefit. If you have information you believe they might want to know about, use this as an opportunity reach out. It is your efforts which will make reconciliation a possibility.

A willing heart sees nothing as impossible. Educate yourself with the information that is available to you. Read from the AGA Bibliography. A great book can change a person's life. Your proactive journey begins when you start to understand. Prepare yourself.

As you read, it will trigger thoughts for strategies. Knowledge is power. Plan your work, then work your plan. Recognize opportunities for communication with you grandchild, then proceed as if you are not afraid. Dare to reach out to the gatekeeper. Try to open a new avenue of communication by reaching out to the spouse of your adult child, even if you are not fond of them. Role model appropriate healthy parenting behaviors.

Reach out to the gatekeeper. Acknowledge all special occasions of your adult child, their spouse, and the grandchildren with a brief loving note. Weakness and fear are the delight of dysfunction. Silence is complicity. It is thru love that a pathway can be found. AGA has had many successes simply because the grandparent kept trying. Your attempts to communicate show them how much you still care about them, so work on that love connection. Though you realize your efforts will be difficult for you, because you are opening yourself up to more rejection, you will be working toward a resolution.

Working your way back into their present time thoughts is a very powerful means of helping your child find some reality in this chaos…Mom still loves me; Dad still loves me. It proves to them that we don't give up on our kids. It demonstrates how your love is that unconditional love only a parent can have for a child. It reinforces that we as parents are forgiving and accepting rational people, and that we understand things have been tough for them.

Everyone has bumpy roads in life. Help your child thru this ordeal. Just show who you are with your words and actions. You be the one to cautiously demonstrate how hard a parent tries to be a part of a child's existence. These life lessons we as parents/grandparents teach even to our grown children. You never stop being a parent. You think you were finished teaching because they grew up…NOPE! Remember what they say, the older the kids get…the bigger the problems. Who knew it would keep going at this age! You now have a difficult student, so keep trying until you find a method that works! Timing is everything. Be patient and compassionate with them. Look at this thru their eyes, because they have been through a lot as well.

Continued efforts to connect with the D-I-L or S-I-L show them you are still welcoming them back into your fold. It shows you are able and willing to follow their lead; that you will do what it takes to have your son or daughter and your grandchildren back as a family.

Hope exists in everyone. Through love a pathway can be found. Periodically make your opportunity and proceed as if you are not afraid. Reach out to them with love. You never know which attempt will be the one to that surprises you. This process requires patience and persistence. Every day is a new day to make a happy ending. Send out positive energy.

For many years you were in charge, just because you were the parent. When your child becomes a parent, the rules change. Now you must abide by the rules of the next generation of parents. When adult children with fragile personalities call upon you, be respectful with your response in order to stay in the game.

(Leslie Stahl, 60 Minutes) has stated in her book *Becoming Grandma,* "I was coming to appreciate that when our children become parents the balance shifts. We grans begin holding our tongues. We turn passive, lest we irk or antagonize. We see clearly that they hold a new card, the power to deny us access to the most precious thing on earth. So, we enter a new precinct of best behavior and walking on eggshells. We live by their rules now, and rule number one is: Do it their way."

Whether your future D-I-L or S-I-L initially worked their way into your heart, or just into your family; you have found yourself in the challenge of your lifetime. There are hopes in the hearts of grandparents that maybe a friend, family member, co-worker or an "influential figure" will find the courage to step forward to offer help in some way. Yet, it seems most are hesitant to do so. It is also not wise to ask your other children to interact on your behalf. Instead, it is now very important to strengthen the relationship you have with each of your other children.

When friends and family ask how they might help you with your situation, let them know they are welcome to tell your alienating child that they themselves have a love and are concerned for both the alienator and the grandparent; that they do not want to get in the middle, but they hope it can be worked out. The bridge person can also mention how family life can have its problems. Their knowing that both the parent and the adult child are good people, they can tell your child that they are willing to help to move things in a positive direction. Do not pressure anyone to do this. But if they are willing, and can find an appropriate time to do so, you would deeply appreciate it. This bridge person may be able to get a message of love to your grandchild for you.

Do the best you can reaching out to your family for now, and accept that this will take time to resolve. Focus your attention on your son or daughter first. Building your relationship with your own child, will build a bridge to your grandkids. This does not mean you shouldn't try to communicate with or see your grandkids. There are locations open to the public where you can possibly get a glimpse of your grandkids, displaying your message of love and trying to be with them. Consider school plays, team sports, graduation, and so on.

We are far more powerful in the hearts and minds of our adult children than we believe ourselves to be, and that they allow us to believe. They may not behave in this manner at this time, or realize it at this time, but they do love you. Never underestimate the power of love. Even if you do not see evidence of their love at this time, have faith that it is there.

Remember, you can only change your behavior, not anyone else's. Do not orient yourself toward what is fair, instead be strategic. Continue to do what you think might work. Change your thoughts to positive ones. Begin thinking, "My child does love me. There is a connection of the heart." By understanding of the complex dynamics of Grandparent Alienation, grandparents become empowered. In fact, after national support group call-ins with AGA Headquarters and the 2019 AGA International Conference, these were the exact words expressed by grandparents who attended, "I feel empowered!" Turn your newly gained knowledge into ideas. The more you learn, share experiences with others, and gain more insight; the better you are equipped to walk your journey. Learn what you need to know. You grow stronger and smarter by educating yourself. Develop a strong sense of self. Set healthy boundaries for yourself to protect your happiness and well-being.

When alienated grandparents are presented with an opportunity to meet with the son or daughter who has cut them off, they express how insecure they feel regarding what to say to their own children. We are talking about educated and wise souls who find themselves not knowing what to say to their own kids. They realize they are being given a rare opportunity, and do not want to mess it up. The majority have already been raged at by these troubled young adults.

(Dr. Caddy 2013 AGA presentation):

> Consider the fact that this is a war not a battle, and that it is chronic. Think of a long-term plan. Make a plan and work your plan. Wait for a strategic moment. Deal with it in a strategic planed manner. Don't be terrified of engagement. Be rational and credible. Be strong and powerful. It's never too late to try again to make this work. Strategize your next move.

There may come a time when you should walk away from all the drama and those who create it. Know when to take a break from this stress. Set your boundaries when needed. You cannot save others by allowing yourself to be destroyed. You are not giving up by not acting now. Stay mentally healthy and be strong enough to win the war, and be there for your grandchildren when the time comes.

If it were easy to be successful in life, then everyone would be. The best successes in life come after disappointments. A willing heart sees nothing as impossible. The prize is worth it! What do you have to lose?

Just as you have been waiting for your grandchildren, they too have been waiting for you. Every child wants the unconditional love of a Gram and Pop. It is because your grandchildren do not want you to give up on them, that you will persevere as best you can. Perseverance is an indication of success. Continue periodically to reach out to your adult child. When you stop, they think you don't love them any longer. In your messages, tell them you love them, will always be there for them, and include something about what you are doing. Keep it happy and upbeat. Do not expect a response, just keep reaching out. You will be planting seeds for the future.

Dr. Baker recognizes how grandparents who have been cut off by their adult children have been burdened with fear, which keeps them from some attempts of reconciliation. She states that If you stop trying to communicate with them, they will be shocked; and that they actually interpret this to mean you have stopped loving them! This is a hugely meaningful concept for alienated grandparents acknowledge. When suggested at AGA support group meetings, it has opened a whole new thought pattern for the grandparents.

Dr. Baker encourages grandparents to find insightful new pathways to possibilities for healing, while realizing it can sometimes be hard to see how your actions are making a difference. In some parent-child relationships, it may take years before results appear from your choices and effort. She doesn't want you to make the mistake of thinking you do not matter to your children; because you do.

If you are experiencing restricted communication, feeling your relationship is in jeopardy, the most important thing you can do is to stay involved. If you receive a message from them, be smart with your response. Be complimentary, and tell them you are open to listening to their thoughts. Even though the gatekeeping spouse may want you, the grandparent, to make all communications through them; do your best to maintain a positive connection directly to your child. The gatekeepers want to feel they maintain the control. Understanding this, and feeling that anything is better than isolation; then choosing limited contact includes calmly abiding by their rules.

In summary, what has contributed most to the successes with AGA is this periodic reaching out with messages of love. Focus your efforts on your adult child first. It is through them that you will gain access to your grandchildren. Work on that relationship. Building your relationship with your own child, will build a bridge to your grandkids. The gatekeeper spouse/partner must be recipients to your efforts as well. Sometimes grandkids can convince their parents to allow contact. By continuing to reach out to your family, you will also be recording your efforts in the minds and hearts of your grandkids.

Reaching out with a lighthearted message monthly brings you back into their present time thoughts. Periodically, but not too often, keep the door open with news about positive things YOU are doing. Keep them informed of and your family, and anyone or anything else they know or care about.

Assure your adult child of your love. Your adult children need this once in a while communication of your love for them. Once again, do not expect a response. This assures them that when the time is right to reach out to you, the door will be open. They will know you love them, and that they can approach you without being subjected to more guilt than they already have.

(Dr. Caddy) Sending a message of unconditional love along with and note of what you the parent is enjoying, places you on their mind in a healthy way.

(Dr. Bone) Keep in mind the fact that alienated children operate under the belief that they are not loved by the targeted parent or grandparent. Reaching out (even over their protest), not obsessively, but with some regularity, flies in the face of that belief. There is no downside to reaching out to estranged adult children. Keep in mind the fact that alienated children operate under the belief that they are not loved by the targeted parent or grandparent. Reaching out (even over their protest), not obsessively, but with some regularity, flies in the face of that belief.

To become a more positive active connection in their lives and depending upon which means of communication is available to you, send a text or an email, leave a voicemail, or mail a postcard. A postcard is more likely to be looked at than a sealed envelope. Have a postcard made from one of your special photos to trigger a good memory of you and your child. Keep the tone of any communication loving but light.

Keep trying. Try again and again. Think of new ways to reach out to them. If you stop communicating to them and stop giving that unconditional love, they will interpret it to mean you do not love them anymore. Communicate to them without expectations, because it might eventually bring the results you so desire. Keep in mind that any response of any nature from your adult child is good; even if it of an unpleasant nature.

Send messages that appear relaxed, positive, and reflect your activity. Your actions tell them you still love them, and assure them that they can approach you without being subjected to more guilt than they already inwardly feel. By sending signals that the door is open, it will allow them at a more vulnerable time in their life to feel more comfortable and welcome to contact you. Use the words, "Hi, it's Mom/Dad. I love you, and I will always be here for you". Next, tell them something positive about yourself. Get back into their present-day mind; become real to them again.

(Dr. Coleman) Going on with your life and doing well can relieve the estranged child from the guilt and worry that he or she may be experiencing. Doing well in your life lets your child know that you are resilient, and creates your best chance of reconnecting at some point in the future.

Stay away from mentioning anything about the conflict or past issues. In time you can eventually offer two choices (so they can maintain a sense of control) asking if they would like to do something together which you have both enjoyed in the past. Keep it lighthearted and happy. Focus on them, not the grandchildren for now. Make it a new start for the two of you. If distance is involved, offer them choices of when you could be in their area. When you do meet up, discuss the next step. Tell them you would like to check in again in a couple of weeks, and that you will send them a text.

As the alienating spouse tries to rewrite history, they are controlling by changing your child's past to make them think it was not a happy or good experience. They are clouding the image of you as a good loving parent and person. You must make the effort to enter their present mind. Become real to them again. Replacing good memories with negative ones is healthy for both of you. By sharing information about things you have been doing or plan to do, and keeping the door open with news about you, your family, and anyone or anything else they know or care about; you are creating new healthier thoughts in their minds. Let them know if you connected with an old friend they knew. Share your travel adventures, great books, movies, sports, and such. Food is a good connecter. Think back to times with your own mom and dad, or your grandparents. Many of those special memories are related to favorite home cooked recipes which they prepared for you. What sparks a good memory? Would it be a picture or text of their favorite meal, a pet, family vacation, holiday tradition, childhood sport, or a hobby? Send good memory photos.

Create a brief message choosing your words carefully. Dr. Coleman explains how in most relationships, telling someone that you miss them would be considered benign-to-meaningful. However, when a disassociation is taking place, telling your adult child that you miss them will likely be interpreted as a demand or a guilt trip, thus working against you. Many family cut offs, at least in part, are a desire to feel *less* in touch with the parent's feelings. This is especially true for those who are working on feeling more separate, less responsible, less worried, and less ruled by feelings of guilt.

This same train of thought applies to those who are less empathetic. Normally saying the words "I miss you" would motivate a response in kind. However, those who alienate interpret this as an attempt on your part of making them feel guilty.

Alienating adult children who are self-absorbed with their own lives break the ties that bind them to their parents. They are very likely married to someone who is difficult and demanding, have some level mental illness, or they are unduly influenced by your ex-spouse. Dr. Baker advises that you may not have control over the others actions, but you do have control over how you respond and how you process the situation with your children.

If you are denied access to your grandchildren, find alternative ways to continue the relationship. When dealing with high conflict situations it can sometimes be hard to see how your actions are making a difference. In some parent child relationships, it may take years before you will see the results of your choices and effort. Don't make the mistake of thinking you do not matter to your children, you do.

(Dr. Coleman) Some adult children take our willingness to keep listening and reaching out no matter what, to mean that we are too weak to take them on. They escalate their behavior to abuse, in part because they are out of control. In addition, sometimes they escalate their behavior as an attempt to have some appropriate limits set on their behavior. Do not criticize, be a good listener. Don't respond in an aggressive way. They want extreme control. Let them think they have control, be a good listener.

These adult children are often in significant pain themselves. You may need to reach out for a long time before there is a reconnect. Even though adult children may say they are unwilling to renew a relationship, they may someday or some year be willing to give their parents another chance. It is up to the grandparent to make those chances count. It is never too late to reach out. AGA's over 200 success stories at this writing include reconnections up to a 17-year cut off. For some AGA grandparents there has been a quick response; for others it can take months or years. By systematically placing yourself into their thoughts, even if only with cards or small gifts, the more chances you have for a reconnect.

When attempting to meet with your adult child, it is important to understand the complexities of alienation which can help you strategize your personal situation. Do not orient yourself toward what is fair, instead be strategic. Do what you think might work. Focus your love on your son or daughter, not the grandkids. They will follow. Should you find an opportunity to meet in person, always conduct yourself with dignity. Do not criticize them, or their spouse. (Dr. Coleman) You may try to be direct with your child in a loving manner. Ask if there is anything you might be doing that is upsetting to them in some way. Let your child know you are willing to listen and view things thru their perspective; then listen without responding defensively.

When you are with them, try to behave as though alienation is not occurring. It is only natural that you may feel anxiety knowing you are about to meet up with the child who has held such control over your situation. Under certain circumstances, you may be able to take someone with you for support. Remember that YOU are still the parent. Lead by example. Demonstrate your best qualities, and show your best listening skills. Be open to their point of view, and show empathy that were unaware how they viewed this. Maintain your sense of self when you are with them. Do not allow them to take away who you truly are. YOU own the truth. What they want you and perhaps others to believe, is not as important as what you know.

Are you open to working on yourself? This is a critical quality in today's parent-adult child relationships. If you have received a criticizing message from them, let them know you heard what they stated loud and clear, and that you would like them to know you are willing to work at it to improve the situation. You might say something like, "I am wondering if there was something in a past that bothered you. I want you to feel like you can be open with me if something bothers you, or if there are things that you would like me to work on."

If distance is not an issue, you may attempt a surprise visit. It would be wise to take a witness with you. Consider scheduling an appointment with the sheriff first to make him aware of Grandparent Alienation. Hand him AGA documents for validation. Focus on false accusations as your reason to meet. This is a means to protect yourself and other grandparents in the community, and to learn about legal restrictions. You can choose to do this anonymously.

As you gather the courage for your visit tell yourself, "I may feel nervous or frightened, but I will survive." You just might be choosing a more vulnerable time in their lives and be invited in, which does happen. As example, an AGA couple flew twice to their daughter's home state. They had success on their second surprise trip. Another couple shared their story of a thousand-mile drive in effort to see their grandchildren, only to be turned away.

Knock on their door. You may get lucky. Your grandchildren may be the ones to answer the door, or you might see them playing outside. (Dr. Caddy) If you have but a brief moment, let your grandchildren know you love them, that you have been trying to see them, and will always be trying to be there for them. If your grandkids are a bit older say, "I am glad you are smart enough to see the difference between right and wrong. I am sorry you have to hear those things. I love you." Never say anything negative about the parents.

If you can travel to their town and want to announce a desired visit, offer them two or three choices that are all agreeable to you. Offering them choice allows them to think they are maintaining the power and control they have been seeking. Then perhaps provide some reason why you would be in the area and could hang out with them for a few hours. It is best to make the suggested amount of time brief. Come to an agreement from the choices you provided which work for you.

When you are given an opportunity to be with the gatekeepers, be complimentary. Do not react with any negativity since this will unsettle them. Do not respond in an aggressive manner. They want extreme control, so let them think they have control by being a calm listener.

They want praise, so give it to them. As your walk your journey back into a relationship with the gatekeepers, and as time passes, your relationship will improve and there won't be as many eggshells to walk on.

When trying to arrange a get together, word your request so their response would provide substance. Do not phrase it so their answer would be a simple yes or no. Ask an open-ended question which requires an answer with information. Begin your question with when, which, where, would, or how.

Example: I would like to take you to lunch. Would Thursday at noon or Saturday at 1:00 work best for you? I will be in your area (give two date choices). Which would be more convenient for you to meet up?

You may need to reach out for a long time before there is a reconnect. Don't give up too soon. When the time is appropriate for them, they will be more inclined to reach out.

The psychological fragility of your son, daughter, D-I-L, or S-I-L, is so important. If granted this time together do not criticize, just be a good listener! Don't respond in an aggressive way. Develop the communication skills necessary to let the gatekeepers know that they have the power, and you are not a threat. They want extreme control, so allow them think they have the control. It is not about fairness; it is about your goal.

If your adult child does agree to meet with you, then returns home and discloses this visit to their mate; you may not be granted a follow up visit. Their spouse may increase the cycle of denigration upon them. In the thoughts of an alienator, anything goes in order to win the game. If your child is stuck in the middle, develop a deeper compassion for them. While you are with your son or daughter suggest they tell their spouse that they have enough love for her/him and for the mom and dad as well. Tell her/

him that having your parents in your life is very important. Say you want to be a whole family, having both sets of grandparents in the lives of the children."

Advances in life are usually first met by fear and skepticism. Your journey toward reconciliation begins with educating yourself and trying. It does take time to accomplish good things. Your character consists of what you do on your third or fourth tries. If you fall short four times, then stand up for the fifth. You never loose till you quit trying. Success is based on your efforts to make contact with your children and grandchildren. Successful people are successful because they think they are. Never doubt your abilities.

Research shows that children of adoption who sought their birth parents at the ages of 20, 30 or 40 have stated that they feel their birth parents did not try hard enough to find them. This scenario may be likened to Grandparent Alienation.

If an uncomfortable or abusive situation occurs when you approach your child, if they rage at you or bully you, do not try to reason with them. It is best to just calmly say, "I will come back another time. I can see that right now is not a good time for you." Then, you be the one to walk away. They can only behave that way if you remain their audience. (Dr. Golly) Your son or daughter deep down inside may want to invite you in, but their unaccommodating spouse is controlling from inside the home.

(Dr. Coleman) If your adult child becomes abusive in tone, it is best to end the engagement. It will not help the situation if you demonstrate angry in return. By retreating, you are reinforcing that you want to make peace.

Carrying this psychological burden around with you 24/7 is traumatic. Try and try again to make it clear to your child that you love him/her, and would like to work it out together. Be selective with your approach. Making a child feel sorry or worry about you usually doesn't work. It can create distance and generate resentment. Making your child feel guilty will likely shut them down and keep them away from you. They don't want to feel the guilt. They don't want to look into the mirror. Many grands suffering serious illness have expressed their deep sadness, disappointment, hurt, and depressed feelings because their own sons and daughters did not respond to their devastating health news. One such granddad sent a message to his son when he was diagnosed with fourth stage terminal cancer. He informed his son of his grave news and asked to see him and his little grandchildren once before he passed. He was denied. AGA has heard similar stories over and over again.

(Dr. Coleman)

> Many parents believe that if they only make their children worried enough, they'll come to their senses, reach out, and express the love and connection that was once so clearly there. While that is, in fact, true for some children, for others, worry is experienced as such a burdensome emotion, that the adult child doesn't know any other way to find relief from it other than to distance himself or herself. Some children become abusive or disrespectful to the parent because they know that their gripe is so mild that it could be ignored or repudiated. In this case, an adult child may treat the parent in a disrespectful or rejecting manner because they're trying to make the parent out to be more of an ogre than they really believe them to be as a way to not feel guilty.

Some adult children just need to be mad and stay mad no matter what you do, therefore reaching out to the gatekeeper in order to time with your grandchild doesn't bring results. Therefore, focus your efforts on your grandchildren. Let your grandkids know you care. The more you can show your grandchildren that you are a kind and loving person, the more they will have those memories in their heart and mind to counter what their parents say. Your grandchildren may reach out to you later in life because they need someone trustworthy to be close to, confide in, or provide them an alternative view of themselves than the one provided by their parents. The more you have stayed in their lives, even if only with gifts or cards, the more chances you have of staying alive in their minds.

Attend school and athletic activities. Do not allow the fear to keep you from trying to communicate with your grandchildren. Find out where their extracurricular activities are, and show up. Always take a witness with you. Find out about school plays, concerts, graduation dates, team sports, or any public event (unless you have been served with a legal restriction). You can schedule an appointment with the school administrator to find out just how much you can do legally. You do not have to give the name of the child. Present the AGA documents including "Dear Educator" form letter at the meeting.

Find out what the laws are in the grandchildren's state. In Florida, it is lawful to tie balloons to the mailbox post; not the mailbox itself. Using magic marker, write their names and your message on the balloons. Knock on their door. Timing is important. Perhaps you will get lucky and actually see your grandchildren. If you do, tell them you love them, and that you are a really good person. They need to hear this because they have not been allowed to develop their cognitive thinking skills. Always take a witness with you.

Presenting at the AGA International Conferences 2017 and 2019, Attorney Jamieson made suggestions to consider. Keep trying everything in a low-key manner. Should you get a complaint letter from their lawyer, it may not require a response from you. In that case, you won't have to admit or deny accusations. Do not harass or offensively interact.

- Go to public school events. If your adult child complains to the school, they will be exposing/showing their true colors.
- Go to public facilities.
- Volunteer as a reading mentor, after school care, homework mentor, or classroom helper.
- Become a sponsor for a party or event at their school.
- Donate supplies such as copy paper or classroom items the students can use.
- Donate a check to the teacher or coach for a healthy snack "I'm _____'s granddad. Would you be willing to take a check for $25?"
- Purchase a yearbook to discover which activities your grandchild participates.
- Use Edline for information on a daily basis.
- Ask for the school athletic department's schedule and practice schedule.
- Sponsor their team with T-shirts.
- School banners can be sponsored by you.
- Go to their place of worship. Do not sit close. Be where they can see you at the back of the room. Volunteer for children's services or serving foods afterwards.

Sometimes the grandchildren can pressure the parents into behaving better than they might otherwise, because they can't adequately justify their behavior to their maturing children.

If at some point, if your grandchild asks you questions about the rupture, Dr. Coleman advises empathizing with what that was like: "Must have been painful to hear your mother/father tell you those things. What did you think or feel listening to that?" If the summary isn't true or only partially true you could say, "Well, that actually isn't what happened," or, "That's only half of the story". I don't really think it's very helpful to you to get into a he said/she said here. "I'm much more interested in hearing how that affected you, and I'm happy to answer any questions that you have about any of this."

Should you have any visitation opportunities or a happenstance sighting where the child exhibits unpleasant behavior toward you, their reaction is the Fear-Fight-Flight response. They may likely have been told mistruths about you. The children understand that they must return home to their controlling parents. They know that if they defy the parent, there will be a penalty to pay. These innocent children who have no one to consult with, try to adjust because they have to live there. This is mind control within the family and child abuse.

When you witness this just say, "I love you, and I always will." Then, depending on the circumstances, walk away. If they are a bit older tell them, "I am glad you know the difference between right and wrong."

(Dr. Caddy) When a grandchild acts nervous or cold toward you, given time alone with you they WILL thaw. They will come to remember how they felt when they were with you.

No one can take HOPE from your hearts—even those who have broken them. No one can deny you this one thing which is keeping you from falling apart.

"Our only message is that we have clung to tiny, yet sturdy threads of HOPE.'

If you don't know where your grandchildren are now, search on Facebook or have a techie friend assist you. If you cannot find them via social media, then consider hiring the services of a private detective. Will your grandchildren know how to find you when the time is appropriate?

Find a sense of peace within yourself that you have tried your very best to reach out.

Accept that this will take time to resolve. If you give up, will you stop thinking about your grandkids? Despite all the misgivings, we must keep our eyes on the prize: our grandkids. It is when you sidestep from the unconditional love for your adult child, that your chances for success diminish.

These adult children can be cold-hearted, and yes you are truly a victim here; but families do reunite. You can become a success story. It is best to work your plan now, because the more time that passes will interpret into the alienator gaining more power, control, and determination.

You must decide what is best for your well-being. There are no rules. If you decide that the attempts have cost you too much psychologically, you can make the decision to stop trying. It is okay to let go. Just realize there is always hope for the future.

27

Memory Box

"My grandson turned 17. He knocked on my door. If had been over a dozen years since I had seen him. He was angry that I had not tried to be with him all these years. I brought into the room the memory box you had suggested. I have been putting things into it for several years for him. He sat down to read and look at every single thing. He then stood up, put his arms around me, his grandpop, and cried."

"I fear he will never know how much he is loved and valued and treasured. I am taking your suggestion to start to save things and thoughts for him in a box that I hope he gets some day so he'll learn how hard I tried to be with him."

"Make a book called, GRANDMOTHER REMEMBERS. This is a very positive book that tells the history of the family. Include pictures. You can have it spiral bound very inexpensively. Although my grandchildren did not meet their grandfather, I wanted them to know about him. They would have been proud to know him. He was a magnificent man."

"Call all the people you know that could give you information about your grandchildren; any news is helpful. You don't need to give these people too much information. I call the grandma and mother of my S-I-L, and the grandma of my D-I-L. I say nothing negative, but I do learn from these friendly conversations."

"ALWAYS photocopy everything and keep it in a file. Give it to someone whom you trust to give to the grandkids after you are gone. I have my photocopied

papers laminated so the S-I-L and D-I-L cannot easily destroy them. Have a NOTARY attached to a letter stating that the S-I-L and D-I-L cannot be in the office when these books and files are delivered to the children. Instruct the person in charge to let the children (hopefully of age 18 and above) be in the office without their alienating parent."

Build a history for your grandkids. Some day in the future they will have this special treasure from you. Let them know you actually tried to be with them. Open your heart to them so they will come to know how much they have been loved from a distance. Give them back the years they have missed with you. They will then recognize the extent of your contact being denied. They most likely have been hearing an entirely different story from the alienating parents who have used them as pawns.

The memory box can include a journal of your thoughts, written narratives, scrapbooks, news clippings, taped stories, legacy letters, memory photos; all things you wanted them to know. Place the cards and gifts you wanted to give to them into the box. Enclose pictures of cards and gifts you did send, but were not sure had been received. Special items you want to pass on to them should be included with a personalized note to explain their significance. It should contain these mementos and anything else that they missed in the years apart. Money you would have spent on them can be placed into an account for their future. Nothing replaces hugs and quality time together, but you will be giving them a part of the relationship that had been denied to them.

Creating an "archived relationship" for future use will someday be deeply appreciated by your grandchildren. They will be grateful for a history from you. Do this for each grandchild. You will be giving them a part of their heritage, and a history of your attempts to connect with them.

The Memory Box has been proven valuable on many levels. It shows them how hard you tried to reach out. If you have been unable to send cards and gifts to them because you have no mailing address, or you have been legally restrained from contacting them, then a memory box of love for each grandchild is an alternative.

Consider including a copy of *From Poppy, With Love…Letters from a Grandfather to the Grandchildren He Isn't Allowed to See* Vol. 1, authored by Rev. Dr. John Killinger. Attach your story to this book. Dr. Killinger addresses his own pain at being excluded from his grandchildren's lives. He passes along the life lessons and loving stories he would much prefer to share in person. The book is a must read - not only for alienated grandparents, but for the grandchildren who have missed out on one of the most special bonds life can offer. Attach your story to this book. You will not only validate what you have been through, but you will be giving your grandchildren a major part of what was lost to them. Tell them what you would have shared if you had been allowed to be with them over the years.

You witness a young child with their grandchild, and all you can think about is how you wish it were you. Friends show you pictures of their growing grandbabies, and you wish you had a photo to share. You watch previews of the newest Disney film, and you wish you could take your grandchild to see it. You're going fishing, and you wish your grandson could tag along. You pass buy a children's shop, and you wish you knew what size to buy; if you even knew their mailing address. You think of relatives and stories from your past, and you want your grandchildren to know about them. Keeping a journal for each grandchild you are not allowed to see, does allow you to place these thoughts in a safe place for them.

You found out about a school concert, and you dared to attend. You watched their soccer game from afar. You waited in your car as school let out. Did you see them? Whether you got lucky or not, write about your thoughts in a journal. Keep a journal of your thoughts and feelings about your grandchildren, and include stories of your life.

Placing special items with notes attached and the very special journal into a memory box, keeps the legacy of the family history alive. It is not only the story or who our elders were, but it defines the future. As you build their history heritage for them, they will come to learn how much they have been loved from afar. They will get to know you, in your own words. Just imagine the day this memory box finds its way into the hands of your very own grandchildren! This documented "virtual relationship" you had with them, will now belong to them. It will help to heal what was denied to each of you. They will deeply appreciate you for giving them the missing part of their family history.

Make every effort you can to have contact with your grandchildren. Document each effort for the memory box. Have that memory box ready for your grandchildren. You never know when that day will come.

"My grandchildren are grown, and unfortunately the damage is done; I have no contact." If your situation reflects this, there is still hope they will come to know your thoughts. The memory box will contain the true love you wanted to share.

AGA received communication from a grandfather whose opportunity to connect came after 13 years apart. At first the grandson exhibited deep disappointment that the grandparent had not reached out to him for so many years. When Granddad handed him the memory box, he took the time to look through everything. Tears began flowing from his young eyes as he embraced his granddad with hugs.

Amanda

These grandchildren would have loved having you during the missing years. Your gift of a memory box gives them your words of wisdom and your thoughts about missing out on milestones you wished you could have shared.

Provide them with the stories of their ancestors' difficulties and sufferings, and how they made it through by staying together! When you give back to them all the history of your/their family, you are showing them how YOU and this grandchild survived a suffering as well. You found a way to pass on the family legacy. You will be forming a relationship thru your written words. Fundamentally, you are teaching them to trust an adult again. Provide a means for the grandchild to receive this memory box, in case you sadly cannot hand it to them yourself.

28

Amends Letters

"After 10 minutes or more of scornful false accusations by my D-I-L on the phone, and my letting her know that I honestly did not do what she was accusing me of having done I finally said, 'I am sorry that you think I did that.' Her response was, 'That's all I wanted to hear...that you were sorry!' Then she hung up."

"It's not the fear of reaching out for me, I am just tired of the rejection."

"It's been 10 years since my adult children have spoken to me. They were coerced by my ex. I took your suggestion, and wrote an email to each of them on the same day. Immediately, I heard from the older one who had so closely aligned with my ex. I am hoping for another blessing."

"With every intention of writing the amends letter when out of the blue I decided to try calling my daughter first. I never expected her to answer the phone, so I was prepared to leave a voicemail. Lo and behold she actually answered! I was so surprised that I didn't respond right away, and she had to repeat, 'Hello'. We ended up talking for a couple of hours. She invited me to come visit that very weekend. When I was there, she invited me to come back for a primary grade school event. I realize it will take time to fully work out all or problems, so for now I'm treading lightly. But, I'm optimistic about the future, and that's a state of mind that I've not known for the past few years. So, thank you AGA. I will forever be in your debt. You can be credited for this particular success story. I am so grateful for everyone involved. You are all doing God's work."

Amanda

"My husband was given an ultimatum by our son, to apologize for something his D-I-L accused my husband of saying. Remembering that my husband apologized before and it didn't help, and after discussing this with our pastor and other AG's, we decided there would be no apology because she will just up the ante."

"After meeting with you, Amanda, I send an email to my adult daughters who had cut me off the past 10 years. I raised them mostly by myself and had a good relationship with them. When we divorced, they aligned with my ex (mostly an absentee father) who encouraged the estrangement. I wrote the things you suggested. That day I heard back from the "ringleader" daughter! Thank you for explaining things to me. We are now moving forward.

It can be extremely painful when your child resists your attempts to connect, or views you as the one at fault. They can be abusive in their blame, and demonstrate a lack of empathy. They keep the door so tightly closed that the parents are faced with ongoing rejection. This abandonment, so strictly enforced, causes many grandparents such hurt and frustration that they feel forced to eventually give up.

Grandparents who have made mistakes or were blamed for crimes they are not aware of committing (dialogue is not permitted) are willing to do what it takes to atone. Yet, their attempts are usually ignored, as they continue to be treated drastically. The majority of grandparents who communicate with AGA believe that they didn't do anything wrong, or that they didn't do anything wrong enough to deserve having their grandchildren removed from their lives. Yet, in the eyes of an alienator, you are the guilty one.

Your child may be married to a troubled controlling spouse, have a personality disorder, need to blame you so that they don't have to blame themselves for their unhappiness, or you may have an ex-spouse who wants to perpetuate the conflict between you and your child.

Alienators position themselves to catch you doing something wrong; or they invent something you did to use it as a reason to severely limit or entirely eliminate you from their lives. Dealing with all of this is not easy. But, keeping the prize in sight makes your repeated efforts worth it!

People make mistakes, and hopefully we learn from them. No one is perfect. No parent and no child is perfect all of the time. Your adult child may see you as having made an error in judgment, and therefore be rightfully concerned; or the punishment imposed (depriving a GP-GC relationship) has little congruity to the fault. Think back to the time you were raising your child. If your son or daughter crossed the line of acceptable behavior, were you careful to match the crime with the punishment? Did you cut your child out of your life with no explanation, and no permit to communicate?

Dr. Coleman explains that perfect parents don't exist. All parents have faced situations that they handled in a less than perfect manner. Offer apologizes for those slip-ups, and learn to forgive yourself. Admit your own mistakes, and apologize for your part (or what they deem to be your part) of the conflict. Hopefully, your child will have respect for your willingness to take responsibility.

(Dr. Baker 2019 AGA International Conference) If you're not guilty and they blame you, make a heartfelt effort to see the relationship from their point of view. Your adult child has an internal explanation for their behavior. You don't have to agree with what's on your child's mind, but you can be loving, understanding, and compassionate as you attempt to identify and deal with the issues your child has. It is important to know the meaning of their behavior for the breech in the relationship.

Learning what's on their mind and identifying their issues, will expand your understanding and compassion. It creates a paradigm shift in the adult child's understanding.'

Dr. Baker recommended writing a letter to create a space, and work from there. She encouraged the grandparents in attendance to build a bridge, as they are the parents, and the onus is on them to try to repair the relationship. She spoke of the adult child wanting to repair in their hearts, even though they cannot say or admit it to the parent.

Love means never having to say you're sorry doesn't cut it with Grandparent Alienation. Offering an apology shows that you love your child deeply, and are committed to listening to them. We hear people's voices, but we don't always listen to what they are saying. Listen to your children, and to their point of view.

Honestly evaluate your part in the estrangement. Critique your own behavior and its impact on your adult child and their spouse. If you are at fault, apologize. Express an apology for the ways in which you might have hurt them, and that you truly feel badly. If you still believe you were not at fault, apologize anyway in a general manner. You could say something simple like," I am sorry if you think I did that. I feel badly that you do". Or, "I can imagine how that made you feel, I wish I had understood." Show interest in their point of view. The most important point is to make the necessary efforts toward restoring relations with your grown child, thereby opening a pathway to regaining contact with your grandchildren.

This doesn't mean you accept all blame and overlook all they have put you through. You still own the truth. It is best to deal with these emotions on your own time before you go one-on-one with your child. By listening and acting out of love instead of anger, you will stand a better chance.

(Dr. Baker) Sometimes grandparents might be hesitant to examine their own behavior. No parent is perfect. Yet, when alienated grandparents do make efforts to make amends, their adult children turn a deaf ear to their pleas. They allow no dialogue, no explanation, no opportunity for a reconciliation. If you're someone who is open to working on himself or herself, this a critical quality in today's parent-adult child relationships.

(Dr. Coleman) Making amends, showing empathy and taking responsibility is an act of humility, not humiliation. It's a position of strength, not weakness. It's the ability to say, "Well, maybe you're right. Maybe I missed something really important about you either in how I raised you, or how I communicate with you. Let's look at that together and figure it out." You may never find out what the child's real complaints are about you, if you don't start with where they are and accept that there be some validity to them. In addition, your humility communicates a willingness to communicate with your child as an equal, which is a requirement in today's parent-adult child relations.

If nothing seems to be working for you, perhaps the time has come to write a letter of amends. There are guidelines to master. Your letter should reflect your sincere apology, or an apology for what you are unaware of having done.

Mental health counselor Anastasia Pollock encourages people to own their own part in a rift, even if it's small. She states that perception is a really important piece of conflict resolution, and that validating the other person's feelings doesn't mean 'you're right and I'm wrong'.

Take responsibility for actions by offering a sincere, heartfelt, empathetic apology. A letter of amends will be about the person receiving it. Include asking if there is anything you can do to reach out to their spouse. What may have seemed loving to you, may have been hurtful to them. Think from their perspective. Try to put yourself in their place to understand how they felt. Let them know if you have come to realize that you may have failed to see earlier that you put them through emotional pain. Consider also what malicious messages may have been told to your son or daughter about you to corrupt their point of view of you. Since Grandparent Alienation is mind control within the family, show an understanding that your son or daughter may be stuck in the middle.

Dr. Coleman indicates that an amends letter to the gatekeeper lets that person know that you realize there must be a reason for taking time away from you, perhaps because they may believe you had done something hurtful to them. He explains how this letter lets them know you will accept any responsibility on your part, and that you would like to know if they would be open to talking with you about it. He emphasizes making them aware that you are willing to listen and try to understand, and that you would like to have a closer relationship with them as well as having visits with your grandchildren. Dr. Coleman states that making amends, showing empathy, and taking responsibility is an act of humility, not humiliation. Your humility communicates a willingness to communicate with your child as an equal.

No two people view an event exactly the same, even within a family. Dr. Coleman calls this a "separate-reality phenomenon." Differences in perspective depend on things like position in the family, age, and relationships with parents or siblings. A parent might view an interaction as conscientious, while the child sees intrusion and control. It helps to recognize we see our own lives typically from our own narrow perspectives.

Dr. Phil has stated, "Try to see the other person's side of the story and make an effort to understand why he acted the way he did. Try not to judge; instead, look at the situation from a bird's eye view. Conversely, examine your role. Ask yourself what you did to contribute to the problem. Did you do or say something hurtful? Did you promise something and then back out of your agreement — even if it was for a valid reason? Keep in mind the other person probably has some valid points that you need to weigh and consider."

You cannot expect your child to believe your apologies if you follow with words that indicate you believe you are right, and they are wrong. Do not take the defensive role. They have the power. They decide if you will see your grandchildren. If they think you are being critical of their behavior, it will only serve to drive them farther away from you. Your goal is to repair the relationship, not fix your grown child. It comes down to the attitude you take with them. Do you want to be right, or do you want to have a relationship? It is the grandparents who have to work harder than they might want to in order to heal the disconnect.

If you are in it to win it, then whether or not you believe you did anything wrong to cause the cut off, keep trying. If you do not receive a response to the amends letter, continue periodically to send a brief message of love, as you find happiness in other directions until your time comes for a hopeful reunification. There is no limit on how long this could take. You may be one of the lucky ones who gets a positive response immediately, or it could take months or even several years. Just knowing you are doing something can help you cope better. The question to ask yourself is, "What is right for me at this time?" If their continuous cruelty is too much to bear, then set your personal boundaries. Decide when you need to take a break, and for how long.

Since the vast majority of grandparents claim to have had a loving relationship with their adult child prior to this cut off, repairing the relationship is certainly possible, but it does take an unknown amount of time. While you may not be the one to blame for the conflict, initiating reconciliation typically falls upon you. Your children are now grown adults, and would like to be treated with respect. Anything less would be undermining the efforts you make.

Educating yourself will help you be more objective, and enable you to think more understandably and clearly. This ability will go a long way in the reconciliation process. Once you have educated yourself in these complex dynamics of Grandparent Alienation, you can reach out to your adult child with a letter. Sometimes a letter works better than a conversation. Words on paper can be read over and over, so your child can absorb what your message implies. You are the one who has to win your child back. If you are cut off from more than one adult child, reach out to all at the same time.

Sending the letter of amends is not for the sole purpose of reconciliation. The grandparent is not taking responsibility for the mistake they did not make, or causing unintended hurt. Instead, a letter of amends is empathizing with a willingness to consider the alienator's perspective. It is evidence of your genuine commitment for change and self-examination.

Writing the amends letter can be agonizing for you on several accounts, but it is a powerful way to show your strength and love. It shows you care. It is a good way to start. You will be demonstrating compassion, and it allows you an opportunity to ask what you can do to move things forward in a positive direction. (Dr. Coleman) The amends letter opens the door for the adult child to respect this offering of taking responsibility for any behavior which may have been hurtful to them, or misunderstood. The adult child who has felt that the parent was the fault for their own shortcomings in life, may now have a pathway for communication to move things forward.

A properly written letter will position your child to tell their alienating spouse that you are trying hard to apologize and that you should be given a chance. If you chose not to write this letter, it is easier for the alienating spouse to position you as the hurtful, defiant, and undeserving person.

Even if your adult child has been unduly influenced by others, this may help you move a step closer. The best reason to do this is that it just might work. Plus, you will have a certain peacefulness knowing that you left no stone unturned.

Amends letters should contain the following:

An opening which is loving and a statement of how precious they are to you

Show that you genuinely care

Acknowledge the distance between you, not where you want to be in the relationship

Expression of mistakes made or perceived to have been made

Empathy for how the mistakes may have felt to them, and how you wish you had understood their needs

Imagining how they felt

Interest in understanding your adult child's point of view

An apology for the ways in which you might have hurt them, and for the things you truly feel bad about.

Your desire for a better relationship in the future

A solution both of you can live with

Nothing to make them feel guilt

No criticism of their spouse or partner

No defensiveness

No anger

No resentment

No self-pity

Dedication to a long-term commitment

Timing of the letter is important. Once the amends letter has been sent, manage your expectations. Any response is a good response. No response is the hardest to deal with, so be prepared. If you receive a negative response to your letter or no response at all, just follow up with periodic light brief messages of love.

Examples:

Happy weekend! I love you and want to make things right between us.

Would you like to get together sometime to: talk, just hang out, or catch up on things?

Offer choices of location, dates, and times which work for you.

(Baker/Fine) In order to avoid despair, it may help to think of your messages of love as watering a plant. When we plant a seed in the ground, we cannot see what is happening beneath the earth, but we water the soil anyway. The watering is an act of hope and faith that one day a flower will bloom. Your relationship with your child is like that flower. It needs attention and care so that one day, perhaps when you least expect it, that flower will bloom and your child will respond to you with the openness of love.

As previously mentioned, often AGA grandparents have reported receiving a list of about 10 demands they must comply with if they want to see their grandchildren again. When you respond, do your best to show your commitment to a reconciliation. When they mention something which you honestly feel no responsibility for, reply as best you can with your goal in mind. Be creative in how you "comply" to that particular difficult demand. Once you have responded to their list, be prepared. The downside of your cooperation to their requests is that oftentimes they up the ante.

If you have been restrained by a court order, then stop.

AGA suggests the following two books for valuable techniques in writing a letter of amends.

Surviving Parental Alienation…a Journey of Hope and Healing, Amy J.L. Baker and Paul R. Fine

When Parents Hurt, Joshua Coleman

29

Reconciliation

"Yay!! There is hope. Love conquers, however sometimes the right psychological approach coupled with that moves the mountain. Not one without the other it seems. Thanks a million!!"

"We conceal the anger and feeling of betrayal that lies dormant within us. We do this because we won the prize…our grandkids."

"Is the journey over? No. Am I grateful, and is progress being made every day? Yes. Do I remember feeling like my son was involved in a terrible accident and he died all those years ago, and I was left mourning and heartbroken? Yes. My grandchildren and I lost 5 years. Those were formative years for the young ones."

"Please remove my email address from the AGA Newsletter list. I'm thrilled to say my daughter and I are no longer estranged, and I spent all day yesterday with my grandson! I have hope this will happen for many others! Thank you, AGA!"

"Once she reached out to us, it was like all the hurt and anger disappeared. We realized that the only thing that mattered was we were a family, and that we were stronger than any alienator could ever be. We have a lot of healing to do. I'm so proud of her strength and determination to move forward. I have been trying to give her support and assure her that she is not to blame for what has happened. She has made some poor choices, but she did not deserve the control and abuse that this man has inflicted upon her and her children the past years.

"Our family survived the alienation, but the reality of having been removed from their life is hard to reconcile. There is a hole in my heart that is closing, but I am forever changed by this experience. My granddaughter (from my other daughter) has been so hurt by all of this, and very well could walk away from this experience in our lives with a sense of what is appropriate or what may be deemed appropriate in any relationship she has."

"There were some opportunities in the past year that held promise of reconciliation; however, our son doesn't have the capacity to do so. His distorted sense of reality and his ex-wife's own mental issues prevent this. We hold the hope that our grandchildren will seek us out when the time is right for them to do so. We will be forever indebted to AGA for providing the ways and means to be grateful or our lives regardless of its trials and tribulations."

"I am beyond thrilled to tell you that we have been reunited with our daughter and grandchildren after not seeing them for four long years! She is in the process of getting a divorce from a narcissistic man that tried to get control of her trust fund. He almost succeeded. It was like she had rewritten her childhood and had Stockholm Syndrome. This has actually s been a 6-year+ nightmare that almost ruined our lives."

"Just wanted to tell you things have taken a change for the better here! My D-I-L finally accepted my apology after many tries. She still doesn't accept that any of it was her fault, but I took the high road because I want to see my grandchildren and my son. The children acted like nothing had ever happened!"

"Thank you soooooo much Amanda for your support. My daughter did call me back, and the conversation went beautifully. My mind was racing to remember ta ask questions which would require answer with information. Thankfully, I remembered questions you suggested to me and the energy changed almost

immediately. Please know I could not have had such a thoughtful and positive conversation with my beloved daughter without your generosity of support."

"Our son passed away, and we had not heard from our grandchild or his mother in almost three years. We sent cards and gifts over the years, but never heard from them. We previously had a loving relationship with our granddaughter for over four years. Yesterday we received a box with so many personal items and photographs of our son! It was like a Christmas miracle."

"Our daughter was killed by her husband and then he committed suicide. Custody of the grandchildren was given to the father of the children from a previous marriage. His girlfriend wanted us to give money to see the children. Basically, after we ran out of those sums of money, we were cut off from seeing the grandkids. Once that relationship broke up, our son was able to have contact with the father of the children. We booked a trip and lots of tears were shed. They had grown so much. When we left, their dad promised that we would get together soon. Our hearts were filled with joy! We can hope and pray that he will keep his word. I can only hope and pray that others will be able to see their grandchildren again."

"I have good news. After fighting for three years, I got the governor to call a meeting. I had been denied my grandchildren because a caseworker had filled my home study reports with false accusations. Lies had been told about me and my adult child. I listened to your advice and have been working closely with the governor and the Police Chief. They have directed me away from to a new lawyer. I will never give up this journey to bring them home."

"My daughter will not respond to my messages. I did as you suggested, Amanda. I have been forming a relationship with her ex who has custody. He now takes my calls and replies to my emails, and we are getting along really well. He knows I support him. The good news… he came to Florida with my grandson for a vacation. I saw them for the first time in three years. It was all wonderful!

His dad and I will keep in touch; my (former) son-in-law now knows I really care about him, too. I am a very happy grandfather. Next I will try again with my daughter."

"Follow up to our phone conversation with you yesterday, Amanda. My husband sent a text to our son (and did mention his health issue), signing it with love. Within three hours he got a return text from our son saying he hoped his health would get better and that he had no idea he was sick. Our son said, 'We are both missing out so I'm hoping this might start some reconnecting between you and me. You're my dad, I love you, I always have and I always will.'

"Amanda, I had taken your suggestion and sent periodic messages to my son. Occasionally he would respond, not always nicely. Fast forward a year (which seemed like a lifetime) and he actually responded to me with a call. I had related something important in my message, and he had just gone through an emotional time. We met for lunch. I decided I would listen and let him do most of the talking. I felt so good that in the midst of a difficult time for him, he made time for me. Seeing my grandchildren will be the next challenge, since he inferred that I would have to make amends with my D-I-L. I will have to do this if I ever want to see my grandchildren. Thank you for all that you do."

"I am so grateful to you. It's been four years of therapy for me trying to hold on. But now I found AGA. I followed your advice and sent a message each week this year telling my daughter that I love her and think of her. Her wealthy controlling husband has kept me away from the daughter I was so close to for so many years, and from the little grandson I love and who loved me so much. Today I left the first voicemail for my daughter, I knew he would be at work, since he did not allow me to call their house. When I returned home, this was the voicemail waiting for me, "Hi Mom. I love you, too. Thank you for reaching out to me. I will be in touch." Afternote – no more contact, but the grandmother now knows her daughter does indeed love her.

"The most important thing is "We are a family again!' Thank you for all you do to help grandparents suffering from a nightmare that is almost worse than a death. Death is something that you know is permanent, you mourn your loss and eventually you begin to heal. However, alienation is almost worse because you can't ever stop thinking about what you might have done wrong, what you could do to change things, and why your children don't want to be with you. Do you ever heal? Unless you have been through this experience, no one could ever imagine the pain and depression associated with it. AGA was about the only source of relief and organization that I felt l could identify with. My heartfelt thanks and appreciation."

"I was reunited with my granddaughter, now 15. When I hugged my granddaughter, I knew a miracle had taken place! I can see how difficult life has been for her during the five years without Grammie. Her relationship with her parents had been the worst. I dare not say anything for fear the worst will begin all over again."

"just wanted to send a happy note for a change. My wife and I went to a Christmas program since public events were the only times we were able to see her. All dressed up we watched her every move hoping she would know we were there. We were hoping to hug her as she came off the stage like so many others were doing. Just in a flash who should appear, none other than her mother and a new great-grandson. Big hugs from all! Our great-granddaughter asked if we still had a big celebration and opened presents on Christmas Eve. With our YES reply she said, 'We sure would like to come!' Talk about HAPPY. This was a 10-minute conversation. We both cried all the way home. So, after 3 years, 10 months, and 24 days our prayers were answered. We have no idea what caused the alienation, but jealousy, the M-I-L, and being??? We know the heartbreak, the depression, the medical problems, and lost feeling of not seeing these beautiful smiling faces that love to see their grandparents. To all of those not there yet, keep PRAYING. Thank you, Amanda. For many months your AGA Newsletter was all that kept this 81-year-old going.'

"It has been five years since I have spoken to my grandson. I kept sending a newsy letter to him, not knowing if he got them. Then, I found his email from a family member who texts with him. He thanked me for writing to him, and apologized for not responding with letters of his own. I now have HOPE. He's almost of legal age and talks about coming to visit me. At least I now know he wants to. I'm OK as long he knows I love him, and that he wants to come to visit with me. I am not sure who is putting the stop on him seeing us, but that doesn't matter anymore either. People would always tell me he will come when he's older; that he won't forget the days and time we had together. I'd tell them that kids have short memories. I wallowed in the negative. I'm not sure who is putting the stop to him seeing us, but the answer doesn't matter anymore. Kids today are different. They are not raised to write thank you notes for a gift. I have to realize that I have to meet him on the media he uses, that's how the breakthrough came. What I want to share is keep trying, don't give up. At some point your grandchild will grow up and ask questions. They will have a faint memory triggered by a sight, sound, or smell. Just yesterday in line at the grocery store the man in front of me bought Juicy Fruit gum, and I immediately thought of my grandma's pocketbook that smelled of mothballs and Juicy Fruit gum."

"After not being allowed to see my grandchild for 1 ½ years, I finally went to their state with a witness and knocked on their door. Her husband let us in. He introduced me to my new grandchild. My daughter went next door to get my firstborn grandchild. We spent a short time together to be respectful. But we did get together a few more times on the trip! My daughter acted as though nothing had ever happened. I knew from AGA not to say anything. I am taking this one day at a time...baby steps as you suggested. Thanks for your help, Amanda."

"After turmoil in my family the past almost two years, and tempted to call the authorities, I was terrified in my heart. I removed myself from the situation and prayed a lot. It was a very hard road. Recently with much prayer, a change

of heart took over and the situation has improved 100%. I am in awe of this, and incredibly grateful. I think AGA is much needed. Please don't disappear. There will always be others out there that need help."

"I wanted to comment on how his return affected our family. I am so grateful for his apology and return. I am so profoundly impacted by how easily he acknowledged his absence. On my part, I never voiced anything about our 3-year separation. I just held out my arms and embraced him. What was there to say? I had what I had longed for, and he had his children in tow."

"I just wanted you to know Amanda that I took every bit of your excellent advice on how to engage with my daughter to heart. I really didn't know what direction to take with the current situation. The perspective and clarity you offered were a great gift to me. My sister and I actually went to her house yesterday with flowers and balloons. She opened the door. You were so right about having her visiting aunt along with me! It was a small miracle! We were able to have a pretty good conversation and all went well. My heart is so much lighter on this lovely holiday, because you took the time out of your busy schedule to offer so much sound advice to me. I greatly appreciate it! Heartfelt thanks and warmest regards from this grandmother."

"I sent messages to our son's office about three times a year. They were positive letters that talked about what was happening in our family. He told me they gave him the courage to call when the time was right. They validated to him that our door was always open for him to walk through. There has been a divorce, so now we travel to enjoy time with our son and grandkids."

"I used a detective as you suggested to find my family. I have spoken with my teenage grandkids, but they still live at home. Still I am blessed that after 12 years I can hear their voices from time to time, and know that they are healthy and sound OK."

"Part of me needs to keep returning to AGA for comfort even though my son has returned. I hope that makes sense. The life event became part of me, and I am hopeful that at some point I will experience minimal conditioned responses to its effects. Thank you for being here for me then and now. I have scars."

"It's like a miracle each time there is a success! What seemed impossible can happen!"

The journey has been difficult, and there is no guarantee of reconciliation. Though it may appear to be an impossible mission since too many years have gone by, or the emotional hurt is too great, it can happen. The most treasured moments often come unannounced, though the causes are seldom completely resolved. Hundreds of AGA grandparents who suffered so deeply, have had their prayers answered. Each is a miracle touched by an angel.

The more you come to understand the complex dynamics of Grandparent Alienation, the better prepared you will be for taking the necessary actions for a hopeful reconnect and reconciliation. Anything worth having is worth working for, and nothing succeeds like persistence. If it were easy to be successful in life, then everyone would be. Successful people learn to use patience. Press on in spite of feeling rejected. We grandparents are treasure chests of talents, insights, and remarkable gifts. It is your passion, tenacity, and commitment which can lead to success.

Alienators make the rules and decide whether they want to let their parents be a part of their families. However, under certain circumstances at more vulnerable times in your adult children's lives, a reconciliation can occur. AGA success stories prove it is possible. Just know that a feeling hopelessness, or the way you have been treated, is not a predictor of whether or not you will reunite with your adult child and grandchildren.

The insight you have gained thus far has better prepared you to understand what is occurring and why it is occurring. You now have greater knowledge, and knowledge is power. These are the tools you will bring with you as you tread the waters of a reconnection. The knowledge you have gained is a recipe for success. You, as the parent, will once again have the opportunity to be a role model for healthy behaviors.

Even after years, take heart that your loved one might naturally come back at big milestones in life. (Sichel) These things can have their own timetable... A grown son may want his baby to have grandparents. One low-pressure way is regularly sending those classics: birthday and holiday cards. If you fear they will put them in the recycling bin unopened, leave off a return address, to pique their curiosity.

So many AGA grandparents who have reunited talk about how they still feel the stress of walking on eggshells. They know all too well what they endured in the past, and are now in silent fear that this once agonizing presence could happen again. It is understandable and normal for you to feel that way. Those who once designed the elimination of a parent could do it again. Remind yourself that your fear is only fear. This fear should keep you from making mistakes of the past. If you become a better listener and more respectful of their boundaries, you should be able to breathe more easily. Put feelings of hurt and anger aside, forgive, stop blaming, and let the past be the past. Gradually begin to build trust, forming a better relationship from the present time and moving forward.

You would be surprised how quickly the joy will come back into your life. Concentrate on expressing positive remarks and feelings, good memories and making new ones, and participating in shared interests. Be respectful of each other's boundaries, allowing for healing from the blockage once placed between you.

Those who have reunited share the actualization that anything is better than isolation. Things may not be exactly as you pictured them to be before this alienation took place. But it certainly is a whole lot better than what you experienced being cut off. Allow yourself focus on the good that has come back into your life. Let go of your grief. Work on healing and serenity. You have been blessed, so leave the past behind. Think about positive and happy things. Start from today, and look toward the future. Enjoy this gift of having your child and grandchildren back in your life. In time you will become more secure about the relationship and your future together.

During the early stages of reconciliation, it is common that the reconnect may be with your adult child only. Be the loving, kind, cheerful, optimistic person your son or daughter would want to spend time with again. Quite any anxiety you will be feeling inside. Remember, there is a connection of the heart. Love has brought you together. Focus first on your son or daughter, not the grandkids. Work on strengthening that new relationship, rekindling the bond you once had. Your child is the key to your connection to the grandchildren.

The reconciliation may begin with restrictions and limits. Just be patient, and allow them to feel they have control. Taking baby steps is essential. Some suggestions to keep in mind:

> Do not be confrontational, demanding, or push for too much too soon.

> Do not criticize your child or their spouse.

> Do not place blame or quilt of any kind on them.

> Avoid conflict, relax, and remain calm in their presence.

Carefully listen to what they are saying or implying, and be mindful of the way you react. Responding in a defensive manner would only fuel the fire for some who have a more fragile personality.

Do what works, not what seems fair to you.

It takes time to re-establish the trust. It will serve you best to avoid topics that could spark any negative engagement. AGA's communications thus far show that most reunited grandparents do not bring up the past. There might possibly come a time and a place in the distant future for discussing what has taken place. It is best to just start from the present day, then move on to the future. Listen with an open mind, empathize, and follow their lead. When and if you feel comfortable, it is okay to ask them to tell you things that might bother them as you journey forward. You may or may not have an opportunity to talk about some aspects of the cut off. For now, show them you will do what it takes to be a family again.

Often siblings of the alienators remain angry and mistrustful. Grandparents, let your other children know that you are willing to do whatever it takes for the family to come together.

If you have built up anger from the way you were treated so badly for long, do not display this when you see them. Instead call a trusted friend, exercise, or journal your thoughts before it is time to meet. Once you are in their presence, if you feel yourself bursting with emotion, make an excuse to walk away for a few minutes. This could be the one and only chance to show you are willing to accept the relationship on its new terms. Develop a mantra silently telling yourself, "Heal don't destroy."

If your child decides to raise subjects related to the alienation, do not allow yourself to react emotionally. If they place blame on you, you might just tell them that you do not see it that way.

Or, ask if there is something you could to make the relationship better. You know your child best. Use your wisdom to handle the matter intelligently. After all, they too are now seeking a reconnect.

The majority of AGA grandparents find it is best not to bring up the past, because they think it will destroy chances for a new beginning. For most grandparents, the reconnect initially feels like nothing ever happened. Some sons and daughters are embarrassed by how they were influenced, and in time apologize for the hurt they caused their parents. Most tend not to bring up the subject.

Communications with AGA grandparents who have reconciled reveal that there are some sons and daughters, who "drank the Kool-Aid", that inwardly still side with the spouse. They still believe the grandparents were the cause of the alienation. Tread lightly. (Dr. Coleman) I have yet to meet an estranged child who didn't feel guilty about the estrangement. Despite the anger, accusations, and self-righteous indignation, most adult children know that their decision to be estranged was very hard on the parent. So, most don't want to talk about the estrangement once they're reconciled. They know, in all likelihood, they don't want to be reminded of that.

If they are openly critical of you, ask how you might make things better from now on. Your objective is to make this process of coming together as easy as possible for them. Try to listen empathically. Do not react emotionally. Do not add fuel to the fire if they attempt to blame you for what has taken place. This is new territory, therefore be sure to choose your words carefully. Stay calm, and respond as little as possible to any accusations thrown at you. Be a role model of good behavior and self-control. If you think you must say something, you might respond with "I'm sorry to hear you feel this way, those were not my intentions. In the future would you please let me know if there is something I can work on to make things better."

In the early stages of the reconciliation, it is not the time to quibble about who did what to whom, and how devastating this has been for you. As Dr. Coleman states, "You be the one to reduce their feelings of guilt or responsibility for what has occurred. Be happy they are back in your life, and be careful not to drive them away again. Concentrate on being the non-threatening parent with whom they enjoy spending time. What is important is that you are in communication and are on your way back together as a family.

Knowing that Grandparent Alienation is mind control within the family, manipulation, and programming by the alienating spouse; do not have expectations that all is well in their thoughts. It is a time when all the players should be cautious. Your sons and daughters have demonstrated that the way things were did not work for them. Their marriage has suffered, and little concern has been given to how this has affected the feelings of your grandchildren. Now is the time for the grandparents to do what it takes to be a family again. Lead by example. You still know who you are, and you own the truth.

Now that they are back in your life, it doesn't necessarily mean that things will go back to normal. There is a new normal… theirs! You may not hear from them or get together with them as often as you would like; but this is the situation with many intact families as well. A new level of power and control enters the picture. They make the rules and you follow them if you want to have a relationship. You are the parent, but they also are parents. They decide when and if you get to spend time with your grandkids. Be respectful of their boundaries. They love you more than they may show, but they do. Take it slow. Just don't necessarily expect too much too soon.

When you do spend time with your son or daughter, suggest a plan for getting together again. Propose an activity you know they would enjoy. Offer them choices so they feel they have the control they have been seeking. Give them choices for dates and times. Phrase your questions so they don't require just a simple yes or no response. Begin your question with words such as what, where, when, or which. These words require information in the answer.

There are times when the adult child agrees to meet with just one of the grandparents. The reason may be that they feel less quilt, or are able to depart from the visit with less emotion. Take the offer since they define the terms. It may be the only opportunity you get. Look at this as a foot in the door. It is a first step to rebuilding your relationship with your adult child. Focus him or her. In time, the other grandparent will be welcome. Take baby steps.

If your child agrees to meet with you, but their spouse/partner is in not a willing participant; accept this. Often times their partner continues to keep your grandchildren from reconnecting with you. When you are granted time together with your son or daughter, keep in mind they may very well go back to their spouse with the details. Be loving and say only positive things about their partner. Meanwhile, since their partner might not go along with the decision to connect with you, take every opportunity to send a thoughtful caring message. Listen carefully to what is said to you. More listening and less talking is recommended. This will give you time to rebuild the bond between you. For now, be grateful that your child is reaching back to you.

Let your child know you are anxious to hear about things in their life. He/she will most likely want to share stories and pictures of the grandchildren. Just remember, it is the redeveloping of a relationship with your child which must be the core of your conversation. You want to be sure they know how important they are to you, and that you are not there only as a means to reconnect with your grandchild. Your child still needs the kind unconditional love they knew with you. That is part of the connection of your hearts. Before you part, ask them for the best means to communicate.

You, the grandparent, has been the one trying to fix this devastation in your life. They are part of the cult that drove you apart. When your son or daughter returns home and tells the toxic partner of the connection you just made, the alienator might increase the cycle of denigration to regain the control they just lost. There is a possibility the gatekeeper's reaction will affect your child continuing to see you.

Some are strong enough to maintain the reconnect. Their spouse may have jealousies, or feel threatened by your son or daughter actually reconnecting with you. AGA has learned, for example, that even very successful, highly degreed, and hugely accomplished husbands have been controlled by insecure, jealous, alienating wives. Try coaching your child to tell their spouse, "I have enough love for you (my wife/husband) and for my mom and dad, too. My parents are very important to me, and I would like for all of us to spend some time together." Hopefully, by repeatedly standing up to their controlling partner and showing they mean business, the toxic spouse will come to realize your child will do what it takes to bring this family together.

Have compassion for your child. They are stuck in the middle. They have just proven this to you by spending time with you. You might not connect again real soon, but you know progress has been made. If you worry how long it will be until the next time, or fear you will never see them again, know this is a natural response. You have been through so much for so long. Think positive happy thoughts, and pray for the best.

When a reconnect has taken place, and you are with their family, just let the past go. Most likely it will feel like nothing ever happened, therefore act like nothing happened. Once reconciliation has occurred, continue to focus your love and attention your adult child. Make them feel loved and welcome without bringing more guilt into the picture. Rekindle the connection of the heart with your child. Once that has been reconstructed, the grandchildren reconnect will follow.

Make it easier for everyone. Appreciate this triumph. Your behavior should role model making the middle generation feel welcome and comfortable when you are together. Offer to help out during your visit. Aware of what it must have been like for the grandchildren, simply show them the loving, gentle, kind, happy, interesting person you are.

When reconciliation takes place due to the break-up of a marriage or partnership, it would be wise on your part as the grandparent/parent to caution your adult child against becoming involved in another controlling partner relationship. Wait till you feel comfortable talking about this topic, but don not wait too long. They may unknowingly be drawn to this type of person. People can be charming, not showing their true colors for quite some time, even years. Set an objective to casually chat about this topic with them before another controlling personality enters the dynamic. Once they're entangled, it's too late. The last thing you and your child needs is for them to hook up with another controlling mate.

Many AGA grandparents share their concerns for their other adult children who have been isolated from their sibling. Grandparents who lead by example and show compassion for those who caused the cut off in the family, appear to make it easier for the siblings to eventually reunite.

Numerous AGA grandparents have shared stories of older teenage grandchildren who have actually come knocking on their doors! This has been every alienated grandparent's dream for years, and it has been happening. If you have had the opportunity to bond with your grandchildren, there will be a better chance of reunification in the future.

Some grandkids have stated that their parents know they are in contact with the grandparents, while others have not told them. A reconnect with the grandchild does not automatically mean a reconnect with the adult child. (Dr. Coleman) Some grandkids are more open to contact with their grands once they move out of their parent's home, when they don't feel as disloyal to the parent for being close to the grands.

Many AGA grandparents have had positive immediate surprise responses due to wording choices and attitude. Sadly, for many, it can take more months or years. "Sometimes reconciliation isn't possible, and you're left to make peace with the loss. You're talking about a real grief, and not just about the person who's gone, says Paul Coleman, psychotherapist. You may be grieving what you never got from the relationship—love, approval, attention."

Continue to handle the gatekeepers with compassion and kindness. Though they may be dealing with unresolved childhood issues, troubled marriages, controlling circumstances, or personality disorders, they may eventually come around. If you do not give up, you may very well be rewarded. At least you know that you are setting the stage for a possible reunification, and that you have left no stone unturned.

These adult children can be cold-hearted, and yes you are truly a victim here; but families do reunite. AGA has had success stories up to 17 years of cut off. That particular grandmother had tried over the years and had all but given up. Through suggestions from AGA, she made an "educated" attempt which resulted in a very happy reunification. The first year was with limited contact. By the second year, there was a comfortable mode of communication long distance. This could happen for you. It is best to work your plan now, because the more time that passes will interpret into the alienator gaining more power, control, and determination. Now that you have read about strategies for success, begin working your plan.

Reconciliation is a celebration of the true gifts in your life. Start making new memories together. Bring new joy to your adult children and grandchildren. Be grateful that you have them back in your life, and that they can experience the wonderful caring person you truly are. In time, you will come to build trust in the relationship. You have educated yourself in the complex dynamics of Grandparent Alienation which will remain within you.

30

Legal Aspects of Alienation

"My son realizes how the family court system works. He realizes that if his spouse makes false allegations of abuse against him, he will most likely lose substantial time with his own children. This is the power that a very abusive spouse holds. At the heart of all this is the family court system which allows for all this. My son is consciously or unconsciously aware of and fearful of what could happen to him if he resists the abuse he is currently experiencing. When the most intelligent among us becomes sheep in such situations."

"I deal with an ex-daughter-in law who has made my life a living hell. My health has been affected. She even set me up to be arrested, claiming false allegations in order to cut all ties to my grandson. I live with the hurt 24/7. I am begging for help."

"They falsely accused me of mistreating my grandchild, when it was actually my daughter-in-law who mistreated me. She had come to realize that our granddaughter was beginning to bond very closely to me."

"My three-year-old grandson had bruises all over his buttocks. I called the law enforcement who did nothing, they actually told her it was OK as long as the bruising was on the buttocks. I contacted Child Protective Services, but they didn't visit the family until 23 days later and the bruising was gone. They had cleaned up the house and put food in the pantry, so the case was closed. I hired a lawyer. The courts saw all of my documentation, and executed an emergency temporary custody order. I had my grandchildren for almost a year. Child Protective Services was a joke. I did more work than they did, and I'm

the one who came up with suggestions to help my daughter regain custody. I requested visitation, and received court ordered visitation. I want more time with my grandchildren, but I fear that if I ask for more time, they could take my precious 5 hours a month away from me."

"We could not have asked for a better person to talk to! The sheriff was so kind. He told me that he was vaguely familiar with alienation, and had come across it 2 or 3 times as a deputy. I told him about AGA and my story, then left some info with him. Here's the best part-he is making sure all the deputies get AGA info, and is putting it on their website!!! He was interested in what had happened to me, and is even going to check these things out. As he listened, he just shook his head. Knowing he could not say much, that gesture was worth a million words! Thank you again AGA for suggesting we take this to the sheriff, Amanda! Your wisdom and guidance have been invaluable!! Blessings!

"My son realizes how the family court system works. He realizes that if his spouse makes false allegations of abuse against him, he will most likely lose substantial time with his own children. This is the power that a very abusive spouse holds. At the heart of all this is the family court system which allows for all this. My son is consciously or unconsciously aware of and fearful of what could happen to him if he resists the abuse he is currently experiencing. The most intelligent among us become sheep in such situations."

Through phone conversations, email communications, support group meetings, and national and international conference calls AGA continually hears that grandparents have been targeted with unjustified criticism. Usually the grandparent does not know they are being bad-mouthed, or what they are being falsely accused of doing. But those who do at some point find out some of the absurd stories that have been told, it is not just shocking but also traumatizing. Grandparents have become the victims with no opportunity granted to defend themselves. The door has been closed. Meanwhile, the alienator strives to gather support from family members and close friends to validate their false accusations and cruel punishment. Convincing others that the grandparent is the bad guy, elevates the alienator to a higher position of power and control.

AGA routinely hears from grandparents who have been threatened or actually confronted with law enforcement issues. Therefore, it is critical that we educate those who make decisions which affect these grandparents. AGA professional consultants travel the country and world to make this issue of alienation loud and clear in the courtrooms. They leave no stone un-turned. And yet, success is not always achieved. It is heartbreaking for the grandparents, great-grandparents, and our innocent grandchildren.

You can help by becoming proactive instead of just the victim or possibly a potential victim. Stand up for your human rights by bringing awareness to family law judges in your district. It is vitally important to bring awareness to law enforcement officials as well.

There are steps you can take within your community to alert and educate those with authority. It is wise to take the steps necessary to protect your position, and on behalf of other innocent grandparents as well. AGA suggests you provide your sheriff and police chief with the following AGA documents: Mission Statement, This is Abuse, and the AGA Professional Board of Directors and Professional Consultants list in order to validate your purpose in representing a global epidemic which is affecting your community and society. Send or deliver these AGA documents to the individual offices of the family law judges at the court house. You may cut and paste these documents from our website, or request them via email from AGA Headquarters and local AGA support group coordinators. AGA brochures are also available by request, and can be mailed to your home or office.

Make an appointment with the local sheriff and police chief to inform them of the dynamics of Grandparent Alienation. Prior to a scheduled meeting, email or send, and also bring with you another copy of the AGA documents to validate your position. First, allow time for them to review the documents. Then, make them aware of the fact that Grandparent Alienation is a global epidemic, and that it is occurring in their jurisdiction. Tell them GA is considered by the experts in the field of Alienation to be a severe form of child abuse, and a severe form of elder abuse.

Focus specifically on law enforcement issues! Your reason for meeting with them is to alert them of the fact that grandparents are frequently wrongly accused of harassment, stalking, and abusiveness in bringing harm to the child. Specify that these false accusations and the pathological lying are common dynamics of GA, as stated by the international experts in this field of study. Tell them how the alienator uses this devious means to justify their behavior. Explain how they tell untruths about the targeted grandparent to their spouse and amongst their social circle to elevate their own standing. In addition, explain the raging by the adult child, and threats being made. Explain how they use the grandchildren as pawns. Suggest they view, at their leisure, our website: AlienatedGrandparentsAnonymous.com

Do not make this meeting about your personal story. If asked, you might end the meeting with a summary of your issue and fears. This meeting will offer you some sense of relief, protection, and safety.

Grandparents fear the possibility of restraining orders. Talk about actual or feared restraining orders against grandparents who are being falsely accused by their adult children. As with PAS-Parental Alienation Syndrome, accusations of sexual or physical abuse of the child are being told to the law enforcement authorizes. These false accusations result in great emotional trauma.

Ask the sheriff what the law in your area states in reference to the process of obtaining a restraining order, and what rights you have to defend your position. Question if a judge should permit a hearing, would the accused grandparent have the right to be heard in the courtroom. If a grandparent is to appear in court, immediately hand the bailiff the same AGA documents requesting that they be handed directly to the judge. Bring along a sizable audience of those who know and respect you.

Grandparents who attempt to make an uninvited appearance to see the grandkids - whether you plan to knock on their door, drop off a present, or go to a public facility or area, know what the law dictates. Always have a witness with you when you make an attempt to see your child or grandchild.

When your efforts to see the grandkids are long distance, it is essential to know the laws where they live. Before you travel any distance for an uninvited visit, take the necessary steps trying to avoid legal problems.

If you have been threatened with lawsuits, or there is a restraining order in place, back off from additional attempts to communicate with your grandchildren and adult child. Never underestimate the power of one who alienates. Contact a lawyer well-experienced in cases pertaining to alienation and the law.

We who know must bring awareness to and educate those who can help our grands and grandkids. We must be the voices of our grandchildren. You can be the one who brings awareness to attorneys who specialize in family and divorce law, and estate planning. AGA Headquarters has participated in amicus briefs by providing the attorneys with significant information for their cases relating to third party visitation rights and Grandparents Alienation.

Florida family law attorney Charles D. Jamieson, a consultant to AGA, presented to grandparents at an AGA International Conferences in 2017 and 2019. Since every case is different, he stated that some or all of the suggestions may not be appropriate for an individual's set of facts. Mr. Jamieson suggested grandparents consult with an attorney before they commence any type of action. He recommended they always consult with their attorney regarding what the laws in the state of the grandchild provide for grandparent visitation and time-sharing, or custody.

Mr. Jamieson discussed numerous opportunities which can offer a means of contact with grandchildren. He cited the religion connection. Find out what faith/denomination and which church/temple/mosque, etc. your grandchildren are attending. Learn about the faith and attempt to attend the same services as your grandchildren. You do not have to make direct contact with them, but you ought to try to make sure that they see you at least once during a service. Attempt to find out which services your grandchildren attend; pursuant to their ages, you may be able to guess which service they may be attending. You may want to go one particular Saturday or Sunday and attend every service that this particular church offers, so that you can try to scope out and determine if your grandchildren are attending the services or not. Try to sit in a location where the children may get to see you at least at one point in time during the service. However, do not sit beside them or in very, very close proximity to them. Attend the coffees/donut gatherings after the services. Meet the minister, rabbi, priest, etc. Try to become acquainted with the youth services minister.

Volunteer to participate in the liturgy, ushering, or in assisting in some other fashion during the service so that your grandchildren will see you. Volunteer for your grandchildren's activities such as confirmation, Friday night post-service refreshments, or Sunday dinner night.

Grandparents wanting to make contact with their grandchildren via the school system may ask the school administrators for facts pertaining to areas where they can lawfully stand to try to see the grandchild, or which activities they can attend. The rules of engagement differ between public and private schools. You do not have to reveal your identity if you believe this would cause more harm to the situation.

When your long-standing attempts to diffuse the situation by talking with the parents have failed, you may choose to seek legal action. Every case must be determined upon its own facts and circumstances. Be sure you are aware of the laws in the jurisdiction of the children before you spend your money. You can call the County Bar Association. Ask for family law specialists who have experience with third party visitation rights.

Presenting to AGA in 2012, Dr. Bone discussed how grandparents have little legal status in most states. Many suffer from the collateral damage of a divorce. It is extremely important that the divorce settlement of your son or daughter include grandparent visitation. He emphasized that any settlement must state your name and frequency and length of your visits. Do not rely on promises. There must be a clause for consequences in the decree. It is imperative that the settlement state that there with be a "consequence to pay" if the alienating parent continues to keep you from spending time with your grandchild. By having this clause in the settlement, it allows you recourse. Be certain to ask the judge to enforce the orders over and over if becomes necessary! This is a very serious issue and should be dealt with promptly to minimize any negative consequences.

Dr. Bone pointed out that it is vitally important these matters are handled with extreme sensitivity, care, and professionalism to ensure the best interests of your grandchild and the continuation of a meaningful relationship between you and your grandchild is maintained. This is a very serious issue, and it should be dealt with promptly to minimize the negative consequences.

There is a serious problem in our society and we have to talk about it – Grandparent Alienation. We have to keep working the challenges of alienation. Morally, it is the right thing to do. We must make this a better world for our young ones. Professionals whose work affects the grandparents and great-grandparents, the middle generation, and the grandchildren must acknowledge the penetrating existence of alienation in our society.

Grandchildren deserve grandparents. Grandparents should be there for the safety and well-being of their grandchildren. Grandparents play a vital role in the lives of grandchildren. Keeping your grandchild safe is their top priority. Keep the focus on what is best for the grandchildren. AGA's professional experts advise that you instantly step in and talk to the parents if you notice any of the following:

- Physical or sexual abuse
- True neglect
- Substance abuse by the parent or a mental health issue
- Imminent harm to the grandchild

If the child is in danger, contacting your local police department or your local Child Protective Services Department is the right thing to do. Abuse is never acceptable; abuse is never OK. Abuse is against the law.

National Child Abuse Hotline: (800) 4-A-CHILD

If you suspect elder abuse, call your state's elder abuse hotline or reporting number. Help is available.

In an emergency call 911, or the local police.

Information and referral is also available from the national Eldercare Locator, a public service of the U.S. Administration on Aging. Call toll-free 1-800-677-1116. This number is available from Monday through Friday 9 AM-8 PM (except U.S. federal holidays).

AGA, Inc. has conducted trainings, providing CLE's for attorneys and CEU's for mental health professionals on the topic of Grandparent Alienation. Presenters at these training sessions have been made by the leading national and international experts in Alienation. Those who have provided this education are members of the AGA Board of Directors, AGA Professional Consultants, or international experts in the field of Alienation. These experts are available for consultations with parents, grandparents, and great-grandparents in-office or via tele-conferencing.

31

Grandparent's Rights

"I can think of few other examples in the field of family problems in which one category of persons is free to inflict misery on another effortlessly, and without social sanction (Charles D. Jamieson, Esq.).

"The intention of grandparents who want to see their estranged grandchildren is not to upset the parents, but merely to know their own flesh and blood. Taking away a grandparent's right to a relationship with a grandchild is elder abuse, and keeping a child from their grandparent is a form of child abuse! We need for parents to stop using their children as bargaining chips against their grandparents, and we need to do this in my lifetime, as I cannot withstand any more of this anguish."

"Imagine our world if we stood up for what we believe and for what is right more often than we do. Think of all the 'bad' things that have happened over and over again because lovers or partners, mothers or fathers, students and teachers, priests and believers, CEOs and employees, world leaders and followers, or neighbors and friends remained silent while a tragic situation or someone innocent screamed for help."

'The thought that no one cares about the kids or the grandparents in Florida is shameful, and has seriously made me consider moving my family away from the state to protect them. As a veteran and having fought for my country, I never not once in my life thought that my own rights to my own family would one day be robbed from me."

Amanda

"I am shocked and disappointed. This judge did not do his due diligence. He simply listened to people he "qualified" as experts. He did not investigate how this will be affecting the young ones...taking half their heritage from them, and taking away their unconditionally loving grandparents which every child needs. The judge reinforces the behavior that teaches our grandchildren the way to deal with conflict is to cut people off."

"Divorce, alienation, bullying, and mass murdering has become the new norm."

"Rights are only necessary when things go wrong. That's why we have/need rights."

"This law is just so ridiculous. Grandparents aren't trying to raise our grandchildren; we're just trying to have a visit or two each month for a few hours.... just the chance to give our grandchildren a hug and tell them we love them. Plus, this would put a little normalcy back into their lives."

"The judge for my case is a typical example of the system. At one time, I found myself speaking to him strongly to impress the importance of grandparents, while he tried to interrupt me. I did not let it happen. However, it got to the point it was *All About the Child's Wishes.* He made me look like the bad guy having gone to court. So, I took the decision to safe guard what I had left."

"Grandparents pay for Florida taxes, and contribute to the Florida economy. We pay the salaries of the legislators. What if this senseless tragedy struck them! Thank you for your attention regarding this terrible, sad, and depressing situation. The state of Florida must get their act together."

"Shame on the state of Florida when an emotionally unstable parent has all the rights, but a sound normal grandparent who has been a school administrator and teacher for 30 years does not have the right to observe the well-being of my grandchild. Does this make sense to you?"

"I struggle alone with the terrible old law which keeps four generations from to meeting each other. I have placed hundreds of phone calls, and sent hundreds of letters to government people

in Florida over the years. I met with representatives and senators several times. All my energies were unsuccessful."

"While I have my own story, it is not about me. This is about the significant bond that grandparents and grandchildren share, and making certain that if this bond were to be severed the grandparents would have recourse. You would be powerless if the bond is severed, unless the laws are in place. Our grandchildren need the positive guidance of their grandparents; it's that simple. Take Action."

"In the end, we must assert ourselves. We must love and defend our grandchildren. And, we must honor and defend both families from which my son and daughter-in-law received positive traits, a great start in life, and many opportunities to live truly fulfilling lives. I love my son. I am his father."

"We have begun steps with a lawyer to gain access to our grandchildren. My son died, and now we don't see our grandchildren. In this state we must show why it is harmful to the child's health, safety, or welfare for the child to be cut off from grandparents. We must show that it is in the child's best interest, and that we had a prior relationship. I have many photos of them with us from birth to show relationships."

"We filed a court case for visitation and won, so we now see our grandchild every other Saturday for five hours. DIL has made these visits extremely difficult. She has made the pick-ups and drop- offs difficult, but we have kept track of all exchanges. The time we have with our grandchild once her parents leave has been priceless, and we have a wonderful time together."

Amanda

"*I was the primary caregiver for my grandchildren from birth, we lived a few houses apart. They spent days, nights, and parent vacations with me. I picked them up and took them to preschool, to the doctor, l and loved and cared for them while their parents worked. That should give me some legal right to see them on a regular basis, I am not an abusive grandmother, just broken-hearted because the parent and step-parent don't care to see the pain they are causing their own children.*"

"*While I have my own story, it is not about me. This is about the significant bond that grandparents and grandchildren share, and making certain that if the bond is severed, grandparents will have recourse. You will be powerless to do anything if the bond is severed, unless the laws are in place. Our grandchildren need the positive guidance of their grandparents; it's that simple. Take Action.*"

"*Having just gone through the court system, I don't think much will change in my case except that my granddaughter will know the truth as she grows up. They know there are no consequences because the law supports this abusive behavior. Only public voice can shed a light MAYBE on deaf ears... however, we can never give up. Coming to AGA has helped me tremendously in dealing with how alienation works. At least I have the knowledge, and I am not doubting myself; and, I spoke up to the judge regardless. Persistency is the only way.*"

"*Wonderful wonderful news. Finally, my son came to my home for a visit and brought with him my granddaughter. WE were all hugging and smiling. All my dreams are starting to come true. She wants to live with my son half the time. My son will petition the court. Thank you for being there for me.*"

"*Coming to AGA has helped me tremendously in dealing with my situation and learning how this alienation works. At least I have the knowledge, and I am not doubting myself. I spoke up in front of the judge regardless of his attitude. Persistency is the only way.*"

(AGA Grandmother 2018):

I would like to share with you what the denial of the petition to grant grandparents the right to visitation resulted in for me (Florida 2018 CRC).

My daughter barred me from visiting her or my grandchild for almost two years. My daughter suffered from bipolar disorder and alcoholism. She denied treatment from the best rehab center in the country. Her behavioral disorders caused many problems in her marriage and eventually visited the damage on her child who was in therapy.

Two months ago, she took her life. Had I been able to see my grandchild, and interact with my daughter, I think this tragedy could have been avoided as it would have given me access to her and my grandchild. As a former behavioral counselor, I would have been able to see her slow decent into despair prior to her ultimate solution. That opportunity was denied me as a result of the committee's decision and current Florida laws – 2017-2018 Constitutional Revision Committee.

I firmly believe that had I access to her mental state; I would have seen the signs and been able to help her past the crisis. Mental illness cannot be detected from a distance. It's important (critical) that grandparents can assess the mental health of their children and grandchildren to prevent tragedies like this one. My grandchild is now without a mother and I have forever lost a daughter.

I would like to inform the entire committee that voted against this bill the consequences of that nay vote.

The biggest losers are children. It is time to seriously consider the kind of adults we are raising when it becomes a societal norm for children to be deprived of grandparents and great-grandparents, and to grow up in ignorance of half of their family. Children deserve to have their rights protected, to be safe, and to know their grandparents. Grands should be allowed to petition the courts for third party visitation rights when a compelling state interest exists relating to the best interest of the child. And, a minor should have human rights when in harm's way.

Being denied contact because of divorce, death of an adult child, or simply because something is going on in the child's household that parents don't want grandparents to know about makes the grandparent, great-grandparent, and the grandchildren victims. Our laws should reflect an attitude that intergenerational families be together. We must focus on showing children that family problems should be worked out, not run away from. Society needs to choose healing and unity instead of having divisive laws.

Never hesitate to use your advocacy voice. Do not allow abuse of children to occur or continue without speaking up. AGA advocates for grandparent-grandchild relationships. AGA is against ending an attachment to an otherwise loving and involved grandparent, and advocates for grandparents who have never been allowed to meet and know their grandchildren.

If trying to have a relationship with your adult child or his or her spouse isn't working, thereby closing the gate of access to your grandchildren, you can try legally pursuing third party visitation rights. Suspecting harm to the child, or when visits are denied due to family conflict and appear to be permanent, and if you believe the court system is the necessary approach in your situation, search the internet to find the actual grandparent visitation laws in place in the jurisdiction of your grandchild. Do this before you decide to take legal action. The legal rights of grandparents differ widely from one location to another. As you investigate your legal right of visitation, take into consideration the possible fallout of using the court system, and how it will affect the likelihood of ever reuniting with your adult child.

It Is important to know if the law is in place before you navigate the court system. If the present law cannot help you, then spending large sums of your money will simply go to waste. Legal fees are not fixed. Many grandparents have spent their entire life's savings on legal fees trying to gain access to their grandchildren. AGA grandparents have shared their stories of retirement funds and tens of thousands of dollars being spent, when in fact the court system did not and could not result in their favor. Grandparent visitation laws are seldom helpful to those who have been targets. We need to take action to change the laws so the judges have the tools to help grandparents, great-grandparents, and grandchildren.

Even if the law does accommodate your particular situation, proving alienation in court is very difficult and complex. The court system process is a source of considerable hardship and pain. It can be a lengthy and expensive process. This is why it is critical to have an attorney well-experienced in alienation and third-party visitation rights managing your case and advocating on your behalf. Call your local bar association to request a referral listing of family law specialists who have these qualifications. Do your due diligence before your select an attorney.

Make an appointment for a consultation. Bring documentation to support that you are doing this in the best interest of the child. Show evidence that bonding and a consistent caring relationship existed in the past. Grandparents should document their relationship with their grandchild closely and follow other recommendations for safeguarding visitation rights. The burden of proof is on the grandparents. Provide the attorney with AGA documents to help validate your position.

The law requires that grandparent visitation decisions be based upon the best interests of the child. The grandchild may have to discuss personal family matters with attorneys, social workers, and judges. They may feel pressure to choose between their parents and their grandparents. The grandchild may feel guilt from being at the center of the conflict, and their living situation may become more tension-filled. The emotional roller coaster of the court system keeps many away from trying.

It is best to try and resolve the family conflict, approaching it from every angle possible. Reconciliation is preferable to litigation for everyone concerned. The option of litigation is used as a last resort if you feel it would be in the child's best interest.

Grandparents who take their adult children to court, regardless of the outcome, should consider they are likely putting a permanent end to any hope of a cordial relationship, and the impact upon the grandchildren can be considerable. If your grandchildren are in harm's way, or if you feel you must have some contact with your grandchildren in order to keep at least a partial watch on their well-being; litigation may be the solution. Grandparents must be the voice of our grandchildren. We must aim to protect our precious youth, and keep them safe at all cost.

You may have no other choice than to seek help from authorities. Who else is there to protect them? Grandparents are the extra layer of protection. Grandparents can keep an eye on problematic or dysfunctional family behavior, and in some cases intervene on behalf of the grandchild. (Dr. Coleman) If parental neglect can and should be considered a form of child abuse, certainly a parent's decision to end a loving and attached relationship between a grandchild and a grandparent should also be considered a form of abuse.

Some jurisdictions offer mediator alternatives. Investigate this possibly. Research shows that mediation can reduce litigation. Neutral mediators can help adults talk out, make a plan, and resolve family problems. What you do not want is to have a mediator or other person of authority unjustly exhibit bias or taking sides. Always provide any authority figure connected to any grandchild related proceedings with AGA documents to educate them. Grandparent Alienation has not been taught in the schools and universities.

Mediation may be a better way to resolve disputes, if both sides agree to the process. It can also be costly. However, it is less expensive, more private, faster than a court action, and less confrontational. The process is generally less destructive to family relationships than a lawsuit. While court hearings are usually public, mediation is usually confidential. For those who live in an area where court-connected mediation is not available, private mediation services are usually available.

The role of the mediator is to guide a discussion of the issues of the dispute, while ensuring a safe environment. A mediator helps participants look forward to seeking workable solutions. Increasing numbers of grands are relying on mediators and the court system to wage court battles simply for the right to spend time together. Grandparent custody and grandparent visitation have become concerns. The courts recognize with increasing frequency the importance of the grandparent relationship. However, the laws may not be sympathetic to grandparents.

If your issue remains unresolved, if you cannot agree or think that you cannot talk about the problem with each other, then grandparents may file papers for obtaining a visitation order. Grandparents only have the right to ask for visitation; they do not have a guaranteed right to visit and see their grandchildren. If you currently have a visitation court order, you have the right to have that order enforced.

(Golly 2016):

> When other remedies fail, alienated grandparents have sought access to their grandchildren through the courts. This approach

has met with varied success. When grandparents first sought access to grandchildren through legal means, the United States Supreme court began to develop a doctrine holding that parents have a fundamental constitutional due process right to raise and parent their children without interference by other persons or the state (Debele, Goldberg, and Mitnick 2014), further minimizing the ability of grandparents to seek access to grandchildren through legal means.

Yet grandparent visitation statutes were enacted in all fifty states over a period of twenty-three years beginning in 1964(Hill2000). These statutes provided standing for grandparent in such cars to petition courts for access. A heavy burden of proof rests with the grandparents to establish "unfitness" of the parent, or to show that the grandchild has special needs that will be ameliorated to some degree by contact with the grandparent. Although there have been various challenges over the years to the fundamental right of a parent to decide who has access to the child, parents continue to retain this right (Debele, Goldberg, and Mitnick 2014).

Another service that may have considerable cost is guardian ad litem. A Guardian ad litem (GAL) is a person the court appoints to investigate what solutions would be in the best interest of a child. GAL's can be lawyers or mental health professionals who have had special training. The GAL will look into the family situation and advise the court. The court will write an order. The court can order the GAL to make an oral or written report. You have the right to know what is in the report. If you are worried that the GAL is not looking out for the child's best interest, you can talk with them. If you are not comfortable talking with the GAL, you can tell the court in writing, or at your next court meeting. You can also file a formal grievance with the Guardian Ad Litem Review Board.

(Warshak 2012) Means of reestablishing a grandparent–grandchild relationship are likely to be more problematic in cases of severe Parental Alienation Syndrome where the relatives of the alienated parent become collateral damage in the campaign of denigration by one parent against the other parent in attempts to influence the children to hate that parent and their relatives. In this case the grandparent could be expected to regain contact if their adult child is reunited with their child (Amy Baker, pers. comm., 2015). Reunification is very difficult to accomplish without intervention because alienated children's thoughts about their parents become highly skewed and polarized, reflecting the views of the parent.

Human tragedies are taking place. Countless numbers of people are suffering. AGA has encountered many heartbreaking situations regarding foster homes, adoption, custody, death of an adult child, and the murder of an adult child.

Children in foster homes have had to endure losses at such tender ages in their lives. An elderly AGA Florida great-grandmother, who was the only family member wanting connection to three young children, was given her day in court. The judge agreed to grant her periodic visitation rights at the foster home. She hired a driver to take her quite a long distant to spend time with her precious young family. She so enjoyed watching their sports, listening to them, and hearing all the stories they were excited to share.

Things went very well for three years; her emails to AGA were happy ones. A few days after Christmas she contacted AGA to report that she had abruptly been called into court a few days before. This great-grandma in her 90's was informed in the courtroom that an adoption had just taken place. She was cruelly and heartlessly told that she was never to communicate with her three little great-grandchildren ever again. She was forbidden to say good-bye.

This happened because a court appointed therapist, unfamiliar with up-to-date mental health studies, was the authority at this sudden turn of events preceding. There and then the judge was informed by this "therapist" that it would be unhealthy for the children to have further contact with the great-grandmother; the one person whom they had grown to know, love, and trust. The judge accepted this long-outdated advice. The kind, gentle, loving great-grandmother, was denied a final good-bye. She was not permitted to tell the children that she loves them. She soon passed away.

(Golly, P.L., MSW, LCSW, RPTS 2018):

> Imagine the kind of losses children of adoption or foster care have gone through in their young lives.
>
> Without their security being disconnected, the children can accept their situation in a healthier way. If they keep this secure base of the grands who love them unconditionally, they would carry this love forward. If a child is to make a successful transition to "another" family (adoption, remarriage), severing the ties that bind would be detrimental to the child's well-being and success in life.
>
> They will lose the trust factor with authority figures/adults. If the grands are denied communications, this disconnect will be carried forward within them for the rest of their lives. Now, yet another severed attachment is taking place for these little ones.
>
> What is the basis that determined this connection to their heritage be severed? The therapist is erasing their past. These young children cannot just start over. That is the old way of thinking. Ruptured attachment makes the children unhealthy emotionally and psychologically. Their grands are established relationships, and the only connection to the heritage of their family. They need

to know those who are their only family of origin. They need to know this great grandmother with whom they have bonded.

Without their security being disconnected, the children can accept adoption in a healthier way if they keep this secure base of the great grandmother, their family of origin. She is the one who loves them, and they would carry this forward. Instead the child thinks, "I must be unlovable if she doesn't say good-bye to me."

In the state of Florida, adoption terminates grandparent visitation rights unless a stepparent adopts the child. The state of Florida should enhance the consideration given to family members in cases of foster and adoptive homes. Keeping families together and kinship placement instead of foster care should be the focus.

An AGA couple had moved to a retirement state. A few years after their grandchildren were placed into foster care. Desperately wanting custody of their grandchildren, they traveled north in hopes of obtaining custody. The children's case worker had told them they could have custody if they would relocate to the state where their grandchildren were living, and buy a house large enough for each of the four children to have their own bedroom. The grandparents sold their retirement home and found a house that would satisfy the requirements told to them. Once the grandparents relocated and settled in, they were informed that the case worker whom they had been dealing with was no longer on that case, and that they could not have their grandchildren. Nothing had been in writing to protect the grandparents.

Other AGA grandparents suffered the loss of their daughter to cancer. The young grandchildren continued a relationship with their maternal grandparents until a new woman became involved with the dad. The maternal grandparents, with whom the children had closely bonded, were cut off from all communication with their precious grandchildren. The link to their mom and her family was severed. Grandma, Grandpop, and the grandchildren have tragically had to live without the love and support for one another. Unfortunately, AGA hears of this scenario all too often.

Grandparent Alienation affects children who need a grandparent's watchful or protective eye due to issues of drugs, alcohol, neglect, or domestic violence in their homes. If the law does not provide for this layer of protection, then the human rights of our grandchildren are being denied.

AGA assists nationally and internationally in the pursuit of improving Grandparents' Rights legislation which presently have sharp limitations. On the positive side, the AGA Grandparent Movement for new and improved laws is making progress. Laws are being written, changed, and amended on a state-by-state and provence-by-provence basis. Having the unity of one national law would be ideal. If a universal law provided all grandparents (who can show cause and prove this harmful to the child) the right to be heard in the courtroom, there would finally be an opportunity for justice in our society.

Keeping the focus on what is best for the grandchildren should be the objective of our efforts. Harm to a child comes in various forms: physical, sexual, psychological, and emotional. Promoting continuity of relationships in a child's life should be considered for the well-being of the child.

(Dr. Coleman) If parental neglect can and should be considered a form of child abuse, certainly a parent's decision to end a loving and attached relationship between a grandchild and a grandparent should also be considered a form of abuse.

Alienation is considered by the experts to be a severe form of child abuse, and a severe form of elder abuse. Abuse is never acceptable; abuse is never OK. Abuse is against the law. It is all too common that the courts refuse to intervene on grandparents' behalf. Great-grandparents are considered to have the same rights as grandparents. The legislators turn a blind eye to the damage that is being done to our grandchildren, by denying them the love and presence of their grands in their lives. We must all bring awareness of Grandparent Alienation to our court system, and educate the family law judges.

Our court system should respect the relationship between children and grandparents, yet little attention is given to the importance of this relationship. Children suffer when they lose their grandparents because of divorce or dysfunctional family circumstances. It is tantamount to abuse. The rights of children are supposed to be paramount, yet the decision for these children has been made for them by their cold-hearted parents and closed-minded legislators.

Providing details from our experience in Florida may enlighten you to the obstacles you may encounter in your locality. Florida is a haven for grandparents and the birthplace of AGA, Inc. During his presenting at the AGA International Conference 2019, Attorney Charles D. Jamieson cited Florida having a more daunting path than the U. S. Constitution. He discussed how restrictive and almost non-existent Florida's Grandparent Visitation Rights are, and how chaotic Grandparents' Rights are across the country. He declared the court as being the worst place to go to try to get relief, and that it is always best to try to fix things outside of the courtroom. His recommendation for grandparents and great-grandparents was to consider every case as being different, and to consult with a lawyer well-experienced in third party visitation rights.

Each of the United States has its own rulings for Grandparent Rights. Each will allow for proving harm to the child and what is in the best interest of the child on an individual basis. Defining harm and best interest remains questionable.

(Arthur Kornhaber, M.D.) We also understand that learning and enforcing your grandparents' rights can be a confusing and overwhelming process. Many states have different laws for grandparents' rights which can make it difficult to know exactly what your grandparents' rights are. Our laws should reflect a different attitude. They should say that intergenerational families should be together. Despite their conflicts, family members need to learn to live together. It shows children that family problems should be worked out, not run away from. Society needs to opt for healing and union of the family, instead of divisive laws and policies.

A court will consider a number of factors when it determines what is in the best interest of the child. None of these factors are determinative or conclusive in and of themselves. In other words, a court would not likely make a decision regarding grandparent visitation based only on the presence or absence of one factor. Instead, a court would look at the presence or absence of all of the following factors before making a ruling:

- The willingness of the grandparents to encourage a close relationship between the child and parents
- The previous length and quality of the relationship between the grandparents and child
- If the child was old enough to express a preference, that preference would be considered
- The mental and physical health of the child
- The mental and physical health of the grandparents
- Any other factors the judge wishes to consider

June 2015 Florida Governor Rick Scott signed into law Statute 752.011-SB 368 allowing grandparents to sue for visitation if the parents of their grandchild are deceased, missing, or in a persistent vegetative state. AGA played an integral part in the passing of this law. We appreciate the devoted efforts of Representative Darryl Rouson who served as sponsor of the bill, and his legislative assistant Jason Holloway. While this law may apply to a minimal percentage of cases, it is viewed as a step in the right direction. Outside of the above circumstances, grandparents have very little legal visitation rights, as many Florida rulings have upheld that parents have the right to choose who has access to their children. The new law will not apply to children who have grandparents residing outside of the state of Florida.

The new law in Florida (2015) can only help if BOTH parents are deceased, missing, or in a persistent vegetative state; OR, one parent is deceased, missing or in a vegetative state **AND** the other parent has been convicted of a felony or an offense of violence evincing behavior that poses a substantial threat of harm to the minor child's health or welfare. If there is one parent who is around and not a violent felon, grandparents have no rights to visitation.

It appears that, to date, there are no cases that meet this criterion that have been heard by the appellate courts. The grandparent for whom this bill was designed does not even qualify for Grandparents' Rights! "Its narrowness has almost been limited to a nullity, that it doesn't even apply to a situation where it was the impetus for us to begin to work to pass it," remarked Representative Darryl Rouson, the sponsor of the statute.

AGA in Florida is hoping to eventually broaden the scope for Grandparents Rights. Florida has 40 senators and 120 representatives. Grandparents must educate those who could potentially help them.

The State of Florida has been resistant due to the Right to Privacy Act based on the Washington State Supreme Court *Troxel* et vir *v. Granville* Decision in 2000. It is a case in which the Supreme Court of the United States, citing a constitutional right of parents to direct the upbringing of their children, struck down a Washington state law that allowed any third party to petition state courts for child visitation rights over parental objections. The Court held that the interest of parents in the care, custody and control of their children—is perhaps the oldest of the fundamental liberty interests recognized by this Court. That fundamental right is implicated in grandparent visitation cases, and as such, it struck down the Washington visitation statute because it unconstitutionally infringed on the right.

State courts considering non-parent visitation petitions must apply "a presumption that fit parents act in the best interests of their children. *Troxel* requires that state courts must give "special weight" to a fit parent's decision to deny non-parent visitation, as well as other decisions made by a parent regarding the care and custody of their children.

The plurality held that "choices [parents make] about the upbringing of children... are among associational rights... sheltered by the Fourteenth Amendment against the State's unwarranted usurpation, disregard, or disrespect. This principle must inform the understanding of the "special weight" that *Troxel* requires courts to give to parents' decisions. Even though *Troxel* does not define "special weight," previous Supreme Court precedent indicates that "special weight" is a term signifying very considerable deference.

The "special weight" requirement, as illuminated by these prior Supreme Court cases, means that the deference provided to the parent's wishes will be overcome only by some compelling governmental interest and by overwhelmingly clear factual circumstances supporting that governmental interest. This is essentially identical to the strict scrutiny standard, in keeping with the fundamental status of parental rights.

Troxel vs. Granville was passed by a slim margin, but its effect on Grandparents' Rights nationally has unfortunately been monumental. The grandparent visitation statutes of most states were jeopardized by the U.S. Supreme Court's 2000 decision in Troxel vs. Granville. This controversial decision gave parents an edge in grandparent visitation disputes and cast a doubt on the constitutionality of most state statutes. The U. S. Supreme Court found that a Washington State statute allowing third-party visitation was unconstitutional. The statute according to the court, was "breathtakingly broad" and did not give parental decisions about visitation sufficient weight.

AGA participated in a Grandparents' Rights case in Washington state several years later. An amicus brief was prepared in cooperation with AGA documentation and consultation. The grandparents in this case won the right for visitation with their grandchildren.

Grandparents would give anything to spend time with their grandchildren. While most states have certain rights with regards to grandchildren, those rights are seldom as robust or as straightforward as grandparents think they should be. This exists because grandparent visitation statutes are part of state law. With such an important issue, many believe this should be covered by federal law. The U.S. Constitution does not mention family law, that area has traditionally been reserved for states. Since lawmakers in each state approach their tasks differently, uniform grandparents' visitation laws appear to be almost an impossibility.

It is usually the state in which the grandchild lives that determines has jurisdiction. The laws of each state define the circumstances by which grandparents have a right to visit their grandchildren. Some being more permissive while others are more restrictive.

In every state, grandparents must prove that granting visitation to the grandchild is in the best interest of the child. Visitation rights are based on pre-existing relationship that has engendered a bond. Some states require that the court consider the prior relationship between the grandparent and the grandchild. This does don't help these grandparents who were never allowed to meet their grandchild(ren).

The main purpose of Grandparents' Rights is to ensure that a child has access to the emotional and developmental benefits of having a grandparent in his or her life. In the best interest of the child: if a grandparent can provide other facts that show that the loss of the grandparents -grandchild relationship will harm the child. This requirement is called the harm standard. Having a journal of proof of quality time during the such bonding, will be an advantage in court. Grandparents who have can provide a time line of photos, family videos, letters, or even a diary would have this advantage. This can be included in the clear and convincing evidence that loss of the relationship has caused, or is reasonably likely to cause, harm to the child. The flaw here is that a grandparent may have been denied contact with the grandchild thus having no opportunity to develop a relationship with the child.

About 15 million residents of Florida are age 60 plus. Florida is a major retirement destination of grandparents. Therefore, Florida should be in the forefront setting an example for rights for the rest of the country. Though Alienated Grandparents Anonymous International Headquarters is in Florida and aggressively pursues rights for grandparents, it is ironically one of the toughest states with regard to winning grandparent visitation. It is embarrassing that the Sunshine State lies at the bottom of the barrel where GP-GC relationships and importance stand. In Florida, grandparent visitation law has been ineffectual for some time, due to the state's stance on privacy and due to the rulings in several important cases. Florida is among other states who has a right to privacy written into the state constitution which awards the wishes of the parent above the desires of the grandparents.

At this time, constitutions in 11 states—Alaska, Arizona, California, Florida, Hawaii, Illinois, Louisiana, Montana, New Hampshire, South Carolina and Washington—have explicit provisions relating to a right to privacy. In addition, more general provisions in other states have been interpreted by courts to have established privacy rights or various types.

Grandparents should be allowed to petition the courts for third party visitation rights under certain circumstances, when a compelling state interest exists relating to the best interest of the child. A minor should have human rights when in harm's way. Loving grandparents can provide the vital safety net for their grandchildren.

You may not think the possibly of not seeing your grandchildren could happen to you, yet that possibility might be on the horizon. If it can happen to so many through no fault of their own, it can happen to you. The laws need to be in place.

When grandparents struggle with substance abuse, mental illness, incarceration, economic hardship, divorce, domestic violence, and other challenges; supervised visits or denial of contact is understandable. Denial of grandparent access should only be used in a situation where the child is in danger from the grandparent, but not as a default position in the acting out of adult anger, desire for revenge, and desire for control. When grands are denied contact because of divorce, death of adult child, or simply because something is going on in the child's household that parents don't want them to know about; it makes the grandparent, great grandparent, and the grandchild victims.

Other than filing petitions or developing new legislation and having our state senators and congressman agree to the needs of the people, Florida is the only state with a Constitution Revision Commission. This CRC is one of the ways Florida can amend the state constitution, but it only happens once every 20 years.

In 2017 Governor Scott, the Florida Senate President, the Florida Speaker of the House, and Florida Supreme Court Chief Justice all named 36 people to the 2017-2018 CRC. The Attorney General was the 37th member. Knowing there would be a major emphasis on Grandparents' Rights, AGA needed to take action, due to Florida's Right to Privacy Act. Unless the Florida constitution were to be revised, Grandparents Rights in Florida would not change. This was the time to be laser focused and connect with the CRC commissioners.

Stakeholders meetings took place for the 2018 Constitutional Revision Committee Proposal. The meeting was attended by advocates for Grandparent's Rights. The Executive Board of AGA, including James Karl, Esq. of Collier County Florida and Charles D. Jamieson, Esq. of Palm Beach County Florida joined Florida Senator Darryl Rouson and his legislative assistant Jason Holloway. These stakeholders had previously drafted the statue for the 2015 GR bill which was passed in Tallahassee in 2015.

The Declaration of Rights, <u>Right to Privacy</u>; Section 23 of Article I of the Florida State Constitution to specify that the right of privacy may to be construed to limit a grandparent's right to seek visitation of his or her grandchildren under certain circumstance.

ARTICLE I: DECLARATION OF RIGHTS, Section 23. Right of Privacy
SECTION 23. <u>Right of Privacy</u>

Every natural person has the right to be let alone and free from government intrusion into the person's private life except as otherwise provided herein. This section shall not be construed to limit the public's right of access to public records and meeting provided by law. This section shall not be construed to limit a grandparent's right to seek visitation of their grandchildren when a compelling state interest exists relating to the best interest of the child.

This proposed amendment included the new wording: This section shall not be construed to limit a grandparent's right to seek visitation of their grandchildren when a compelling state interest exists relating to the best interest of the child.

AGA's Proposal would amend the Right to Privacy:
CRC Proposal # PUB 700709: Rights of Grandparents
https://www.flcrc.gov/Proposals/Public/700709

The CRC Commission held public hearings throughout the state where citizens could attend, and share ideas and feedback on potential proposals for the general election ballot. After gathering public input, the commission recommended proposals for the 2018 ballot. Only ten proposals were to be placed on the ballot, and voters would ultimately decide what passed. Proposals require 60 percent of the vote in order to pass.

Thousands of Floridian grandparents who suffer the negative impact from not having contact with their grandchildren, placed phone calls and sent emails to the CRC committee members focusing on the best interest of the child. AGA's proposal was one of a few selected from approximately 2000 proposals to be heard in Tallahassee. The goal was to move the AGA proposal through the Declaration of Rights Committee, and into the Judicial Committee where it would face its greatest challenge. Once the first challenge was met, ongoing continued amendments would eventually provide help for more varied circumstances, so that more grandparents and grandchildren would have the opportunity to be reunited.

Ultimately, the proposal was temporarily postponed, with Senator Rouson vowing to fight for it on a later day. James Karl, Esq. stated, "Our proposal received a temporary pass for a second hearing. Attorney Karl recommended, we adjust the proposed language to, "Nothing in this provision should be construed to prevent an immediate family member from seeking timesharing in a case where there is demonstrable harm being done to the child (including other family members' rights to visitation)", in hopes to get more votes.

Having presented at the first CRC hearing in Tallahassee, Attorney James Karl stated, "There is a strong general opposition on the part of some committee members to amend the constitution relating to privacy rights. This is a 'when in doubt, no amendment attitude'. The committee also expressed a strong opposition based upon the belief that statutory relief is possible and therefore no amendment is needed. This second position, of course, ignores that fact that statuary relief has been impeded by an overly broad right of privacy clause in the Florida constitution."

(James Karl, Esq.) The committee reiterated that the right to privacy is a cherished fundamental right founded upon more than 200 years of federal and state law, and it should not be compromised unless absolutely required. The government interest essentially requires showing, by clear and convincing evidence, that demonstratable harm is being done to the grandchild. Some committee members seemed to believe that dependency court and adoption provide sufficient protections for children in dysfunctional families. On the other hand, some members seemed to understand that there are states which have meaningful grandparent statutes with constitutional safeguards. Our sponsor, Commissioner Darryl Rouson, articulated that the Florida constitutional provision is too broad and has led to a grandparent right to timesharing statute, Florida Statute Section 752, that is so narrow that it is meaningless. This is embarrassing for our state and tragic for our grandparents."

Presenting at the AGA International Conference 2019, legislative assistant to Senator Daryl Rouson, Jason Holloway, a professional consultant to AGA stated, "The attitude of those who legislate believe that no one should change the constitution but them. They want to make it harder for you to change the law. They want you to find the way to work out your situation between you and your children."

Florida rulings have consistently upheld that parents have the right to control who has access to their children. The old Florida statutes exist no longer. Grandparents, in reality, have no rights in the state of Florida. It is time to remove those in office who oppose grandparents having the right so visit with their precious grandchildren. Participate in the AGA Grandparent Movement. This could blindside you and eventually become your story, too.

At the CRC hearing a Florida grandmother told the committee how her daughter disappeared years ago and remains missing, while her daughter's fiancé – the only suspect named by police in the case - has refused to let this grandmother see the couple's twin children since the incident five years prior. "How can a primary and only suspect for murder who takes the Fifth get the upper hand?" she asked the committee. "I need your help so that we don't run into the stop sign, the Constitution as it is written now."

AGA has communicated with several other grandparents in Florida whose daughters have been murdered, where the only suspect is the boyfriend or husband. They have each been denied the right to have contact in order to keep a watchful eye over their grandchildren.

The following story was presented by a grandmother at the AGA International Conference 2017 In her own words she shared her story which she had presented in Tallahassee;

On December 3, 2012 in North Carolina, my daughter was shot in the head by her husband who then shot himself in a murder/suicide. Visiting from California at the time, I was the person who discovered their bodies.

My stepson in Tennessee took custody of their three children. He suffered a heart attack, and keeping the children proved too difficult since he had three children of his own. At that point, he granted custody to Robert's sister who resides in Florida. I thought my relationship with the new parents was amicable, but I recently discovered that they have adopted my grandchildren and will no longer permit me to see them. I have even been threatened with a restraining order if I go to their house, to the schools, or try to contact the children. I don't understand their viewpoint since I come from a place of serving, and have only had the best interests of the children at heart.

Three attorneys have advised that I, as a grandparent, have no visitation rights in Florida. How heartbreaking it has been to lose my only biological child and now my three grandchildren. Laws need to change, particularly for the elderly population in Florida who shouldn't suffer such anguish.

I would like to testify before all committees and subcommittees considering HB 149: "Rights of Grandparents and Great-Grandparents" to convey the importance of granting grandparent visitation rights. My grandchildren and I have lost so much, and they DO want me to continue being part of their lives. WE had a great pre-existing relationship which would still be intact had my daughter not been murdered. I know she would want me to be close to the children, and I want very much to watch them grow and prosper.

When the CRC 2018 Declaration of Rights hearing decision was announced to by Chairwoman Lisa Carlton, and the Co-Chairperson John Stemberger, a grandmother who had testified to a similar situation found her way outside the courtroom door and collapsed in complete anguish. This grandmother had pleaded before the committee for this proposal to pass. Her daughter had been murdered by the spouse and the remains the prime suspect. When Lisa Carlton announced the decision she so profoundly influenced, this grandmother left the chambers crying hysterically and collapsed onto the floor. Her daughter had been murdered, and now the grandmother was denied the human right to spend time with her grandchildren. There will not be another constitutional revision committee for 20 years. The Right to Privacy Act remains.

Link to CRC Declaration of Rights Committee Meeting on P64: *https://thefloridachannel.org/videos/1-19-18-constitution-revision-commission-declaration-rights-committee/*

(James Karl, Esq.) It is important to reiterate that there are many safeguards currently in place (under federal and state law) to protect a parent's right of privacy (and the corollary right to rear their children as they see fit), and the proposed amendment does not change this. On the other hand, there are virtually no grandparent rights in Florida to protect grandchildren in imminent danger. Such a danger could be avoided or reduced by giving grandparents the right to seek time sharing in an appropriate. There is a strong argument to be made that the Florida legislature has a duty to protect these children. It seems certain that the support for same by the voters would get even stronger as time goes on and Florida takes no meaningful action.

In a last-minute effort to kill our proposal, Chairperson Lisa Carlton requested Tallahassee attorney Shannon Novey provide testimony to the committee regarding legal rulings on the issue. She said there was a serious problem with giving standing to grandparents, but not other "third-parties" such as aunts, uncles, and neighbors who established relationships with children. She said this violated the Equal Protection clause of the 14th Amendment.

When it was Attorney Karl's turn to present before the committee at the hearing the rules changed. The chairwoman announced there would be an eight-minute limit for his presentation, and for those (the grandparents) who followed.

At the close of the session for AGA's proposal, The Declaration of Rights Committee Chairperson Lisa Carlton emphatically stated, "I cannot support expanding the rights of grandparents to visit their grandchildren." The co-chairperson John Stemberger stated that he absolutely couldn't support the proposal. Under their leadership, the votes of the committee members who had supported our endeavor turned to the other side.

Many grandparents lost hope of rights in the state of Florida. Harm continues to be done to the children. Who better than a loving grandparent could watch over abused children? (Karl) It is perplexing why anyone would put up resistance to grandparents petitioning the court to visit their grandchild on a case by case basis.

(James Karl, Esq. 2018):

> Eight hundred thousand families with minor children are led by grandparents in this state. We give them nothing. No standing. No ability. That's not what the federal right of privacy is all about. It is tragic that the state stands alone when it comes to the rights of grandparents' visitation rights. We learned a lot during the constitutional amendment process. It was disappointing to see that the pollical climate is not yet ripe for a meaningful grandparent

visitation stature in the civil (family court) arena. Florida is way behind other states in this regard. There are remedies for Florida grandparents in other areas, such as dependency when grandchildren are in harm's way and the parents are unfit. There are no perfect remedies. In the meantime, for good grandparents, we continue to hope that the Florida politicians get with the program, and do something to expand grandparent rights in family court.

We need to have a primary focus in keeping the extended family unit intact; to deal with the evermore troubling world around us. It's perplexing why anyone would resist grandparents petitioning the court to visit their grandchildren on a case-by-case basis.

If we are to restore hope for justice and human rights, YOU must be diligent when it comes to making a decision to whom you give your vote. New leadership by the right legislators can bring about change. Investigate names of legislators who voted against Grandparents' Rights. Vote them out of office.

Grandparents are 70 million strong in America, and the AGA Grandparent Movement worldwide is moving to action. Together grandparents are continuing to connect with legislators. We believe that if you want something changed, then gather support and change it. Grandparents will campaign for the human right of grandchildren to have loving grandparents in their lives. Kind and caring grandparents should have the right to go to court to stand up and be heard.

We must protect grandchildren from harm in the form of physical and sexual abuse, and from drug and alcohol addiction in the family. Grands deserve the right to protect these precious young ones from dangerous parents. If they are kept away because their jurisdiction does not provide the laws necessary for grandparents' open-eyed observance, and to offer them love, safety, and security they deserve as human beings; then we must stand up and be their voice.

When there is contact with grandparents, our youth has an extra layer of protection from those who truly love them. But when alienation affects minors who need a grandparent's attentiveness due to issues of drugs, alcohol, neglect, or domestic violence in the home; then the human rights of our grandchildren need protection.

When grandparents are denied visitation, severe child abuse in a family goes undetected. From time to time we sit in horror of national news coverage regarding the shocking discovery of horrifying child abuse. It is often an abuse that has been taking place in the home for years. Follow up coverage eventually reveals that the grandparents had been denied contact. A likely scenario would find circumstances where the children having been sheltered from social contact, possibly home schooling, and no scheduled pediatric evaluations. These unprotected children have disappeared under the radar. Meanwhile, grandparents are grieving from the isolation, and from not knowing of the welfare of their grandchildren.

Who is there to help these young ones? If new grandparent visitation laws are enacted, and only one child is saved from this horrific experience, all our efforts have been worthwhile. If our legislators continue to deny grandparent visits so they can periodically check on the circumstances of their grandchildren, then it is our legislators who have failed to protect our minors. All too often we hear of the overload of cases for social workers. Who better than children's own loving caring grandparents to oversee the well- being of their youngest generation? This is happening in America. Let these U.S. elected officials then be the ones to carry the heavy burden of the harm done to these unprotected children. Let them live with the blame, not the grandparents who begged for laws to help them and were denied every time.

Will you help a grandchild who misses their grandparent, and a grandparent who is broken-hearted? We must campaign this issue to the top of the political agenda to achieve justice and legal rights. The laws must be adjusted to ensure these grandparents of not losing contact, and to be reconnected as a member of their family. Elect legislators who will not turn a blind eye to this great social injustice and the damage that is being done to our grandchildren by denying them a presence and the love of their grandparents. Stand strong for what is good, what is right, and what is the truth. Do not let the" restrict access" stand.

Grandparents who do turn to the courts for assistance are likely to find that the laws are not in place, leaving the judges without the tools to help. If we do nothing, we may never see our grandchildren again. It would be bad for grandparents and much worse for our grandchildren as time passes.

Team AGA is a strong force in leading this Grandparent Movement. Grandparents are millions strong. Together we can make history! Let your voices be heard in the courtrooms and halls of justice across the country and around the world. Lift your voices in unison to raise awareness about the Grandparent Alienation phenomenon which has become increasingly common among families today.

As grandparents and great-grandparents, we have faced challenges over the years. We have met those obstacles head on, and we survived. We must now be the voice of the unprotected grandchildren. We must stand up for human rights.

If the laws in place are not favorable to your personal situation, then perhaps it is time for you to take action. If the judges do not have the tools to help you and your grandchildren, there are things grandparents can do to promote laws that will allow us to restore our relationship with our grandchildren. Don't allow the abuse of children to continue without speaking up. The way things are now is not the way they must remain.

Grandparents need to stay connected to their grandchildren not only for the safety and well-being of the child, but also because "positive family connections" are important to everyone, especially children. Should a child have a loving relationship obstructed due to a conflict the parents may have?

Marilyn Daniels, PhD conducted one of the first ever studies of the Grandparents Rights issue. Remarking on this terrible ordeal, and noting that it can happen to any grandparent, Dr. Daniels stated that she was amazed by the apparent senselessness of the withholder's actions. "Many withheld them with little or no provocation. I think of few other examples in the field of family problems in which one category of persons is free to inflict misery on another effortlessly and without social sanction."

(Rev. Dr. John Killinger) Perhaps through the efforts of AGA and other organizations, there will be changes in the state laws regarding the rights of grandparents, and future generations of Grammys and Poppys – our oldest grandchild's favorite names for my wife and me- will enjoy more protection from 'grandparent abuse' than ours."

There is an urgent need for updating and creating legislation for Grandparents' Rights, whether by state or for an entire nation. Efforts to establish a uniform law that applies nationwide so far have failed. You can begin by contacting your state representatives and senators. Ask to speak with their legislative assistant. Request email addresses. Email or send AGA documents to validate your situation. Make an appointment with your local legislators. Perhaps they will make Grandparents Rights their platform for the next election. Also bring with you the AGA brochure, AGA Letter to Legislators, AGA Professional Board Members and Consultants, and the AGA This is Abuse document to validate your situation. Then, tell your story.

AGA will be a strong voice for one of the most tragic yet often forgotten victims in the family law arena. In conversation with Attorney James Karl, he hopes that with time, diligence, and patience more voices will come out. Grandparents will more openly share their stories, then others will start to listen and understand.

Grandparents play a vital role in the lives of grandchildren. Grandparents, stand up for your human rights. It is time we are proactive with our legislators. We must work toward providing the judges with the tools needed to help grandparent and grandchildren. We must educate our judges, attorneys, and legislators. Seek out these people. Set up appointments with them. Remember, legislators work for you. You pay their salaries. YOU VOTE! Elitist legislators are refusing to listen to those they are supposed to be serving. They are supposed to represent us! We need to find out who the legislators are that are anti grandparent, and do something about it! Take a stand with your legislators who stop the courts from intervening on your behalf.

We as grandparents must address our concerns and help our society. We must be involved. If a grandparent has spent months or years raising a grandchild, a special bond develops between them. That special relationship should not be cut off because of disputes between the parent and the grandparent.

Ask your legislators for cooperation in writing a new statute for Grandparents Visitation Rights. We need to elect and allow into office legislators who will vote to help our grandparents and our grandchildren who are suffering. This is about the significant bond that grandparents and grandchildren share, and making certain that if the bond is severed, grandparents will have a recourse. Our young ones are waiting to be with us. They need others to stand up for them.

Do citizens really understand who they are voting for? Do we really know what these politicians' actual views are? We can no longer live in a situation with old style thinking. We need to become aware of how each is voting, then make it our duty to inform others. Our votes and our voices should count. Young lives matter. We must not allow this society to deteriorate more than it already has. We must strive to restore the democracy in our families and in our society.

Due to the widespread recognition of the roles played by grandparents in grandchildren's lives, and because of the pain caused when contact has been denied, states have recognized some limited degree of grandparent rights with legislation. What is needed are updated laws to reflect some modern societal norms. We need laws which benefit minors. Grandparents Rights laws are being written, changed, and amended. Aim to make the legislative process simple, inexpensive, and powerful to uphold. By actively engaging in this mission, you will make a strong statement to your grandchild, "The whole time we were apart, I never stopped trying to find a way back to you."

Walk on with hope in your heart. You are not alone.

APPENDIX

AGA Documents to Share

- **AGA Mission Statement**

Alienated Grandparents Anonymous, Inc.
www.AlienatedGrandparentsAnonymous.com
AGAInternationalHeadquarters@gmail.com

AGA originated in Florida in 2011.
International Headquarters is located in Florida, U.S.A.
AGA was established as a 501c3 Non Profit in 2012.

In the United States, statistics show that 71% of grandparents state that being a grandparent is the most important part of their lives. Yet, Grandparent Alienation is a global epidemic. This abandonment by our adult children is endemic in our society. It has no socio-economic boundaries. At this time, AGA has a presence in 50 states and 22 countries. Grandparent Alienation is a Human Tragedy.

Alienated Grandparents Anonymous Incorporated focuses on the struggle so many grandparents have in being part of their grandchildren's lives. AGA provides support and information in a safe environment, and helps validate the feelings of those suffering the effects of being cut off from access to their grandchildren. AGA serves toward bringing alienated grandparents, parents, and grandchildren together.

Alienation is something that no grandparent/parent should face alone. Grandparents are suffering serious emotional and physical consequences. It has been stated by the experts in the field of complicated grief, and studies show that the best form of help for us is to have peer led support groups.

AGA support group meetings are a place for those of us who are experiencing this devastating emotional trauma, to share their circumstances with those who "get it". AGA recognizes that each situation is unique; however, many commonalities are shared. Simply knowing that you are not alone helps you cope better with the heartbreak and frustration of being a targeted grandparent.

Grandparents are an intricate part of raising and loving unconditionally our young ones and preparing them for society. Grandparents provide a balance in grandchildren's lives that no one else can replicate. Studies have shown that multi-generational contact between children and their grandparents provides a special unconditional love and nurturing which is healthy for children. The quality of attachment is very strong, and contributes to our grandchildren's sense of self.

At AGA main events, international experts offer explanations why this occurs and strategies to help relieve the pressure and heal relationships with adult children. They offer coping skills to help manage the devastating emotional pain of being disconnected from our grandchildren.

These featured international guest speakers impart valuable knowledge and insight from their field of expertise. Qualified consulting experts help grandparents/parents come to understand the varied dynamics involved in the complex realities of Grandparent Alienation-GA and Parental Alienation Syndrome-PAS. An interactive discussion is included. Grandparents may remain anonymous so that everyone feels free to openly share their plight.

This incredibly destructive alienation creates an unnatural psychological distance between the grandparents, adult children, and grandchildren. Information from the experts helps grandparents develop strategies to form plans for improving family relationships, and in dealing with the excruciating emotional pain of the chaos they experience.

Understanding the complexities of Alienation helps grandparents. Knowledge is Power. When we hear an expert say something with which we can personally identify, a light bulb goes off in our minds, and a new piece of the puzzle comes together. If you take away with you even one piece of information from each meeting, process it, and then apply it to your adult children and grandchildren; eventually, you will begin to see a clearer picture of the bewildering phenomena of our own children not wanting us to have a place in their lives and in our grandchildren's lives.

Alienation is a willful intimidation. Experts on Alienation state: Alienation involves such issues as underlying personality disorders - delusional disorder, anti-social, borderline, narcissism, etc. and it includes unresolved childhood issues, neuro-linguistic programming, manipulation, brainwashing, and cult-like behavior. It is about Power and Control. It is mind control within the family.

Thru AGA grandparents come to realize that if they did not cause this, then they alone cannot fix this campaign of denigration and domestic violence. Grandparents come to understand that they should not be embarrassed by this estrangement, and that they can stop blaming themselves. Healthy minds want to fix things, while unhealthy minds do not.

The unjustified abusive behavior of our adult children is creating a lifetime of emotional problems for our grandchildren. It is considered by the experts in Alienation to be a severe form of child abuse, and elder abuse. Abuse is never acceptable; abuse is never OK.

A number of suicides have been brought to the attention of AGA. This is not fair to the grandchildren who are anxiously awaiting reconnection with their grandparents. Grandparents must realize that our grandchildren are waiting to see us, too! Would you help AGA bring awareness Grandparent Alienation so those who suffer will learn they are not alone? AGA is here to help those in need of support.

AGA advocates in seeking legislation for Grandparents Visitation Rights worldwide. The Right to Privacy Act in many U.S. states severely limits Grandparents Rights. Baby Boomers comprise about one-third of our national population. We vote, and we need to be granted Human Rights. Grandparents must be the voices of our grandchildren, especially when a watchful eye is needed to determine if they are in harm's way.

We must elect legislators who will give judges the tools to help our grandparents and our grandchildren. Grandparents suffer deeply. Our grandchildren are suffering, too. Grandparents must be the voice of our grandchildren who have had to go emotionally underground with their feelings. Grandparents can seek help, but who is there for our grandchildren as they live this emotional chaos?

- **Dear Educators:**

Too many grandparents are walking around our community needing help to cope with Grandparent Alienation issues. Too many grandparents are being denied or severely limited access with their grandchildren. Grandparents and grandchildren who have had years bonding with each other, sharing this most precious of relationships, have become isolated. Some grandparents have never even been allowed to see their grandchildren. There is no socio-economic group unprotected from such devastation.

Unfortunately, alienation has become endemic in our society, and globally. Ask those around you, and you will discover they have this in their own extended families, or know of someone close to them who is emotionally traumatized due to Grandparent Alienation GA or Parental Alienation Syndrome PAS. This is considered by the experts to be a severe form of child abuse, and a severe form of elder abuse.

Alienated Grandparents Anonymous Incorporated focuses on the struggle so many grandparents have in being part of their grandchildren's lives. AGA provides support and information, and helps validate the feelings of those suffering some degree of estrangement, alienation, or isolation. AGA serves toward bringing alienated grandparents, parents, and grandchildren together.'

It has been brought to our attention that children under your watch in your school are experiencing this personal trauma. Would you PLEASE be aware of what children in your school are trying to cope with each day. Would you please care for and protect them for us. Give them a voice. Listen to them. Encourage them to share with you. Someone needs to tell them their grandparents still love them, and would be with them if they could.

Once you review our website www.AlienatedGrandparentsAnonymous. com; would you please take a moment to think about our precious little ones.

As adults we can seek advice from clergy, mental health professionals who have knowledge of alienation, inform our physicians of the emotional devastation which affects us 24/7, read self-help books, ask a friend for support, attend AGA support group meetings, etc. BUT who is there to help our grandchildren? They live with this chaos in their lives. They have no one to whom they can turn. They must go emotionally underground.

Grandparents are supposed to be there to comfort them as they grow up in this world. Love and caring should flow through generations.

- **This is Abuse**

Alienated Grandparents Anonymous, Inc.

This is Abuse
Grandparent Alienation is considered by the experts to be a severe form of elder abuse, and a severe form of child abuse.

Read Chapter 23 for validation that Grandparent Alienation is harmful to the grandchildren, the grandparents, and the great-grandparents.

- **AGA Board of Directors and Professional Consultants**

AGA, Inc. Alienated Grandparents Anonymous
501 C3 Non Profit I RS U.S. Government
AGA, Inc. Florida State Department Division of Corporations

AGA, Inc. Board of Directors

Amanda, Founder / Director AGAInternationalHeadquarters@gmail.com

Carol Golly, PhD, P.L., MSW, LCSW, RPTS
Doctoral Dissertation: Intergenerational Conflicts-Grandparent Alienation
Child Adolescent Family Therapist Collier County Florida
PAS/AGA Specialist
Frequent Court-Appointed Child Therapist

James L. Karl, II, Esq. Marco Island, Florida
Cornell University, J.D., 1983
Oxford University, Oxford England, Bachelor of Comparative Law Program, 1979
Washington College, B.A., 1978
Bar Admissions: Florida, Connecticut, New York, Massachusetts

Vickjo Letchworth, Elder Abuse Advocate Child Advocate
Collier County Residential Shelter Advocate
Domestic Violence Child Welfare Specialist
Collier County Leadership Council on Aging, Chairperson
Certified Trainer FL Coalition Against Domestic Violence
Facilitator; Support Groups for Seniors Who Are Victims of Elder Abuse
State-wide Speaker: Elder Abuse

Suzi Krig, R.N. AGA, Inc. Grandparent Advocate

AGA Professional Consultants
Leading International Alienation Experts

J. Michael Bone, Ph.D.
www.jmichaelbone.com
Michael@jmichaelbone.com Florida

Glenn Ross Caddy, Ph.D.
www.mind-experts.com
drglenncaddy@mind-experts.com
Florida Australia

Joshua Coleman, Ph.D.
www.drjoshuacoleman.com
josh@drjoshuacoleman.com
California

Charles Jamieson, Esq. P.A.
www.cjamiesonlaw.com
cdj@cjamiesonlaw.com
Florida

Rev. Dr. John Killinger
www.johnkillinger.com
drjohnkillinger@gmail.com
Virginia

Abe Worenklein, PhD
Clinical Psychologist
Québec Canada
abew@videotron.ca

Rev. Robert Winn
Mid.Nebraska.AGA@gmail.com

Jason Holloway, Legislative Assistant to Florida Senator Daryl Rouson

Printed in the United States
by Baker & Taylor Publisher Services